FANDOM, NOW IN COLOR

FANDOM & CULTURE
Paul Booth and Katherine Larsen, series editors

Fandom, Now in Color

A Collection of Voices

Edited by RUKMINI PANDE

UNIVERSITY OF IOWA PRESS
Iowa City

UNIVERSITY OF IOWA PRESS, IOWA CITY 52242
Copyright © 2020 by the University of Iowa Press
www.uipress.uiowa.edu
Printed in the United States of America

DESIGN BY TERESA W. WINGFIELD

Printed on acid-free paper

LIBRARY OF CONGRESS CATALOGING-IN-PUBLICATION DATA

Names: Pande, Rukmini, 1984– , editor.
Title: Fandom, Now in Color: A Collection of Voices / edited by Rukmini Pande.
Description: Iowa City: University of Iowa Press, [2020] | Series: Fandom &
    Culture | Includes bibliographical references and index. |
Identifiers: LCCN 2020017600 (print) | LCCN 2020017601 (ebook) |
    ISBN 9781609387280 (paperback; alk. paper) | ISBN 9781609387297 (ebook)
Subjects: LCSH: Mass media—Social aspects. | Mass media and minorities. |
    Fans (Persons) | Ethnicity. | Racism.
Classification: LCC HM1206 .F36 2020 (print) | LCC HM1206 (ebook) |
    DDC 302.23—dc23
LC record available at https://lccn.loc.gov/2020017600
LC ebook record available at https://lccn.loc.gov/2020017601

In solidarity with all the bravehearts around the world

who are striving against the forces of structural injustice

in order to forge a more equitable and hopeful future.

For All Fankind

EBONY ELIZABETH THOMAS

WE ARE ALL THE INHERITORS of long traditions of struggle. As the Black American descendant of people who were captured from West and Central Africa, enslaved in first the British North American colonies, then in the nascent United States of America, I know that every part of my education and lived experience has made me keenly aware of US-centric histories of exclusion, erasure, and marginalization. And thus far in fan studies, that perspective has been dominant in the few works that have considered race.

To look beyond academic fandom scholarship toward science fiction, fantasy, and horror studies, recent key critical works on race and speculative fiction of the 2010s include Ytasha Womack's *Afrofuturism: The World of Black Sci-Fi and Fantasy Culture*, Sheena Howard and Ronald Jackson's *Black Comics: Politics of Race and Representation*, André Carrington's *Speculative Blackness: The Future of Race in Science Fiction*, Michelle Commander's *Afro-Atlantic Flight: Speculative Returns and the Black Fantastic*, Kinitra Brooks's *Searching for Sycorax: Black Women's Hauntings of Contemporary Horror*, Diana Adesola Mafe's *Where No Black Woman Has Gone Before: Subversive Portrayals in Speculative Film and TV*, Sami Schalk's *Bodyminds Reimagined: (Dis)ability, Race, and Gender in Black Women's Speculative Fiction*, and my own *The Dark Fantastic: Race and the Imagination from Harry Potter to the Hunger Games*. Taken together, these and other critical works form an essential new canon for the study of race in contemporary science fiction, fantasy, and horror—although a canon centered almost entirely in the Global North and, as this volume notes, written exclusively by scholars who hail from minoritized and/or marginalized communities in the West.

When I was first asked to write the foreword to Rukmini Pande's new and indispensable collection, I wondered what I could provide, since I had learned much from these pages. Although I am a longtime fan of literature and media, I entered academic fandom studies through the worlds of children's literature criticism and educational research. Over the past twenty years, my primary considerations have been the diversification and decolonization of literature for young adults written, published, and circulated in the United States, Canada, and the United Kingdom. Two book series structured much of my thought about audiences and reader response—starting with *Anne of Green Gables*, written by Canadian author Lucy Maud Montgomery, and *Harry Potter and the Philosopher's Stone* (published in the United States as *Harry Potter and the Sorcerer's Stone*) by British author J. K. Rowling. Anne and Harry bookmarked the twentieth century's dawn and dusk as much as they laminated the years of my youth and young adulthood. Both texts have been adapted into multiple genres, modes, and formats, and both texts anchor imagined communities of readers, viewers, and fans who use digital media to communicate across space-time. The vast majority of those fans are nonwhite and hail from non-Western cultures.

Fandom, Now in Color is a book I wish I had had access to while writing *The Dark Fantastic*. After reading it, I found myself concurring with Pande's observation that "race is seen to be relevant to an analysis of fandom only when controversy entails overt and identifiable racist behavior . . . or when the fans or fandoms under analysis are explicitly framed as nonwhite. . . . Equally crucially, this kind of scholarship is then seen to be significant only to similar studies rather than making an impact on the foundational texts of fan studies." This critique of the West/Global North as a locus for fan studies is well taken, and this volume provides an important first step toward decentering Western perspectives in several areas of fan studies that will be useful for scholars, researchers, and the academic fandom community alike.

The first section of essays, "Methodologies," speaks to the necessity of decolonial frameworks in inquiry, pedagogy, and practices in the field. The next section, "Otherness," interrogates a term that is increasingly used when discussing race, identity, and difference without reference to its roots in postcolonial studies, which raises the unvoiced question, "Other to whom?" and demands attention to subjectivity and positionality. The volume is rounded out by two sections that tour the state of contemporary fandoms— "Affirmative/Transformative" and "Identity/Authenticity"—and provide a window onto the experiences of fans challenging a media landscape that inscribes whiteness onto the collective popular imagination.

Fandom, Now in Color reminds us that those who produce media are not the only ones who consume it, that fans in the wealthiest and most dominant parts of the world aren't the only creators of transformative works, and that in order to achieve the decolonial landscape of the imagination that we seek, we must broaden our lens beyond inclusion within dominant frameworks and move toward analyses and critiques that are one small step for a fan, one giant leap for all fankind.

THE MAKING OF THIS EDITED COLLECTION has been a long and challenging process. After I initially proposed the project, I was convinced that I had bitten off far more than I could chew. And indeed, at many points in this journey, that definitely seemed to be the case. Challenges came not just from the process of putting together the collection itself but also from the increasingly turbulent social and political events around the globe. Even as I put the finishing touches on these acknowledgments, students in India—my current geographic location—are leading the resistance against very troubling crackdowns by the state. Though they are not part of this project in an overt way, their spirit certainly suffuses all my work at the moment, and so I think it is appropriate to thank them for their courage and perseverance here.

Further, as I make the final edits to this collection, I must also mark the havoc being wreaked across the world by the COVID-19 pandemic. Among the almost incalculable loss of lives and livelihoods, I would like to use this space to acknowledge the fact that the toll of this global tragedy on higher education will be disproportionately borne by those least equipped to handle it. I therefore register my personal note of mourning for all the marvelous work on race and racism in fan studies that will now be inevitably delayed or, in some cases, abandoned. It is my hope that readers of this book—as one of the lucky manuscripts that did make it to publication—will make greater efforts to boost critical voices who now have even more hurdles to overcome to be heard.

I would also like to thank the series editors at the University of Iowa Press, Kathy Larsen and Paul Booth, for their patience and their extremely helpful advice through the process. I'm very grateful to my coordinating editor, Meredith Stabel, for keeping everything on track even in trying times! My deep gratitude also goes out to the peer reviewers of the manuscript, whose insightful feedback made this volume infinitely stronger. And of course this volume would not have been possible at all without the wonderful work of all its contributors, and I would like to thank them for their excellent scholarship and for trusting me to steer this ambitious project to fruition.

Finally, I'd like to thank my family—Amma, Devika, Radhika, and Naina—without whose unwavering support and belief I would never be able to move forward in the world.

AMONG THE ISSUES THAT INEVITABLY ARISE in a book such as *Fandom, Now in Color* are disputes around language, particularly when it comes to labels and descriptors. Individuals may adopt or resist specific identifiers for a variety of reasons, including geographic location, language use, and geopolitics. In order to accommodate these varying claims, I have included this explanatory note. The use of these terms is specific to each contributor and in no way can be taken as universally agreed upon.

Color-blind/postracial: Nonacknowledgement of race is commonly referred to as race blindness or color blindness. However, in this book we have chosen to avoid the term due to its ableist roots and use the term "postracial" where possible instead.

Hispanic: This term is used in the context of the United States. The census exercise has defined it as referring to a person of Cuban, Mexican, Puerto Rican, South or Central American, or other Spanish culture or origin. In recent years, there has been some dispute about its usage, because it is seen as having been imposed by government authority and also because of its association with Spanish colonialism. Within this book, some individuals chose it as a self-identifying label.

Latina, Latino: These terms have been used within this book to refer to Latin American inhabitants of the United States, distinguishing Latin Americans living in North America from those living south of the border.

Latinidad: The Real Academia Española specifies that the word "Latinidad" can be used to refer both to *tradición cultural latina* (Latina cultural tradition) and to *conjunto de los pueblos latinos* (the body of Latino peoples).

Person of color/nonwhite: There are numerous issues with the terms "person of color" and "nonwhite." Each uses whiteness as a monolith by which to define itself and subsumes all other ethnicities into a singular Other, regardless of their specificity and historicity. However, due to the complexities of the ethnicities represented and the lack of time and space within which to flesh out a singular argument for each, we have chosen to use the general terms, and we apologize for any offense.

FANDOM, NOW IN COLOR

Introduction

TO ANNOUNCE A COLLECTION ON RACE, racism, and racial identity in fandom is to be immediately confronted with a series of questions. What exactly does each term mean? In what context are race and racial identity being discussed? Are Western-centric, generalized, and essentialist categorizations such as white and nonwhite being taken as the default? What kinds and forms of fandom are being encompassed within such a description? Can the operations of a category as slippery and controversial as racial identity be mapped with any degree of accuracy in today's transnational and globalized world? What about the intersections of race with other aspects of identity like gender, sexuality, class, religion, and disability? There obviously cannot be any one satisfactory answer to all these questions. Nor should there be. In line with this approach, *Fandom, Now in Color* offers multiple answers to each of these questions. Each answer in turn pushes the boundaries of the original questions significantly, seeking to displace not just binary divisions of identity but also assumptions about the circulation and intersections of power as well as the linear modes of representation in pop culture.

But perhaps it will be helpful to try to lay out at least what is meant by race and what is meant by fandom within this collection. To address the first part of this question, with regard to race, racism, and racial identity the essays in this volume emphasize the need to approach these categories as contingent, shifting, and localized. At the same time, they are also cognizant of the fact that these localized categories are structured by a hierarchy of power in the Global North that is progressively being allied with the logics of a globalized white supremacist identity politics. These logics are increasingly evident in different facets of geopolitics, from those at the level of international relations such as the implementation of Fortress Europe and the rising militarization of borders against immigrants as embodied by Donald Trump's Wall against Mexico to the increasing evidence of collusion among transnational white supremacist organizations, which coin terms like "white genocide" when referring to such issues as white farmers being asked to participate in reparative social justice in South Africa (Berg 2012; Daniels 2009; De Genova 2016; Giroux 2017; Linke 2010; Lipsitz 2006; Maskovsky 2017; McVeigh 2010).

This volume therefore balances the need to talk about location-specific modes of racialization as they intersect with questions of ethnonationalism, religion, and cultural identity and with their own specific histories as well as with the interactions of these modes with both intra- and intercultural exchanges as US-centric ideas of race are being globalized through multinational media distribution models. Indeed in some cases, as was seen in the explosion of cultural criticism around *Black Panther* in 2018 that was written by African American, African, and diasporic Black critics, *all* these facets can be relevant to the discussion at the same time (Haile 2018; Mehri 2018; Mohale 2018; Okeyo 2018; Serpell 2018).

To address the second part of the question, the contributors to this volume are cognizant of the ways in which the term "fandom" itself has been contested by fan scholars. These discussions have largely revolved around questions of attachment and approval (do antifans count as fans?), degrees of investment (what are the differences among audiences, consumers, and fans?), modes of fandom (what kinds of fandom are authorized and monetized?), and ways in which gender and sexuality influence all these questions (Alters 2007; Booth 2015b; Busse and Gray 2011; Coppa 2014; J. Gray 2005; Gray, Sandvoss, and Harrington 2007; Hills 2002; Sandvoss 2005; Stein 2015). However, what has been less attended to are the ways in which the discipline of fan studies itself has constructed a default referent for that term—mostly white fans located in the US and UK and organized around English-language texts. Other fans and fandoms are usually siloed off into categories like transnational and global fandom and seen to be somewhat othered by language, geographical location, or media text—K-pop fans in Brazil or fans of *Star Trek* in Russia, for example (Madrid-Morales and Lovric 2015; Mikhaylova 2012). Indeed, fans who depart from the default positioning even within anglophone fandoms are also marked off, such as Black cosplayers or Asian American comic book fans.

This is not to dismiss the importance of specific situated studies of these fans and fandoms—it is vital that their histories and practices be explored—but to point out that the whiteness of the default fan is rarely marked off. As Kristen Warner has pointed out, these logics order the "people who are allowed to be visible within fandom and imagined to be fans by the media industries" (2015a, 33). In response to these invisibilized yet extremely powerful structuring logics, perhaps the most radical step this collection attempts is to put vastly different modes and categories of fans and fandoms in conversation with each other without placing any in a default or privileged position. The fandoms taken up for consideration include those around films (including documentaries), television shows, theater, video games, and music. This diversity also extends to the modes of fan activity being explored, which span cosplay, tabletop gaming, the creation of fan fiction, racebending, fan meetups, meet and greets, and so on. Inevitably, there are some omissions, traditional sports fandoms being one of them, but I hope that the scholarship showcased in these chapters will provide contexts and linkages to scholars studying those spaces as well.

This volume is by no means the first examination of either fans of color or fandoms of color. There has been a rich tradition of work on non-white audiences and consumers of popular media, both within and outside anglophone cultures (Benwell, Procter, and Robinson 2012; Bobo 1995; Carrington 2016; Gopinath 2000; H. Gray 2004; Punathambekar 2007; Puri 1997; Rao 2007; Smith-Shomade 2013). However, it is equally true that the simultaneous presence and absence of race as an analytical category within fan studies as a discipline are glaring. This has been noted with increasing frequency in contemporary scholarship. Rebecca Wanzo has named race as that which "troubles the claims—and desires—at the heart of fan studies scholars and their scholarship," while Benjamin Woo has called it a "yawning void" (Wanzo 2015; Woo 2017). I have described whiteness as an "unexamined structuring force" in work on media fandom (Pande 2018a 13). In the editorial of a special issue of *Transformative Works and Cultures*, Abigail De Kosnik and andré carrington also affirm as "indisputable" the fact that "fan studies was founded, and has been dominated up to this point, by white scholars" (2019). Henry Jenkins has called the present stage a moment of reckoning as the field struggles with these critiques (2019).

Despite these repeated affirmations, this acknowledgment is certainly not universal within the field, and there is very little consensus around what concrete efforts the discipline needs to take, if any, toward decolonizing itself. Indeed, there cannot be only one approach to such a project. The first impulse has been an increase in attention to work by scholars like those just mentioned. This is certainly a necessary and important step, but it can also create the impression that due to the hypervisibility of some scholars, who are still in a minority and whose work is still seen as new, the problem can be considered solved. It is therefore vital to trace on which aspects of scholarship this emergent attention to race is being registered most clearly and where it is seen to be less urgent.

Race is seen to be relevant to an analysis of fandom only when controversy entails overt and identifiable racist behavior—Gamergate, for example, or the targeting of nonwhite actors such as Kelly Marie Tran or Leslie Jones—or when the fans or fandoms under analysis are explicitly framed as nonwhite—Bollywood, for example (Desta 2018; Punathambekar 2005). Equally crucially, this kind of scholarship is then seen to be significant only to similar studies rather than making an impact on the foundational texts of fan studies. For instance, while the work of Henry Jenkins or Matt Hills or Kristina Busse is seen as universally relevant and indeed crucial to new fan studies scholarship, despite focusing primarily on white fans in anglophone fandoms, it is very possible to go through an entire monograph or special issue of a journal or edited collection and not come across any work by scholars like Jacqueline Bobo. This is not to slight the aforementioned scholars, whose work is indeed critical, but to point out how the logics of whiteness structure the assumptions of both fans and scholars in these spaces. Therefore, while work on nonwhite fans and fandoms has certainly proliferated, it is important to recognize the contexts within which it is being circulated.

The second impulse adheres to what Sara Ahmed has termed a politics of declarations of whiteness (2004). This may take multiple forms, but here I will discuss it as a practice of deferral. This occurs when scholars, usually at the beginning of their presentations or essays, declare an absence or footnoting of race in their analysis. As a rhetorical strategy, this implies that discussing race as an analytical category, while important, does not intersect meaningfully with the aspects of identity (usually gender and sexuality) that they *do* discuss. This is demonstrably inaccurate, as has been established by decades of critical scholarship (Bailey 2012; Barnard 2004; Bérubé 2001; Frankenberg 1993; Hull, Bell-Scott, and Smith 1982; Moreton-Robinson 2000; Thomlison 2012). Of course, this continued elision is possible only when the same logics continue to structure publishing practices with white research supervisors, peer reviewers, and editors failing to push back against such assumptions and thus reinforcing hierarchies of citation.

This ties into another impulse, what Mel Stanfill, among others, has called the unbearable whiteness of the field, which is maintained by a refusal to name it as such (2018). That is, white scholars continue to claim that they are not equipped to talk about race or that it is not their place to engage in these discussions. However, by doing so they (re)establish whiteness as the default and ignore the fact that it is also a racialized identity that has a key effect on their research. Ironically, this places the burden of making whiteness visible squarely on those scholars who wish to engage with questions of nonwhiteness, especially within the anglocentric fandoms that have formed the core canons of the field. In my personal capacity as a scholar whose work on race has received attention, I am often told by my white colleagues that they also hold back from such engagements for fear of "getting it wrong" and therefore becoming a target of criticism. To that I would point out that nonwhite scholars run an equal risk of being criticized for their analyses, especially because fans of color are not a homogeneous group but instead have many conflicting and contested opinions, any one of which can become a flash point for debate. Indeed, I would argue that nonwhite scholars often struggle with an increased burden of "getting it right" because their own overlapping identities are erroneously seen to give them unique insights.

In the chapters that follow, each section heading articulates a focal point that brings multiple, seemingly different projects into conversation with each other and with the field as a whole. The authors in the first section, "Methodologies," seek to continue the critical interventions by previous scholars that have exposed the undeclared whiteness of fan studies genealogies. One of the most important ways to address this gap is for fan scholars to widen their knowledge of the theoretical frameworks that produce nuanced studies of fans and fandoms. It is also important to understand that frameworks that center approaches like critical race studies and postcolonial theory are relevant and powerful tools to use when approaching *any* fandom space, not just those marked off in some way. This collection aims to demonstrate this through case studies that insist on foregrounding the operations of race, racism, and racial identity (including whiteness) in diverse fandom spaces, including the classroom.

The first chapter, Elizabeth Hornsby's "A Case for Critical Methods: Sense Making, Race, and Fandom," uses methodologies grounded in critical race theory to analyze the online fandom of the US television show *Sleepy Hollow*. Hornsby draws upon Brenda Dervin's theoretical framework of sense making to examine fan reactions to flash point situations around the show's treatment of its nonwhite characters, particularly Abbie Mills (Nicole Beharie). She approaches race as a "meaning-making agent" in the fandom to disrupt "the idea that affect toward the object supersedes personal, cultural, and societal identification." Because fandom so often sees race only as relevant to discussions around nonwhite characters, it is crucial to be able to parse the ways in which these discussions proceed. Through the use of a multisited methodology to analyze interview data as proposed in the sense-making framework, Hornsby argues that race is unembedded and challenged instead of remaining unexamined.

Next, in a move outside what is constructed as traditional fan studies, Sam Pack disrupts multiple disciplinary boundaries in his analysis of differential audience reactions to four films about the Navajo people of North America. Pack pushes hard against the boundaries of whom and what can be considered to be fans and fandom, but his discussion of authorship, authenticity, and affective engagement expands these categories both productively and provocatively. This chapter also provides the opportunity for fan scholars to reflect on their own preconceptions of whom they consider to be legitimate examples of fans and engaged audiences. When it comes to looking at ideas of reception, audiences, and fandom with regard to underrepresented communities (or indeed communities that have never been seen as fans), I believe that scholars need to become almost radically creative and flexible in order to expand the discipline. Any discomfort around whether this chapter fits into the overall scope of this collection is therefore a very necessary one. Pack's use of a methodology of ethnographic reception studies also intersects with how anthropologists and other scholars could approach media studies, while bringing these ideas into conversation with fan studies by interrogating notions of "us" within imagined communities of fans and audiences.

In the final chapter in this section, "The Absence of Race: Teaching Practices and Inclusion in the Fandom Classroom," Katherine Anderson Howell examines the ways in which whiteness can operate within pedagogical practices, particularly those that use methodologies, texts, and conceptual framings sourced from fans and fan studies. This study is situated in the context of US higher education and provides an insightful case study into the ways in which, once again, whiteness works to invisibilize itself in formal educational structures. Howell's self-reflexive methodology, as well as her inclusion of nonwhite student voices, makes the piece a truly multivocal reflection on which modes of reading, writing, and thinking can be assumed to be deracialized and which ones are never given that unmarked space.

The second section of this collection, "Otherness," focuses on how fandom participants negotiate insider-outsider status in physical spaces where their embodied selves are often subject to differential modes of racialization. Fans are often seen as othered bodies that disrupt normative ideas of appropriate behavior in public spaces. The figure of the screaming fangirl at pop music concerts is a common example. However, the reactions to specific bodies that carry further markers of otherness—pertaining to race in this case but also intersecting with ideas of disability, fatness, and so on—by fellow fans, public authorities, and the media at large vary vastly. This section seeks to interrogate these variations further.

The first study, "Raceplay: Whiteness and Erasure in Cross-Racial Cosplay" by joan miller, relocates ideas of embodiment, authenticity, and appropriation to the context of transnational cosplay communities that focus on characters in US-based media texts. Specifically, miller takes up the problematics of literally embodying the Other in terms of racial identity by taking on the personae and appearances of popular characters in fandom. Due to the fact that the fan body and its public presentation are core aspects of cosplay, its fandoms have frequently been at the forefront of debates around safety in collective fandom spaces, cultural appropriation, use of blackface and yellowface, and issues of harassment of nonwhite cosplayers both offline and online (Gooden 2016; Romano 2014; Stubblebine 2018; Sura 2018). For miller, the cosplay of canonically white characters by Black and Brown fans can be seen as a political act because it serves, ironically, to highlight the (so far) invisible whiteness of the original. By taking up cases of both white fans and fans of color engaging in cross-racial performances, she explores the ways in which these moments can lead to either an expansion or a foreclosure of understanding of racial identities within transnational communities. Once again, the circulation of images that carry US-centric racialized categories through globalized media flows is an important aspect of this discussion.

Next, Miranda Ruth Larsen's chapter, "'But I'm a Foreigner Too': Otherness, Racial Oversimplification, and Historical Amnesia in Japan's K-pop Scene," rounds off this part of the collection by tracing the ways in which racialized interactions in this transcultural fandom are shaped significantly by histories of conflict, colonization, and uneven contemporary geopolitical relations while they continue to overlap with circulations of whiteness as aspirational. Larsen argues that due to Japan's strong monocultural ethos, both the male Korean idols who perform there and the perceptions of their female fans are shaped by particular racial, xenophobic, and patriarchal scripts. Indeed, the fans themselves often further reinforce these scripts in their interactions with the idols. Larsen's carefully situated analysis draws attention to the ways in which modes of othering can proceed along seemingly contradictory lines of attraction and repulsion, functioning both as an impulse toward ridicule and as objectification. Her mediation of her own position as a multiracial, visibly othered body in Japan and the reception of her specifically nonwhite American identity are also key parts of her analysis. Indeed, many of the authors in this volume have reflected on the ways in which their own raced identities as fans, researchers, and participants in these spaces mediate their work significantly.

The next set of chapters is grouped under the title "Affirmative/ Transformative." This division in approaches to modes of fannishness was first articulated by a fan, obsession_inc (she used the terms "affirmational/ transformational"). This framing has been taken up by scholars of fan fiction, fan art, podfic, and so on. In this construction, members of affirmative fandoms are "creator-centric" and do not wish to engage in fanwork that changes the relationships, characters, and worldbuilding of a narrative text. In contrast, members of transformational fandoms engage in full-scale changes and are "all about laying hands upon the source and twisting it to the fans' own purpose" (obsession_inc 2009). This was also elaborated by another fan, Skud, who argued that affirmative fandoms are associated with male fans (broadly) attached to notions of hierarchy and faithfulness to a particular authorized canon; transformative fandoms were marked by female participants interested in fanwork that revises source material in various ways (Skud n.d.). These categories were also discussed by Karen Hellekson and Kristina Busse, who saw fans in transformative modes as engaging more actively and taking "creative" steps "to make the worlds and characters their own" (2014, 3–4). This division has since been complicated by scholars like Matt Hills in his coinage of mimetic fandom, while others like Henry Jenkins have pointed out that male-centered fandoms may seek to transform texts in ways that further ally them with patriarchal codes (Hills 2014; Jenkins and Scott 2013).

An example of this was seen when a fan produced "*The Last Jedi* De-Feminized Fanedit." This was, as is perhaps obvious, a version of the film *The Last Jedi* that cut out all the female characters of the original (Cooper 2018). In response, another cut of the film, this time with all its male characters removed, was also produced (Ferber 2018). While both versions created controversy, the latter was broadly seen as a progressive production. However, one of the problems with the no-men version of the film was that it lost a significant portion of its central characters of color, most notably Poe (Oscar Isaac) and Finn (John Boyega), since the *Star Wars* franchise has an abysmal record of casting women of color. This incident puts into focus the problems with the overt linkage of positivity and subversion to transformative fandom and its associated fan spaces, which are assumed to be dominated by fans who are white women and white people of marginalized genders. While the second cut of the film arguably was made in response to an overt act of sexism, it must be noted that the transformative fandom of the newest *Star Wars* trilogy had already elevated even its tertiary white characters over its nonwhite leads in fanwork (Pande 2018a). Poe Johnson has also provocatively argued that even the simple inclusion of Black bodies and characters into fanwork without careful reflection on the histories of their representation in US pop culture holds the potential for continuing the legacies of violence and minstrelsy embedded in those histories (2019).

It is in these contexts that the chapters in this section make their arguments around the intersection of race, racism, and racial identity in the creation of stand-alone fanworks as well as through the "playing" of racialized scripts in tabletop gaming. In "Alpha/Beta/Omega: Racialized Narratives and Fandom's Investment in Whiteness," Angie Fazekas takes up a specific genre of slash fan fiction that focuses on romantic and sexual relationships between cisgender male characters: that of the omegaverse. Omegaverse stories, which are extremely popular, have been analyzed around themes of its largely (white) female creators and creators of marginalized genders exploring gender identity and essentialism as well as the effects of rape culture (Busse 2013). Its roots can be traced to the *Supernatural* fandom—which seems to be the case for many things in contemporary fandom spaces—but omegaverse stories have now crossed cultural and linguistic boundaries.

It must be noted that omegaverse stories are also written around cisgender female characters. However, the specific focus of Fazekas's analysis is on anglophone and slash fandoms. She argues that the genre's promise of "queer futurity" is foreclosed by its whiteness—not just in terms of its overwhelming focus on white characters but also through its mobilization of tropes around slavery narratives (Muñoz 2009). This, she states, "effectively decenters the lived experiences of Black people, trivializes historical and intergenerational trauma, and foregrounds white feelings and experiences within a specifically racialized narrative." By also interrogating survey results, her analysis effectively demonstrates the importance of interrogating the stories that fans tell on multiple axes, as those occupying marginalized positions can and do replicate structures of white supremacy while laying claim to a broader progressive politics.

Next, Indira Neill Hoch advances the conversation to focus on the activities of anglophone video game fans and fandoms through the construct of the original female character (OFC), also known (somewhat derogatorily) as the Mary Sue. Hoch's analysis reflects on the imminent failure associated with the figure of the Mary Sue in fandom more generally and how this continues to influence perceptions even in video game fandom, where it could be assumed that the creation of original characters is an integral part of fan practice. As she argues, the nonwhite OFC occupies an even more vulnerable position in this frame. Hoch takes up her own fanwork and experiences in the *Dragon Age* fandom to explore how racial scripts continue to shape the ways that OFCs are allowed to function within a narrative. As she notes, the burden of racialization is almost always placed on nonwhite OFCs, who then must indicate this difference from the established white norm in some overt way.

In the following chapter, "Waiting in the Wings: Inclusivity and the Limits of Racebending," Samira Nadkarni and Deepa Sivarajan continue the conversation around the complexities of "playing" with identity categories in fanwork by focusing on the fandom around Lin-Manuel Miranda's hit musical, *Hamilton: An American Musical*. The discourse around *Hamilton* as a text has moved through various stages, from rapturous praise of its subversive postracial casting to criticism around its brownwashing of historical personalities who owned slaves and participated in atrocities against Native American peoples (McAllister 2017; Monteiro 2016; Nathans 2017). Nadkarni and Sivarajan use this frame to examine the fandom practice of racebending, in which characters of one racial identity (usually white) in a canonical text are reimagined as having another. Racebending has been broadly seen to be a subversive practice because it can question the white default and reframe assumedly universal white narratives around the specific experiences of nonwhite people in societies where they occupy marginalized positions (Fowler 2019; Pande 2018a). However, as Nadkarni and Sivarajan note, racebending in fandom can also participate in a flattening out of identity, where simple inclusion is valued over the questioning of the dominant societal structures that continue to operate in subcultural spaces. This creates scenarios "wherein identity is both presented and abstracted on these raced bodies, creating them as interchangeable and nonspecific." This flattening out can also extend to a playing down of tensions and histories of violence between nonwhite and Western cultures to appeal to a largely toothless sense of racial liberalism. The chapter takes up trends in the fanwork created around *Hamilton* to examine these threads of critique further.

The final chapter in this section, by Carina Lapointe, takes up the idea of fan play and the potential (re)fashioning of racial scripts thereby within the constructs of the popular tabletop role-playing game *Dungeons and Dragons*. As Lapointe argues, through the influence of fantasy writers such as J. R. R. Tolkien, *D&D*'s narrative universe draws upon very specific racialized scripts for both its initial framing of fantasy races and their subsequent roles within gameplay through the assigning of innate characteristics, abilities, behaviors, and so on. She traces the tension between the structures of the game itself, with its established conventions and narrative movements, and the rules established around interactivity and what counts as success, which often reinforce reductive and stereotypical racial associations with various characters. However, the open-endedness of gameplay itself can also enable the interrogation and subversion of these rules. Lapointe examines the work of R. A. Salvatore, an influential fan-turned-writer for the *D&D* universe, to trace the latter potential in more detail. Salvatore is also an interesting example of a fan and author troubling the affirmative/transformative categories of fan activity.

The fourth and last section is titled "Identity/Authenticity." As I write this introduction, it seems that both fan spaces and fan scholars are grappling with increased levels of conflict around questions that broadly concern identity and representation and how these interact with shifting ideas of authenticity. These conflicts mirror, to some extent, struggles taking place in broader sociocultural arenas—from the rise of right-wing populist rhetoric in global politics and anxieties around differential gender and sexual identities to debates around the role of homonationalist discourses in the advancement of neo-imperialist agendas, to name only a few (Bhushan 2015; Puar 2007). None of these struggles is new, but their increased visibility in the shaping of geopolitics on a global scale makes them seem more urgent than ever before. I do not wish to make direct connections between these vastly heterogeneous and complex issues and the debates currently seen as urgent in fandom, but there is certainly a similarity in the kinds of anxiety being articulated in these spaces around fan identity, notions of belonging and communities, ownership of media texts, and ideas of representation. Indeed, these threads have been taken up in some way by multiple scholars in this collection already. However, in this section, these ideas take center stage.

The first chapter questions the ways in which ideas of representation and authenticity are being debated in fandom spaces that have been seen to value a more progressive or radical politics, such as those formed around the production and circulation of queer fanwork. In "Whose Representation Is It Anyway? Contemporary Debates in Femslash Fandoms," Swati Moitra and I highlight the fault lines within these fandoms as both queer white and queer nonwhite characters gain (some) ground in the canons of pop culture texts. Through our examination of incidents in the fandoms of *The 100*, *Black Lightning*, and *Supergirl*, we argue that fans often use "representation matters" as a catchphrase to support specific characters or romantic relationships but that this often papers over the contested nature of notions of representation and authenticity. These notions also interface with questions of racial identity in differential fashions that cannot be traced in a linear analysis. Some conflicts are sparked by the continual marginalization of queer women of color, both in terms of fanwork and in physical spaces such as "inclusive" convention environments. Others concern the narratives of "authentic" racial casting, where showrunners (and sometimes fans themselves) engage in a flattening out of racial, cultural, and ethnic specificities in their discourse. Therefore, while "representation matters" remains a powerful idea, this chapter argues that it is time for fan studies scholars to push past this claim to interrogate *whose* representation gets the most traction both in primary texts and within fandom spaces.

In the next chapter, "Jane the Virgen or Virgin? The Dis-United States of (Latino) Fandom," Jenni Lehtinen examines the multiple fandoms of the US-produced television show *Jane the Virgin*. She throws light on the ways in which racial, cultural, ethnic, and linguistic identities interact with the reception and interpretation of specific genres of popular media. This is especially true when US-centric texts circulate through globalized media flows. Lehtinen argues that the show's depiction of Latino identity—implied by plot structure as well as by linguistic, social, and religious references— is often contradictory. These contradictions then play out in the fandoms of the show, and the linguistic politics in particular plays a crucial role in shaping intrafandom hierarchies. Lehtinen's study is also illuminating because it traces the ways in which fandoms of a single text, even when divided by language, continue to influence and interact with each other. This is an important step because, too often, researchers tend to approach these linguistic divides as being totally separate.

In the next chapter, McKenna James Boeckner, Monica Flegel, and Judith Leggatt also interrogate fandom conflicts around identity, this time in the US-centered Marvel Comics fandom. The context for the study is the backlash against the so-called diversity push seen in 2015, when Marvel Comics announced that it would be diversifying its original (mostly white and male) lineup by focusing on characters like Miles Morales (Spider-Man), Kamala Khan (Ms. Marvel), and Sam Wilson (who would take up the shield of Captain America), among others. Boeckner, Flegel, and Leggatt examine the ways in which fans opposed to this move framed their objections in terms of charges of forced identity politics and bad writing, while being anxious to maintain that they were not motivated by racism or misogyny (or both!). The chapter delves into fan narratives as constructed in comment sections and fan forums and performs an important example of discourse analysis that pushes past fan claims to make the underlying ideological arguments more explicit.

In the last chapter, Al Valentín turns to the world of anglophone Let's Play videos on YouTube—the part of video game fandom in which gamers post streams of gameplay as well as reviews and personal content. Let's Play has become a highly lucrative and influential part of fan cultures and has been in the eye of several storms (Burgess and Matamoros-Fernández 2016; Chess and Shaw 2015). Valentín argues that success in Let's Play videos is highly determined by how closely gamers can adhere to notions of authenticity that dictate who is a "true" gamer. Unsurprisingly, these scripts are highly influenced by factors such as race, gender, and sexuality. This is seen not just in the success of gamers who present as white and male but also in the reproduction of these scripts by gamers who are in a marginalized position in Let's Play culture due to some aspect of their identity. Valentín also traces the importance of examining YouTube's algorithms as active agents in how fandom cultures often function on the platform by promoting the harassment and toxicity that drive engagement metrics.

The contributors to this collection are in conversation with all the intersecting and seemingly contradictory narratives around the (in)visibility of race, racism, and racial identity in fandom and fan studies. They undertake differential tactics of decolonization: diversifying methodologies, destabilizing canons of must-read scholarship by engaging with multiple disciplines, making whiteness visible but not the default against which all other kinds of racialization must compete, decentering white fans even in those fandoms where they are the assumed majority, and showcasing models of fan behavior that question the validity of divisions between transformational and curatorial fandoms as well as the valorization ascribed to the former. Although no model of categorization can be complete, I hope that readers will discover connections among all of them.

ONE. METHODOLOGIES

1. A Case for Critical Methods

Sense Making, Race, and Fandom

ELIZABETH R. HORNSBY

CONVERGENCE CULTURE HAS ALLOWED the practice of fandom to explode in online spaces. Online fan communities are ever-growing sites of social construction and participatory culture. Fandom functions in the wider context of socially constructed realities, and fans find points of identification across multiple social identities. Because of this, examining how participation in fandom affects and is affected by social identity needs to be a crucial part of fandom scholarship (Duffett 2013a). Fandom has been researched in terms of a collective othering operating outside the normalized power structures (Jenkins 1992). Social discourse concerning fandom culturally constructs fans as white, even though existing research shows that this does not hold true (Bacon-Smith and Yarbrough 1991; Coppa 2006; Jenkins 1992; Stanfill 2011). Scholarship focusing specifically on issues of race, culture, and ethnic identity has challenged issues of othering and marginalization within fandom (Carrington 2016; Pande 2016a, 2018a; Wanzo 2015; Warner 2015b; Woo 2017). Furthermore, scholars are addressing issues of transcultural and transnational fandom, again expanding the notion of who and what constitutes fandom (Chin and Morimoto 2013; H. K. Lee 2016).

Media and community are each powerful agents in the meaning-making process. Combined, they are formidable in creating a space where culture can be constructed, reconstructed, and deconstructed for fans. Henry Jenkins and Lisa Lewis pioneered the research situating fandom in the audience as a community concept. In Jenkins's description of fan cultures, he describes how a fan's relationship with a television show serves as the foundation for participation in a fan community, which serves as a site of meaning making and interpretation. The concept of fandom as a community has become even more complex as fandom communities have moved online. The internet has made fandom communities more easily accessible and has also provided a rich research site (Andrejevic 2008; Baym 2000; Jenkins 2006; Shefrin 2004). Kristen Warner, in her article discussing ABC's *Scandal* and Black women's fandom, emphasizes the distinction between "fandom as a space for the othered and marginalized and fandom as a space for common interests untethered to race, culture, or identity" (2015a, 34). Benjamin Woo explicitly addresses the empirical and ideological work that has led to the invisibility of race, culture, and identity in fan discourse (2017).

The convergence of the internet and media is most visible in media fandom, resulting in a productive and distinctive culture; however, this culture does not erase racial identity. Fandom is not devoid of the personal or the politics of identity; conversely, fandom is filtered through identity, which includes a racial lens. Studying fans allows us to explore how interactions with mediated worlds intersect with "our social, political, and cultural realities and identities" (Gray, Sandvoss, and Harrington 2007, 10).

In this chapter, I suggest sense-making methodology as a way to examine fans' meaning-making experiences to interrogate the racial politics embedded in fandom through individual narratives, which describe specific situations or moments within an online fan community. Using Brenda Dervin's theoretical framework of sense making as it pertains to media provides a structure for rich, qualitative inquiry into the meaning-making practices of media consumers and addresses some of the issues concerning fans and race. Sense making allows audience members to place themselves in the context of the larger media collective and articulate the experiences that occur in those spaces (Reinhard and Dervin 2009). Sense making's emphasis on the politics of identity and location provides a framework for investigating racial constructs as they relate to meaning making. First, I briefly discuss the design of my own research project with fans of the television series *Sleepy Hollow*. Next, I discuss the intersection of the sense-making interview data and race. Finally, I discuss ethical considerations in undertaking sense-making research and reflect on my own personal experiences conducting this research.

—Welcome to *Sleepy Hollow*

Sleepy Hollow (2013–2017) premiered on the Fox network on September 16, 2013, as a supernatural drama series centered on the life of Revolutionary War hero Ichabod Crane and police officer Abigail Mills. In the first season, the television series was critically acclaimed not only for its story lines but also for its racially diverse cast, specifically the casting of African American actor Nicole Beharie as Abigail Mills. The series quickly developed an active online following in part fostered by cast member Orlando Jones. The second season was marred with controversy highlighted both in fan communities and in television criticism as story lines began to center more on Ichabod Crane and his white wife and less on Abigail Mills. Tensions hit maximum levels when news broke that Orlando Jones would not be returning for season 3 of the series.

Sleepy Hollow and its subsequent fandom provided the perfect situation to examine the racial politics of fandom as it relates to fans using race as an act of meaning making. Of particular interest was how the first season's accolades regarding diversity and the second season's criticism concerning lack of care for the diverse cast created a situation for race to be used as a meaning-making agent (Fitzgerald and Marquez 2015; Prudom 2013). Fandom here is imagined as media fandom, more specifically as the online interactions of people connected by affect toward media objects. This is a very generalist approach to fandom; however, this is intentional. I want to highlight the fact that even in the most generous interpretations of what constitutes fandom, issues of race, culture, and identity are still present. Particularly, I hope to continue the work of disrupting the idea that affect toward an object supersedes personal, cultural, and societal identification.

Borrowing from the research of Laurence Parker and William Tate, I used the sense-making interviews to specifically locate the intersection of racial discourse and the sense-making process of *Sleepy Hollow*'s fans, most located in the United States. I attempted to go beyond the dimensions derived from sense making to accentuate the fans' "voices or experiences" as a way to "name [their] reality" (Ladson-Billings 1998, 13). What I found was that fans from diverse ethnicities brought their experiences, prejudices, and ideological lenses to the fan experience and discursively created a space for meaning making in terms of making sense of *Sleepy Hollow* as well as contextualizing the fan discussions within the larger social discourse.

—Methodology

Brenda Dervin's sense-making methodology has developed since its 1983 presentation. Sense-making methodology is both a participatory and a dialogic methodology based on the premise that communication is a series of participatory and dialogic steps (Dervin 2008). Dervin's sense-making work is grounded in the disciplines of communication and information science but is used as method, methodology, and metatheory across disciplines (Dervin 1998). Sense making is based on the idea that humans seek information when they experience discontinuity or a gap. To make sense of the discontinuity or bridge the gap, individuals will seek out information, revise methods, and search for new approaches to help build the bridge. Sense-making methodology consists of the following key concepts: the situation involved, the gap encountered, the bridge constructed, and the helps or utilities that resulted in bridging the gap. Five dimensions are typically used to categorize sense-making methodology data: past experiences, expectations, questions, helps, and hindrances.

Critical race theory is considered both a modern and a postmodern approach that involves the following tenets: counterstorytelling (Matsuda 1995), permanence of racism (Bell 1992; Harris 1995), whiteness as property (Harris 1995), interest convergence (Bell 1980), and the critique of liberalism (Crenshaw 1988). I used it to further interrogate the sense-making data provided in the interviews, shifting the focus from experience to racialized experiences.

I conducted sense-making interviews with self-identified fans of *Sleepy Hollow* located mainly in the United States as part of a larger research project. Of the 40 participants, 24 (60%) were female and 16 were male (40%). The sample was ethnically diverse, with 10 participants (25%) identifying as Caucasian, 12 (30%) as African American, 8 (20%) as Hispanic, 8 (20%) as Asian, 1 (2.5%) as Indian Canadian, and 1 (2.5%) as Somalian. With regard to education, 25 individuals (62.5%) had a college degree; 5 (12.5%) had an advanced degree or were currently in pursuit of an advanced degree; and 10 (25%) had attended some college. Their ages ranged from eighteen to sixty-plus. I interviewed participants who lived in New York, New Jersey, California, and Louisiana face to face. Due to the locations of the remaining participants—Florida, Canada, Colorado, Wisconsin, Sweden, Massachusetts, Idaho, Michigan, France, North Carolina, Kansas, and Pennsylvania—I conducted phone, email, or Skype interviews with them.

Using sense-making methodology as my guide, I asked fans to recall specific experiences pertaining to *Sleepy Hollow* during seasons 1 and 2. The interviews were open-ended, which encouraged fans to construct a view of reality from their own perspectives. I probed their responses, focusing on gaps, bridges, and helps so that each fan could construct the event and its personal significance.

In my research, the five dimensions frequently used in sense-making methodology emerged, though I deviated from CarrieLynn Reinhard and Brenda Dervin's 2012 research in that I combined past experiences and expectations because past experiences were intrinsically tied to future expectations. Issues related to racial identity expanded the conventional understanding of sense making. By examining how critical race theory complicates our understanding of sense making, the interviews provided insight into the "meanings and messages about race from the analysis and interpretation of the words" of the fans as they relate to *Sleepy Hollow* as well as insight into "sense-making on race in relation to the broader concept of race" (Evans 2007, 167).

—PAST EXPERIENCES AND EXPECTATIONS During the interviews, past experiences included not only the experiences fans had prior to the ones I asked about but also the expectations their experiences produced. Several fans discussed their previous interactions in other fandoms as predictive of their expectations. While most of the fans' discussions of past experiences and how they affected expectations focused on previous fandom or genre experiences, several fans specifically addressed issues of race. The lack of characters of color, specifically in science fiction, was consistently mentioned. I interviewed Jesse, an African American female, via telephone. (All names of the participants are pseudonyms per their requests.) Although Jesse briefly mentioned her previous fandom experiences with *Buffy the Vampire Slayer* (1997–2003), it was the lack of Black women in the *Buffy* series and the subsequent casting of Nicole Beharie as a co-lead in *Sleepy Hollow* that drove her expectations. Jesse specifically mentioned her excitement: "It's not often you have a nondamsel female lead in the horror-supernatural genre, at least not on mainstream TV, let alone an African American woman! The last one I can remember was when *Buffy* introduced the new slayer, but that was only for one episode, I believe."

Discussions of previous fan experiences also touched on how other fandoms such as *The Vampire Diaries* (2009–2017), *Doctor Who* (1963–present), and *Merlin* (2008–2012) seemingly disregarded race. Particularly, the fans of color I talked with discussed their experiences in previous fandoms stemming from the perceived mistreatment of characters of color versus the treatment of white characters as well as the treatment of advocates for characters of color in fandoms. For many fans of color, their experiences contributed to their hesitancy with regard to expectations of both the television series itself and the fandom. Jessica said, "I was scared . . . honestly. Black women have never been treated well in sci-fi or in sci-fi fandoms. I was nervous about how the writers, viewers, and fans would treat Abbie Mills."

Interview discussions that focused on past experiences and how those experiences shaped expectations of both the television show and fandom interaction highlighted the multiple influences that constructed avenues for sense making. For most fans, previous exposure to science fiction television or fandom was the driving force in shaping expectations of *Sleepy Hollow* and its fandom. However, discussions of race were frequently mentioned during the interviews. Several fans felt that the lack of racial diversity in science fiction television shaped their expectations, attributing it to both individual and institutional racism. This coincides with what critical race theory describes as the permanence of racism. Other fans expected *Sleepy Hollow* to function as a form of counterstorytelling, a way for marginalized voices to be seen and heard on television in the characters of color and in the fandom. Past experiences and expectations shaped the questions that the fans formed while viewing and interacting online about *Sleepy Hollow*.

—QUESTIONS. The questions dimension derives from the sense-making methodology term "gaps." According to Reinhard and Dervin, gaps are "conceptualized operationally as confusions, desires, needs, questions, or any time a person is stopped, even if just momentarily, to consider what is potentially missing from what lies ahead" (2012, 42). In the interviews, most of the gaps—the questions—centered on depictions and discussions of race. Jennifer, a self-proclaimed superfan of *Sleepy Hollow*, was confused by how much race dominated discussions about the show: "During season 2, it seemed like all the talk about the show was about race. The media was talking about how Black Abbie was being replaced by white Katrina. Fans were mad at white fans that didn't like Abbie calling them racist."

While some fans were confused about why race was even an issue with regard to the television show and the fandom, other fans' questions stemmed from not understanding how other fans could *not* see the importance of race in the discussions. Leanne, a fan I interviewed in New York, placed her questions about Abbie's "diminishing role as a lead" in a broader context regarding the lack of diversity on television. She asked, "Why are characters of color considered interchangeable to some fans? Why do white people act like it's a crime to have a mostly or all POC cast when television is 99.9 percent white in the first place?" ("POC" stands for "people of color.") Leanne's questions exhibited a direct intersection of the critical race theory tenets and sense making. She addressed the permanence of racism within media institutions in that most decision makers in the television industry are white and tend to cater to white audiences outside of niche markets. Furthermore, she questioned postracial rhetoric by stating, "If white people are uncomfortable with seeing other races on TV that's the problem of white people and not POC. Just because you choose to live in a color-blind vacuum doesn't mean everyone else does. We shouldn't need permission or a reason to be represented on TV." Leanne's questions invite a critique of postracial attitudes, exposing them as a function of racism that reinforce racist thinking instead of dismantling it. Her comments point to the steady frustration of fans trying to address invisibility not only in the macrocosm of media institutions but also in the microcosm of the fan spaces they participate in.

Most of the fans' responses correlated with three tenets of critical race theory: permanence of racism, interest convergence, and the critique of liberalism. Several questions arose between the fans who could not understand the discussions regarding race and *Sleepy Hollow* versus the fans who could not understand dismissing the discussions of race and its impact on *Sleepy Hollow* and how fans responded to it. Oftentimes, the questions about race were framed using postracial rhetoric as a way to not see race and therefore not discuss it (Gotanda 1991). Some fans critiqued this ideology, in essence challenging the permanence of racism by actively unembedding race from the discourse. Finally, a set of questions emerged from the interviews that focused on what diversity means, how it is marketed, and how it works in media institutions. Here fans voiced the idea of interest convergence, in that the attention and labor dedicated to promoting diversity in the media occurred only in a way that benefited white network executives and white audiences.

—HELPS. The helps dimension deals with constructing bridges to overcome the gaps. For my interviews, the helps dimension involved what processes or steps the fans took to answer the questions that arose during their experiences. Questioning one's standpoint was a common method used by the fans to help answer their questions. Lisa discussed feeling "silenced" as an Asian American in society and in her fandom interactions: "People are more likely to be critical of women or people of color, but they will be a lot more critical of women of color. Listen first. Understand that your perspective is limited. Understand that there are times when your voice is not necessary."

Melissa, during our interview sessions, credited "POC-friendly spaces" for helping her interrogate the racial politics at work in the writing of the show as well as in the fandom. She credited the *Sleepy Hollow* and sub-set *Shady Hollow* online communities for exposing her to "something new every day, whether that's about a style of acting or an aspect of intersectional feminism or an incredibly filthy joke." She described the importance of inter-acting in the fandom, saying, "I am white and have spent most of my life in white-dominated spaces, [but] I've learned a huge amount from the women of color in the fandom about representation and racial politics. The things I've learned in the fandom are making me a better person in other parts of my life."

Fans also used advocacy as an active way to answer questions. Jamie noted how aggressively advocating for what she wanted was the best way to have her questions answered and overcome obstacles. Citing the "racial bias both in Hollywood and in the viewers," she strongly suggested advocacy as a way to get her questions answered: "I think that characters of color and the shows that feature them require more proactive participation and full-throated support than other shows." Jamie's advocacy stemmed from her belief that fans of color cannot afford to be passive about voicing their viewing tastes: "Fans can't just sit back and enjoy passively—that's a privilege for the viewer whose expectations are constantly catered to. So the life lesson is that racism and sexism have to be actively fought even in the most trivial and unexpected of places, like *Sleepy Hollow*." Advocacy is then reimagined as counterstorytelling, as a way for marginalized voices to be seen and heard. Advocating for diversity in *Sleepy Hollow* was then transformed into advocating for diverse television media in general, and counterstorytelling was used as a form of pushback against the permanence of racism. For Jamie, campaigning for better treatment of Abbie showed that "we want diversity, and we're willing to fight to show the higher-ups in prime-time media that we are tired of seeing the same stories by the same kinds of people that are not reflective of our real life."

Several fans mentioned that exposure to the online discourse about race within the fan communities helped them answer their questions. This is not to say that all the fans embraced the discourse as productive—some fans felt that the constant discussions of race were futile. Regardless, the discussions helped answer individual questions about the importance of race as well as issues of diversity.

—HINDRANCES. Originally termed "hurts" in Brenda Dervin's 1983 presentation, the hindrance dimension deals with the gaps that are not bridged. In later discussions of the dimensions of sense making, the term "hindrance" is used instead of "hurt" (Dervin and Frenette 2003). For my research, I used "hindrance" instead of "hurt" as a way to neutralize any hegemonic connotation the term might invoke in the context of racialized discourse. "Hurt" in this context could be inferred as "victimization," a label I as a researcher was not comfortable implying, nor did the data suggest it.

The comments that fell into the hindrance dimension dealt with stumbling blocks to sense making more than hurts.

As seen earlier, online interaction provided a help to answer questions for some fans; for other fans, it was a hindrance. Jacob, in our interview session, discussed how during the first and second seasons of *Sleepy Hollow*, his activity online was limited because he did not want a ton of outside voices to cloud his view of the show. He limited his participation in the fandom to creating and posting fan art on Tumblr but did not interact with other people. However, when describing his current online interaction, he discussed how increasing his online participation hindered his understanding of what was going on. For Jacob, season 2 left him "bewildered" in terms of the confusing narrative shift from "what made season 1 so great." After a brief online hiatus after the season 2 finale, he reentered the fandom hoping to find some answers to the questions he had regarding the previous season, only to be met with "a clusterfuck of people being called racist and haters and it was all just too much." For Jacob, the environment of the fandom was "just too toxic." When I asked him if he ever got his questions answered, he responded that he had not. Jacob's perspective highlighted a gendered aspect of the research in that most of the male-identifying fans I spoke with felt this way. Although gender was not the focus of my research, future investigation into how gender and race intersect in terms of sense making is warranted.

Jamie found that the overuse of certain terms, even if well intentioned, hindered the overcoming of obstacles and prevented questions from being answered because they "gaslit" the arguments. Jamie understood the importance of the discussions concerning race and *Sleepy Hollow* but was leery of the overuse of terms. "One thing I learned was that 'diversity' is an easy word to throw around. As is 'representation in media,'" she explained. She said that as a Hispanic woman, she knew that she had to try to be the best she could be, regardless of what was on her television screen, seemingly acknowledging that true representation is more myth than reality. Jamie points to the complicated politics of representation, specifically, where does representation end and tokenism begin? Tokenism "glorifies the exception in order to obscure the rules of the game of success" (Cloud 1996, 122). Even in an ever-changing mediascape, representations of people of color are exceptions that are often offered as tokens of change or progress. Jamie's comments highlight the tensions between celebrating visibility while living under the pressure of what that visibility supposedly represents.

For many fans, the constant references to race and racism muted valid points and felt overwhelming, which caused them to detach from the show and disengage from the fandom. For others, the discussions caused a desensitization to racial discourse instead of encouraging productive debate.

—Sense Making as an Act of Unembedding Race and Fandom

The experiences described by the fans in their interviews showcased the specific sense-making properties used to make sense of the happenings both on the television show and in the fandom. Most gaps or questions that the fans encountered were related to race, either explicitly or implicitly. Furthermore, the helps and hindrances used in relation to bridging the gaps involved participating in and contributing to the fandom through discourse. Elements of critical race theory emerged from the fans' descriptions that helped contextualize the racial discourse on a macro level. The resistance rhetoric to discussions of race echoed liberalist ideologies of color blindness, while the advocatorial sense making functioned to dismantle racist ideology and attempted to challenge permanence of racism and disrupt interest convergence. The interview data also provided answers to the question of how *Sleepy Hollow* fans discussed race as it relates to the show. The physical diversity of the cast made discussions of race prevalent during the interviews. When fans were asked to discuss their initial experiences of watching *Sleepy Hollow*, almost all mentioned the diversity of the cast, especially the interracial co-lead pairing. For some, this was seen as positive and produced positive expectations of the show, while others commented that the diversity caused them to be more cautious in their expectations, and a final group of fans did not seem to understand why the diversity was even a talking point.

The responses given during the interviews were often complex and pointed out the pervasiveness of conscious and unconscious racialized discourse in fan communities. While interview responses differed over whether discussions of race helped or hindered the meaning-making processes, most responses acknowledged that race played a significant role in the discourse. Furthermore, while I was interviewing fans, several referenced current racialized events or phenomena happening in the United States, such as the Black Lives Matter movement, when discussing their online experiences. Fans, specifically those who took a special interest in defending Abbie Mills (Nicole Beharie), referenced connections to protests around the country that drew attention to Black lives. Conversely, some fans felt that in light of the inundation of racialized discourse in the news, the discussions of race pertaining to *Sleepy Hollow* were burdensome. These fans felt that television acted as an escape from the real world and discussions of race erased the escapism of entertainment. Fans used discussions of race in *Sleepy Hollow* to contextualize race relations in the United States by either closely associating themselves with the national racial discourse or distancing themselves from it.

In my research, convergence was the conduit for race to be used as a meaning-making agent for several *Sleepy Hollow* fans. By analyzing the sense-making data through a critical race lens, I was able to unembed race and challenge "fan studies' unexamined whiteness" by highlighting racial discourse (Stanfill 2018, 314). As stated earlier, my research takes a generalist approach to media fandom: fandom connected by affect toward the media object. However, what emerged from the intersection of sense-making data and the tenets of critical race theory were issues of identity, particularly racial identity as present in fandom discourse regarding past experiences, expectations, questions, helps, and hindrances. During the interviews, it became obvious that in discussions of the object of fandom—*Sleepy Hollow*—racial and culture-specific views were embedded.

—Ethical Considerations

Adopting an open-source ethical framework allows for adaptability and flexibility based on the specific needs of the research project (Bruckman 2001). Maria Bakardjieva and Andrew Feenberg put forth another approach that has "respect for the intent with which online communities have generated content [and that] emerges as a fundamental ethical principle of social life online" (2001, 235). This means that the researcher must understand the purpose of the community and the artifacts produced within the community before making decisions to appropriate and analyze the artifacts as research data. At the forefront of my research was the principle that the community and its cultural artifacts must be respected.

Briefly, I want to discuss the journey that I, as the researcher, traveled during this research process. My standpoint as an African American female informs my position as a researcher. Furthermore, as a researcher, I identify with feminist understandings of communication, language, discourse, and, more specifically, womanism. A major tenet of womanist methodology is that it "strives to make research practical, accessible, and empowering for the informant, the researcher, and the communities of which both are part" (Few, Stephens, and Rouse-Arnett 2003, 206). Because a second tenet of womanism recognizes that "sharing certain identities is not enough to presume insider status," as a researcher I never assumed that my shared racial identity presumed a more intimate understanding (ibid., 207). During the interview process, I was specifically aware of how my own identity and social location could affect interactions with participants. Finally, attentiveness to language helped in the reflexive process. Language, written and oral, can connote a privilege that could become problematic in the research process. I tried as much as possible to neutralize any hegemonic tendencies that can occur in cross-racial qualitative inquiry.

Reflexivity, positionality, and identity all converged when my research moved to the phase in which permissions were needed and I had to make contact with fans. Several times fans assumed that because I am a Black female, I aligned myself with certain ideologies within the fandom. I worked incredibly hard to maintain a neutral presence online to avoid any perception of bias; however, for some fans, the color of my skin automatically caused me to seem biased. Even when I was able to gain permission to interview fans who were hesitant, there were more than a few uncomfortable moments when the participant assumed I advocated for certain characters or story lines or, even more generally, believed that all white fans were racist. There was constant negotiation on my part to ensure that I did not come into the interview process or the analysis process with preexisting biases. Even though I managed my online presence in the *Sleepy Hollow* fandom to not specifically align with any faction within it, I still encountered resistance and hesitancy because of my race.

The goal of my research was to highlight the meaning-making experiences of *Sleepy Hollow* fans to interrogate the racial politics at work. It is important to showcase the rich cultural and ethnic tapestry that creates fandom communities. The tensions I observed in the *Sleepy Hollow* fandom affected fans, particularly fans of color, attempting to normalize their experiences while championing the diverse and unique nature of their object of fandom. This discussion of fans bringing their experiences, prejudices, and ideological lenses to the overall fan experience and discursively creating a space for meaning making, as well as contextualizing fan discussions within the larger social discourse, serves to further the development and scope of fan studies to include investigations of race. I hope that moving forward, sense making will be considered a methodological tool in the critical toolbox to investigate how fans use race and racial discourse as a way to make sense of self and others and how these discussions reflect and relate to the larger societal discourse on race.

2. The Intended vs. the Unintended Audience

Deconstructing Positionality in Fandom

SAM PACK

UNTIL RELATIVELY RECENTLY, studies on audience reception among Indigenous peoples have all but been ignored within anthropology. This absence is ironic in light of the often quoted Malinowskian dictum that the goal of ethnography is "to grasp the native's point of view, [their] relation to life, to realize [*their*] vision of [*their*] world" (1922, 25). Anthropologists in industrialized countries have paid scant systematic attention to the production, distribution, and consumption of mass media in their own societies and even less attention to mass media in nonindustrialized societies (Lyons 1990). While there are emerging wide-scale debates on the subject of anthropology and film within the field of visual anthropology, discussions concerning the topic of anthropology and television have been scarce (Weicker 1993).

This glaring lack of reception studies within anthropology reflects the unacknowledged assumption that all viewers process information in a similarly unproblematic manner. Studies have demonstrated, however, that there is an intrinsic link between culture and communication and that each culture socializes its members' own viewing habits and interpretive strategies (e.g., Caldarola 1990). Simply stated, the media does not affect all equally or in the same fashion. The dynamics of image interpretation are magnified when the producer of the image and the consumer of the image come from different cultures. Messages encoded in the first world may be aberrantly decoded wholly or partially in fourth world countries, or they may not be fully accepted (Lyons 1990).

Precisely because of these inadequacies, an anthropology of mass media is uniquely qualified to enter into the discourse on audiences. Traditional methods such as questionnaires or watching people watch television in a controlled environment for a few hours at a time are insufficient to understand the fluid, shifting constellations of audiences. Instead, reception studies require the Geertzian thick descriptions made possible only by ethnography. Ironically, calls for an ethnographic turn in fan studies have been frequent, especially among cultural studies scholars (Hughes 2011). Timothy Gibson, for instance, advocates an audience ethnography that productively investigates the relationship between social and historical determinations and the practice of media consumption within the contexts and routines of everyday life (2000). Although cultural and media studies scholars may employ ethnographic research techniques such as participant-observation and interviews, their research strategy is not ethnographic because they fail to recognize that ethnographies are produced by particular practices (Virginia Nightingale cited in Peterson 2003). Further, there has been a tendency to lump all these techniques together, thereby blurring the distinctiveness of the anthropological method (Coman and Rothenbuhler 2005).

An even more troubling tendency in fan studies conceives of the audience as a singular and monolithic entity. Rebecca Wanzo notes the ubiquitous absence of race, in particular, as an object of analysis. For instance, the first edition of the seminal text *Fandom: Identities and Communities in a Mediated World*, edited by Jonathan Gray, Cornel Sandvoss, and C. Lee Harrington in 2007, did not contain a single essay that focused on racial differences among fans (Wanzo 2015). The editors rectified this glaring lacuna in a second edition published a decade later by challenging the field of fan studies to "explore how fandom changes in mode and type across demographics and globally, so that the 'us' expands" (2017, 10). By focusing on an unintended audience, this essay challenges the boundaries of who (and what) constitutes a fan.

The ethnographic approach is to seek people in places where they are engaged in meaningful action: "This involves a shift from texts and their imagined spectatorships and from interviews in which people tell stories about their own media practices to the presence of ethnographers in the . . . venues where media consumption actually takes place" (Peterson 2003, 127). Unfortunately, researchers have either been reluctant to heed the call or simply content to make recommendations without doing anything on their own. In the classic Geertzian dilemma between just thinking about ethnography but never doing it or doing ethnography without thinking about it, most media scholars have opted for the former. There has been a great deal of theorizing about the effects of mass media but comparatively little actual audience research until recently. Instead the academic, who is presumably able to understand precisely how audiences will interpret particular television programs or movies, speaks on behalf of the viewers. Obviously this is problematic, since an academic who has spent his or her career analyzing films and their ideological content will see details that others might not.

Anthropologists are entering media studies at a time when the field has posed the kinds of questions that our methods and theoretical approaches are especially well equipped to answer (Dickey 1993). The notion of audiences that has emerged from anthropological media scholarship since 1990 is not a unified, homogeneous object but one that is "contested, disparate, multiple, and constantly being redefined in a kind of territorial struggle over its representation and meaning" (Hughes 2011, 310).

This essay is based upon my experiences conducting research (approved by both the Institutional Review Board at Temple University and the Navajo Nation's Historic Preservation Department) among members of the Benally family, a matrilineal network of clan-related kin. All names have been changed to conceal my informants' identities. However, this anthropological relationship was preceded by a personal relationship with the Benallys that spanned over a decade. There is an old joke that a typical Navajo family consists of a mother, a father, children, some sheep, and an anthropologist. I suppose this is true in my case as well, but I must add that I was considered a member of the family long before I ever thought of becoming an anthropologist. In fact, I have maintained a continual presence on the reservation for so long that many Navajos not only assume that I am from there but identify me as an actual member of the Benally clan.

From the moment I first arrived on the reservation in 1989, more than thirty years ago, I felt strangely comfortable. Such a reaction is extraordinarily rare since I usually do not adjust well to a new environment, especially one so different from anyplace I had ever known or seen. Yet I noticed that these Navajos and I shared certain similarities. The first was the most obvious: we looked alike. I am Korean American, and my Asiatic features often pass for Navajo. Moreover, I know better than most what it is like to be on the other side of the anthropological gaze. Based on the mistaken impression that I am Native American, missionaries have attempted to convert me, tourists have asked to take my picture, benevolent professors have offered me special benefits not available to my peers, and once an anthropologist actually tried to recruit me for an interview. In all these cases, the perpetrators treated me in a very distinct way difficult to describe. Given their overly polite manner of speaking, exaggerated enunciation, and friendly body language, I can best compare this treatment to the way adults speak to mentally challenged children. When they discover that I am not Navajo but "just another Asian," I invariably witness the dramatic transformation from obsequious respect to betrayed insouciance. For a more detailed description of how my relationship with the Benallys influenced my research, see my 2006 essay, "How They See Me vs. How I See Them: The Ethnographic Self and the Personal Self."

I would now like to discuss two reception studies that I conducted, the first with both Navajo and Anglo viewers and the second with a Navajo-only audience. I used two sets of films about Navajos in order to compare and contrast viewer reactions to insider and outsider perspectives of the same subject matter. The first study used a set of films that addresses the forced relocation of Navajo families from their ancestral homeland as presented by a Native filmmaker and non-Native filmmakers. In this study, I screened the films to both groups to determine if either was able to distinguish cultural authorship. The second study used another set of films—one a documentary and the other a television drama—that chronicles the journey of Navajos who were adopted by white families as infants and then reunited with their biological families as adults. Unlike the very structured nature of the first study, this one replicated a more natural viewing environment, and the films were screened only to Najavo viewers. Interestingly, any historical and cultural inaccuracies in these visual reproductions did not detract from my viewers' enjoyment of the films.

—In the Heart of Big Mountain vs. Broken Rainbow

Both films in the first set tackle a similar subject matter from different points of view. While a Native American filmmaker completed the first film, *In the Heart of Big Mountain* (1988), non-Natives produced and directed the second, *Broken Rainbow* (1985). Robert Aibel conducted a similar reception study among Anglo university students to see whether they could distinguish between a Navajo-made film (by Johnny Nelson) and an Anglo-made film (by John Adair) about the same topic, Navajo silversmithing. By virtue of a self-fulfilling research design, he found that informants could correctly determine cultural authorship. However, he acknowledges that it would have been "particularly valuable and revealing" to conduct the study with a Navajo audience, especially in light of the comment by a Navajo woman during a screening of the Navajo Film Project films that she "cannot understand English"—despite the fact that all the films were silent (Aibel 1976, 27; Worth and Adair 1972, 130).

This reception study does precisely that as it was undertaken with *both* Anglos and Navajos. Anthropologist Elizabeth Bird has pointed out that very few scholars have studied "how White audiences respond to representations of Indians, but also how Indians respond to, and imagine representations of themselves" (2003, 88). I originally completed a study in 1999, using the aforementioned films in an introductory anthropology class I taught at Temple University with eight Anglo college students. Two years later, in 2001, I repeated the study with five Navajo informants as part of my dissertation research, in which I investigated the crucial role television plays in the formation and contestation of social and cultural identities.

Methodologically, presenting the films to these two constituencies posed a unique challenge because the cultural baggage that each group brought to the viewing was very different. Since most of my students knew little to nothing about Navajo culture before taking my class, it was imperative for me to provide some context for what they were about to watch. As such, I assigned relevant readings and dedicated two class periods to lectures describing Navajo history as well as the issues and ethics of (self)-representation. For obvious reasons, my Navajo informants did not require such background information. All five were already familiar with the relocation controversy to varying degrees.

The viewing contexts for the college students and my Navajo informants also varied tremendously. All the students watched the films together in a classroom as part of an assignment, and all were made aware that their responses might be included in a published study. Although I emphasized that they would not be graded on their responses to the films, their participation was undoubtedly motivated by academic coercion. Several of the students, for example, scribbled notes during the screenings. My informants, on the other hand, took these films a lot less seriously. With the exception of Grandma Annie, who required an English translator, the other four family members watched the films individually and at their leisure. They often paused the films to get up and do something else. Several ate during the screenings. None wrote down any notes.

For both groups, I introduced the films by stating that each addressed the same topic—Navajo relocation—from different perspectives. I cued each film to start at a point where the title and the credits would not be visible. I distributed questionnaires immediately after each screening and instructed the viewers to fill them out. Both groups were allowed a brief intermission before the next screening.

The questionnaire was divided into four components. For each film, respondents were told to provide a summary, describe what they learned from the film, numerically evaluate ten separate filmic qualities, and devise their own titles for the film. After both screenings, they were also asked to explain which film was better made, which they liked more, and which was made by whom. While the college students wrote down their answers, my Navajo informants verbally responded to the questions.

Before discussing the results of the reception study, I want to emphasize that neither group can be essentialized as constituting a homogeneous entity. Members from both groups exhibited significant differences and contradictions. There were also common cultural threads. Although I may generalize findings from each group for the sake of brevity, readers should keep this intragroup diversity in mind.

A highly polished film narrated by actor and activist Martin Sheen, *Broken Rainbow* won the Academy Award for best documentary in 1985. The film details the relocation of Navajo families from their homes in the Big Mountain area of Arizona by compassionately portraying the devastating impact on the forcibly removed Navajos and by implicating the federal government's role in creating the Navajo-Hopi land dispute.

Navajo-Hopi borders were nebulously defined before the reservation era. Strife between the two tribes resulted in a federal partitioning of the commonly claimed land in 1974. As a result of this ruling, over ten thousand Navajos had to be relocated to government housing in cities off the reservation. Many traditional Navajos who had lived on Big Mountain for generations refused to leave. Those who were forcibly removed have had great difficulty adjusting to a radically different way of life. The film makes an impassioned plea for the relocation process to be overturned in order to prevent the impending ecological destruction of a sacred land as well as the cultural destruction of a proud people.

Like *Broken Rainbow, In the Heart of Big Mountain* addresses the forced relocation of Navajos as a result of the land dispute. The major difference is that the latter was made by a Native American filmmaker. Sandra Osawa provides thorough background information for those unfamiliar with the history of the land dispute. The strength of this film lies in Osawa's emphasis on the emotional and human aspects of the issues. She shows how the land dispute has adversely affected the lives of various Navajos from Big Mountain who have become afflicted by alcoholism, mental problems, physical illnesses, and even death because of their separation from their homeland.

The film is divided into two sections, the first of which focuses on a Navajo matriarch, Katherine Smith, who was born and raised and continues to live on Big Mountain. The second half describes Katherine's daughter, Nancy, who was relocated to a Department of Housing and Urban

Development house near Tuba City, Arizona. With these two individuals, Osawa juxtaposes the traditional and modern worlds. While Katherine washes her face with water from a bin and cooks fry bread over an open fire, her daughter enjoys the amenities of running water and electricity. The dichotomy is overly simplistic, but it serves its purpose.

The dominant description among the Anglo students was that *In the Heart of Big Mountain* depicted yet another instance of the government mistreating Native Americans. In their questionnaires, most students recycled familiar clichés along the lines of "Oh, these poor Indians." Colleen, for example, wrote:

> The film was about the problems brought on by the forced relocation
> threat imposed by the government: namely, increased death
> rate, alcoholism, mental problems. The government has created
> boundaries and split up the land between two groups of people.
> However, in doing so, they have divided land that is sacred. Because
> there are no statues or huge churches built on the land does not mean
> that this is not a place of prayer.

Colleen's comments clearly reflect that she has learned something about cultural relativism. A self-proclaimed devout Catholic, she recognizes that the Navajos' religious beliefs are just as valid as her own. Karen's remarks are interesting because, in the space of only a few sentences, she proceeds from feeling sympathy for the Navajos to proclaiming admiration for their strength of character:

> I feel this film was made primarily to generate sympathy. It worked.
> I felt really bad for these people. What right do the whites have to
> come in and drive those people from their homes? I greatly admire
> Katherine and the others who stayed where they belonged regardless
> of what the government said.

The majority of the students referenced *In the Heart of Big Mountain* when summarizing *Broken Rainbow*. The general consensus was that the second film approached the topic of relocation in more historical detail. Mary wrote:

> Like the other film, it was about the government trying to take away
> Big Mountain from the Navajo in order to exploit its resources.

Only this time, the film gave time to the Hopi to show how they are affected by this as well. Not as much time spent on their bond with the land, but more on the whole litigation process.

But what this film gained in comprehensiveness, according to the students, it sacrificed in a personal connection to affected individuals.

In terms of the film's educational value, the students' responses varied most in this category. Some, like Dave, found *In the Heart of Big Mountain* to be a valuable learning tool:

> I really learned a lot from the film because I can understand that the Big Mountain is an important place for the Navajo. I am angry that the government forced the people to move out. I would support Navajo people to have their rights to stay . . . I would like the Navajo to maintain their standards. I really want them to be left alone.

Others, like Mary, were not as impressed:

> I didn't learn a whole heck of a lot. I know from papers I wrote earlier in college that the Navajo religion is based on the land and that each element of the land has its own "spirit," and I knew from the readings that land inheritance was a "female thing." Also, it didn't surprise me that mental illness and suicide was on the rise among the Navajo. It makes sense given what they're going through. The deaths did surprise me, although it can be argued whether that's really based on the relocation or if it's purely medical.

A similar juxtaposition applied to *Broken Rainbow*, which was well articulated by Scott: "Basically what I learned was a pretty solid history of the Indians in that region. But most of the info about whites taking advantage and manipulating I was already aware of."

As part of their evaluation of the films, I asked all the respondents to give a numerical score from 1 to 10 (lowest to highest) for a series of different filmic qualities: artistic, smooth, intelligible, complete, interesting, funny, educational, good, unusual, and likable. On the whole, the students ranked *Broken Rainbow* higher in terms of intelligibility, completeness, and educational value, while *In the Heart of Big Mountain* received a slight nod for being more interesting and unusual. Both films were rated as being evenly artistic and smooth, and none of the students found either film to be particularly funny.

For the final component, I gave the students the opportunity to demonstrate their creativity by proposing their own titles for each film. For *In the Heart of Big Mountain*, their titles tended to focus more on the deleterious impact of relocation: "The Effects of Forced Relocation on the Navajo" (Mark), "The Heartache of Relocation" (Karen), and "Big Mountain and How the People Can't Live without It" (Gena). Suggested titles for *Broken Rainbow* concentrated more on the underhanded tactics of the government: "Manipulation and Destruction of the Hopi and Navajo" (Scott), "The Navajo, the Hopi, and the Government: Whose Land Is It?" (Mary), and "The Government's Destruction of Indian Lifestyles" (Dorian).

Unlike the college students, my Navajo informants spoke in broad generalizations and rarely provided specific examples from the films. For instance, this is the way Isabelle, a middle-aged mother of ten, summarized *In the Heart of Big Mountain*: "It was about the Navajo people being relocated out of Big Mountain and how it's working on them psychologically. And all the problems they're having up there with their family dying and all that."

Isabelle's college-educated daughter, Regina, employed similarly sweeping strokes when describing *Broken Rainbow*: "This film gave a brief history of the origins of Navajo relocation. Then it also included the Hopis. This one was more spread out to a whole group of Navajos living on Big Mountain." Such lack of detail may indicate that they did not pay very close attention to the films. But I have noticed that many Navajos I have come to know over the years have difficulty precisely answering vague and open-ended questions like "What did you think about it?" or "What was it about?" Instead, general questions invariably elicit general responses.

Of course, the main reason they might not have paid very close attention to the educational value of the two films was because they were already familiar with the subject matter. Although bothered by the travesty of justice perpetrated against the Navajos of Big Mountain, none expressed any surprise—they have come to expect this type of unethical behavior from the government. Sixteen-year-old Chucky first heard about the issue in his high school class:

> I knew about Big Mountain from taking Navajo Government this semester. He didn't tell me about the relocation, though. I got a white guy. He don't know nothing. He just goes by the book. The part I

was surprised about was where people died because of it and how it affected their minds and stuff. I felt sorry for the people but, then again, it was expected. Because the government, man, they're always going to do you like that. Sooner or later, they're going to kick us off our land. Watch.

An underlying apathy also characterized their reactions to *Broken Rainbow*. In Isabelle's words:

> I never really paid attention to the relocation because it didn't affect me. It used to be a big thing about ten years ago, but now people kind of just forgot about it. Even when all this was going on, nobody really cared or they would have been out there supporting those relocatees. I don't think the outside people really got involved.

All five members of the Benally family maintained an emotional distance from the issue of relocation since neither they themselves nor anyone they knew was directly involved. But Delbert, an unemployed silversmith, acknowledged that the situation would have been different if he had been personally affected:

> Being way over here, I heard it all on the radio and newspaper. I couldn't really do anything about it. What if they come over to where *I* live? "Hey, man, this whole doggone valley ain't yours." That's when you get a little bit more about how these people feel. And it could happen this way, too. They can easily say, "Forget about these social services anymore. No more hospitals. Run your own show."

These unsympathetic remarks are consistent with the "every man for himself" ethos that I have found to be common among contemporary Navajos such as the Benallys.

As a means of evaluation, assigning a numerical designation to various traits seemed to be an entirely foreign concept for my Navajo informants. Unlike the college students, they were not accustomed to isolating specific traits and then ranking them on a relative scale. Grandma Annie, the Benally family matriarch, had an especially difficult time understanding the ranking system no matter how many times and ways that her son, Delbert, and I tried to explain it to her. Ultimately, I believe she appeased me by rattling off an arbitrary series of numbers.

The arbitrary nature of the evaluation is most evident in how inconsistently they ranked the different traits. Delbert, Isabelle, and Chucky all felt that *Broken Rainbow* was the more intelligible, complete, and interesting film, yet they gave higher scores in all three categories to *In the Heart of Big Mountain*. Another interesting tendency was how several of the Navajos supplied two different numerical scores: one for the general public and the other for themselves. So, for example, Chucky gave *In the Heart of Big Mountain* a 7 for being unusual, but he quickly noted that it rated only a 3 from his own point of view. Similarly, Isabelle and Regina both thought the films would be much more educational for non-Navajos.

Asked to propose their own titles for these films, the Navajo informants were predictably uninspired given their generally lackadaisical approach during the viewing. Unlike the case with the Anglo students, there was no discernible difference between the titles for either film. In fact, Delbert and Chucky unknowingly gave practically the same title to both films. Perhaps this is because the films were ultimately about the same thing in their eyes: how the federal government has once again victimized Navajos. It is a story they know all too well.

As with the college students, the titles basically fell into two camps. The first addressed sadness and heartache: "Brokenhearted Dine" (Grandma Annie), "Emotional Crisis at Big Mountain" (Isabelle), and "The Psychological Effects of Navajo Relocation" (Regina). The second group focused on anger aimed at the federal government and Anglos as a whole: "Screwed Again by Uncle Sam" (Chucky), "Stealing Indian Lands" (Regina), and "The Corrupt White Man" (Delbert). Significantly, the two camps were almost equally divided according to gender lines.

When asked which film was better made, each group of viewers provided responses that reflected their own cultural biases. While the college students unanimously agreed that *Broken Rainbow* was the much slicker production, a higher budget did not necessarily translate into superior overall quality. Scott elaborated on the pluses and minuses of each film:

> For entertainment value, the second was made a lot better and gave more of a historical background. But the film was done in the "voice of God" method with the narrator speaking for the people. While the first film was not very artistically pleasing, it did seem to be more believable. So as far as an ethnography, the first seemed to have less flaws.

Similarly, Dorian hailed *Broken Rainbow*'s "informational nature and multiple perspectives" but ultimately decreed that *In the Heart of Big Mountain* was "more anthropological" because of its focus on individuals rather than groups.

The Navajo informants unanimously nominated *Broken Rainbow* as the superior film in terms of production quality. Compared with *In the Heart of Big Mountain*, this film was longer, more detailed, and more informative. Taken together, my informants easily gathered that the documentary was the more expensive film to make. *Broken Rainbow*, observed Grandma Annie, "looked like it cost a lot more money." For Annie, there was a direct correlation between cultural value and its monetary counterpart.

Surprisingly, several of the students who decided that *Broken Rainbow* was the better-made film nevertheless liked *In the Heart of Big Mountain* more. Karen, for example, sided with the Oscar-winning documentary as the superior production because it was "more informative and educational," whereas *In the Heart of Big Mountain* was "only about one woman and her life." Yet when it came time for her to cast her vote for the film she found more appealing, Karen preferred the smaller production precisely because of its human touch:

> I enjoyed the first better because it was on a more personal level.
> I know the view of one person does not represent all Navajo, but
> I sympathized with her. The second film was too full of facts and
> statistics. It doesn't matter to me that their sheep are a gift from the
> Holy People—I could care less. I was interested in how relocation
> affected their everyday lives and the first film showed that well.

Dorian, on the other hand, had the opposite impression:

> While I feel the first film was better made, the second provided
> me with more information that was obviously lacking in the first. I
> needed things to be placed in a historical timeline and the second
> film provided adequate info mixed with varying opinions and
> imagery. Film 1 acted as a more focused version of Film 2.

As these divergent comments illustrate, there is no accounting for personal taste.

Perhaps because of their greater familiarity with forced relocation, the Navajos were far more critical of both films' content. In contrast to the college students, my Navajo informants were not as susceptible to the emotional

THE INTENDED VS. THE UNINTENDED AUDIENCE   41

underpinnings of either film in its portrayal of the relocated Navajos as help-less victims. Through the reservation grapevine, Isabelle had heard that the Big Mountain residents were offered a significant economic incentive to move: "Those guys received funds to build brand-new houses and they also got moving expenses. There's a lot of other people that had their arms wide open to the money. You know how Navajos are. Ninety-nine percent of the time, they're thinking about the money."

While the goal of both films was to elicit sympathy for the displaced Navajos, several of the informants viewed the financial settlement resulting from the relocation as a blessing in disguise for those involved. Perhaps because neither film showed this perspective, the Navajos did not express a strong preference for either. They seemed to agree with Chucky's one-word response when I asked him which film he liked better: "None."

Finally, the all-important question, Is there anything uniquely Native about Osawa's version? Other than smaller production costs, is *In the Heart of Big Mountain* really that different from *Broken Rainbow*? Would a casual observer or even a fellow Native be able to tell the difference? After the screenings, I asked respondents from both groups to select which film they thought was made by a Native filmmaker and which was made by a non-Native filmmaker.

The majority of the college students based their judgments on aes-thetic quality rather than content. Scott, Dorian, and Gena attributed the personal nature of *In the Heart of Big Mountain* as being a Native quality. Dave, Karen, and Colleen cited the strong antiwhite stance of *Broken Rain-bow* as being characteristic of a Native American filmmaker because he or she would understandably be upset at the harsh treatment of their people. In other words, there was no clear consensus: all the students felt strongly that *their* perception was the correct one.

My Navajo informants, however, experienced much less uncertainty in determining cultural authorship. For them, the simple fact that *Broken Rainbow* looked like it was more expensive to put together necessarily meant that it had to have been made by Anglos. By comparison, a Native Ameri-can could never gather enough funding to travel to all those different places, much less hire a famous actor to serve as a narrator. Furthermore, "all those politicians and businessmen wouldn't have talked to no Indian" (Isabelle), and "only a white man would do that much homework" (Chucky).

Sufficiently impressed by the Native filmmaker's privileged status, none of the students noticed or cared that Osawa is Makah and not Navajo. Operating under the apparent assumption that all Native Americans are essentially the same, my students did not attribute any importance to the tribal dissimilarity even after I specifically brought this fact to their attention. Osawa seemed to be granted the preordained right to speak for all other Natives.

In contrast, the fact that Osawa is not Navajo made a significant difference to my Navajo informants. Delbert, for instance, attributed the glaring omissions in *In the Heart of Big Mountain* to his conclusion that the filmmaker, although perhaps Native, did not know enough about Navajo culture to make a thorough and convincing film:

> They should have put a little bit more about what the Hopis thought about it and what the US government really had to do with it. The United States government is not something you mess around with. I think at the time Peter MacDonald was chairman and I feel like he sold the people out. They didn't say anything about what the council's reaction was. It should have been more about getting the whole tribe involved and asking them what they thought about it. That film right there was just about one person. What they should have done was they should have got another family that had a mother and father and see what the father thought about it. And the kids, they come back and just feel sorry. They should come out and speak. It seemed like this family just kind of folded.

Regina also speculated that the individual behind *In the Heart of Big Mountain* was not from the reservation: "I think he was an urban Navajo. He probably based the film on just a few relocatees that he may have interviewed but not a lot." After I informed her that the filmmaker was actually a Makah woman, Regina thought for a moment to choose her words: "Then I don't think she should have made this film." What this statement suggests is that Osawa, as a non-Navajo, did not have the *right* to make a film about Navajos.

— *The Return of Navajo Boy* vs. *The Lost Child*

Quite the opposite of the structured nature of the first reception study, my second study, in 2001, was based entirely on observations within a natural viewing environment. Instead of watching my Navajo informants individually watch a videotape, taking notes during the screening, and then asking a series of prepared questions afterward, I decided just to go with the flow and see what happened. No tape recorder, no list of questions, no notepad, not even a pen. For *The Return of Navajo Boy*, I simply inserted the tape into the living room VCR during a time when the trailer was full of people and, within minutes, a crowd of curious onlookers began to assemble in front of the television. I did not limit viewing to my five Navajo informants but opened access to whoever was interested in watching the documentary. Various people came and went and came back again.

The Lost Child was screened under even more informal circumstances. One evening, when a large group of people came over to play cards, Isabelle suggested that I "play the tape," ostensibly as supplemental entertainment. So while a couple of dozen people were crammed together around a makeshift gambling area, the made-for-TV movie played in the background (or foreground, depending on one's perspective). Every now and again— between shrieks of laughter, cheering, and cursing over the card game— various members of the Indigenous delegation would sneak a peak at the television to follow along with the plot. Granted such divided attention seems far from ideal for a purported reception study, but this is the way the Benally clan typically watches TV as a group.

Analogous to *In the Heart of Big Mountain* and *Broken Rainbow*, *The Return of Navajo Boy* and *The Lost Child* also tackle a similar subject matter: the abduction of Navajo infants by outsiders and their subsequent reunion with their biological families as adults. But this is where the comparisons end. While the former is a heart-wrenching documentary, the latter is a cheesy television drama.

The Return of Navajo Boy (2000) chronicles a serendipitous chain of events that began with the appearance of a silent film reel and eventually led to the reunion of a long-lost brother with his Navajo family after four decades. The Cly family has a long and storied history in pictures. For nearly a century, family members appeared as unidentified Native Americans in countless photographs and films shot against the backdrop of Monument Valley. But it was the sudden appearance of a 1950s silent film reel called *Navajo Boy* that would affect the Clys the most. Bill Kennedy, the son of the man who shot the original footage, wanted to return the film to the people in it. Cly family matriarch Elsie Mae Begay delighted in seeing herself as a young girl, but she also sadly recognized her infant brother, John Wayne Cly, who was adopted by white missionaries and never heard from again. Amazingly, John Wayne read about the return of *Navajo Boy* in a newspaper article, and he learned that the Clys were the family he had never known. Suddenly, *The Return of Navajo Boy* took on a literal tone.

The Lost Child (2000) also follows an individual's path to self-discovery, but this Hallmark Hall of Fame presentation ultimately gets lost in trying to do too much. Although based on the 1999 autobiography *Looking for Lost Bird: A Jewish Woman Discovers Her Navajo Roots*, by Yvette Melanson with Claire Safran, the film's fish-out-of-water narrative still feels like a stretch. The movie is about a middle-aged Jewish woman living in Pennsylvania who discovers that she was stolen at birth and that she is actually a full-blooded Navajo. Like most screen adaptations, there are numerous discrepancies between the book and the film.

After learning of her roots, Rebecca (played by the non-Native actor Mercedes Ruehl) uproots her family to move to the reservation. While she retraces her ancestry and adapts to her new family, her Anglo husband and two daughters experience bitterness and prejudice from the locals. In fact, after continual teasing, her older daughter is assaulted at school by a male student. At this point, the film suddenly switches gears altogether by turning Rebecca into a crusader. (Needless to say, none of this occurred in the book.) While the first half is an almost interesting portrait of birthrights and cultural clashes, the rest of the movie is reduced to a predictable fix-the-system melodrama.

Perhaps it is unfair to compare these two films, since one is a documentary while the other is a Hallmark special. We are talking about apples and oranges—or, more appropriately, fry bread and Wonder Bread. Although *The Lost Child* was inspired by a true story, the producers have taken obvious creative liberties and fictionalized certain parts in order to package the film for mass consumption. But herein lies the problem: by virtue of being telecast on broadcast television, *The Lost Child* reached a much larger viewership than *The Return of Navajo Boy*, a documentary distributed by PBS. As a result, the inaccurate version is more likely to shape the general public's attitudes about Navajos in particular and Native Americans in general.

In spite of the chaotic circumstances surrounding the screening of *The Return of Navajo Boy*, the documentary was compelling enough to captivate the attention of nearly everybody who originally sat down to watch it out of curiosity. Such a high retention rate is exceedingly rare for most television programs or videos, as it is customary for these viewers to watch only for a few minutes before losing interest. At the documentary's heart-rending climax, when Elsie May is finally reunited with her younger brother after forty years, there was complete silence in the room. Intermittent sniffling and eye rubbing soon followed. I noticed that even the men were choking back tears.

The key to the documentary's appeal among the assembled viewers was its authenticity. Members of the Benally family could identify with

THE INTENDED VS. THE UNINTENDED AUDIENCE 45

and literally relate to the film's characters. (The Clys are clan relatives of the Benallys.) Everyone recognized familiar locations such as the new museum at Window Rock and Richardson's pawnshop. (In fact, a brief shot of a photograph of an elderly couple at the pawnshop showed my research assistant's girlfriend's grandparents.) Isabelle and Regina saw people in the documentary whom they knew. Grandma Annie remarked that one of the older women shown speaking at the museum bore a striking resemblance to her. Tom and Todd elbowed each other during scenes of "rez kids" playing outside as these idyllic images surely reminded them of their own not-so-distant childhood.

Isabelle referred to the Monument Valley Navajos depicted in the documentary as "hard-core traditionals" because of their remote living conditions. In one particular scene involving footage of the original Navajo boy happily riding around a desolate canyon on a horse, Jerry (who is about the same age now as that boy was then) asked his mom if "that's how it was back then" and if she had ever experienced those types of moments herself. Ironically, the documentary includes a scene of a young Navajo girl clad in a basketball jersey looking at old postcards of her relatives and inquiring of her grandmother, "Did you always put your head in a bun?" and "What did you do for fun?"

Grandma Annie particularly enjoyed this film because a large portion of the dialogue was spoken in the Navajo language. But she was also able to follow along with the parts in English with only minimal translation. (Later, she stated that this was "the first movie I ever understood.") At the conclusion of the documentary, her comment was simple but fitting: "*nizhoni*," the Navajo word for "beautiful."

However, *The Return of Navajo Boy* did not garner unanimous praise. Isabelle objected to the powwow music at the beginning of the documentary because powwows, a ceremony of the Plains Indians, are not culturally indigenous to Navajos. Nate voiced disagreement with scenes of a Yeibechai song and dance not so much because it is a sacred ritual but more because the ceremony is performed only during the winter months and is not intended to be shown at any other time. (This viewing took place during the summer.) Regina, who had already seen the documentary at a screening sponsored by Fort Lewis College in Durango, expressed mixed feelings. While she found the reunion to be deeply touching, she resented the fact that John Wayne Cly was abducted from his family in the first place: "It was the white man who took him away and the white man who brought him back." Meanwhile, the members of the Cly family spent four decades with their lives shattered.

The Lost Child elicited very different reactions. Although the movie depicts a similar scenario of a Navajo baby adopted by Anglos who returns to her Navajo roots as an adult, members of the card-playing gathering immediately dismissed it as inauthentic. Scattered throughout the screening were frequent protests of "Those aren't Navajos!" Trisha ridiculed the actor who played Yazzie, the Navajo father, for the way he tied his hair as well as his loosely fitting concha belt. The most vocal scorn, however, was reserved for the characters' persistent mispronunciation of common Navajo words. They repeatedly said "Dee-NAY" instead of "Din-EH"—the name Navajos traditionally call themselves. The actors even pronounced the more mainstream tribal moniker as "NAH-vah-ho" when no self-respecting "Na-(long a)-veh-ho" would verbalize it that way. Similarly, the characters kept referring to the Navajo girl's puberty ceremony as a "key-nal-da" when it is supposed to be enunciated "ki-na-al-DAH."

The assemblage also took issue with the movie's corny New Age dialogue. From Rebecca's sappy testimonial that "I don't know why I walk the path I walk, I only know I have to" to Aunt Mary's melancholy proclamation that Rebecca's biological mother's "spirit returned to the great creator," none of the Navajos in the room talk in these aphorisms or know of any other Navajos who speak in such a manner. In a similar capacity, Adrienne Keene laments the appropriation of Native spirituality with the infusion of Indigenous magic into the Harry Potter universe (2016a). When Rebecca's daughter begins attending the reservation school, her classmates tease the blond-haired girl by calling her cornhead. The gathering suddenly erupted in laughter, as they had never before heard such an insult. For the rest of the evening as well as for the next several days, the members who were present at this screening would teasingly call one another cornhead or corny for short.

Although *The Lost Child* played to a steady soundtrack of mocking laughter, none of the onlookers appeared angry or offended by the inaccurate representation of their culture. Rather, it seems as if they have all become immune to these mass-mediated stereotypical portrayals. The Hallmark special is just more of the same standard fare. Whether Native Americans are depicted as the cold-blooded murderers in the old westerns or the noble victims in more recent films such as *Dances with Wolves* (1990), none of these misrepresentations is taken personally. Whenever I ask members of the Benally family why they react to these films in such a detached manner, they give me the same answer: "It's so stupid." In other words, they seem to be saying, "Why get hot and bothered over something so trivial that you have no control over anyway?"

The recruited Navajo spectators disagreed with the basic premise of the film: since medicine men are the only ones with the power to repel the witchcraft caused by skinwalkers, they have no reason to fear them as the movie shows. Their criticisms of the film ranged from the anecdotal (e.g., Jim Chee's "non-Navajo" wood-chopping technique) to the more factual (e.g., again, the mispronunciation of Navajo words). Yet none of these discrepancies seemed to prevent them from enjoying the movie. The Navajo viewers did not nitpick about these details, much less act offended by the inaccuracies. In fact, they seemed surprised and even somewhat grateful that their culture was even portrayed on film at all. It is important to remember that Navajos have not experienced too many cinematic moments of seeing a familiar landscape or hearing their language (albeit not enunciated correctly).

This does not mean that the Navajo viewers in my study did not challenge the rights of both Anglos and non-Navajos to undertake such films. In varying degrees, they displayed an awareness of wider historical contexts that problematize the filmmakers' narrower points of view. But as my reception studies confirm, the viewers' criteria for production evaluation are not the same as those for enjoyment. The reported reactions of my viewers suggest a window onto what criteria are most salient for their enjoyment, engagement, and evaluation, as well as what factors contribute to the point of view that they express. My findings might also be interpreted as a glimpse of film as a mode of cultural exchange in a period of rapid social change, as indicated by the increasing personalization of media content and use caused by "the unparalleled accessibility of digital content, the ubiquity of personal individual and mobile (screen) media, social media, customer relation management, and the general 'algorithmization' of digital media encounters" (Sandvoss, Gray, and Harrington 2017, 9). Watching their cinematic counterparts provided these real-life Navajos with a clearer understanding of how they are seen through the eyes of the mediated mainstream.

3. The Absence of Race
Teaching Practices and Inclusion in the Fandom Classroom

KATHERINE ANDERSON HOWELL

IN 2008, I TAUGHT A COMPOSITION COURSE at a community college in Mississippi. My students were mostly Black recent high school graduates. One day none of my students had received a message I had sent via the learning management system Blackboard. Frustrated, I told them, "This is the problem with Blackboard." As I finished the first syllable of "Blackboard," my class sucked in its collective breath, then audibly relaxed when I finished. In a split second, I registered their tension. "What," I asked, "did you think I was going to say?"

A young man responded, "We thought you were saying, 'This is the problem with Black people.'" He said this casually, as if it would have been common. I asked the class if teachers and professors had said things like that to them before. All the students, even the white students, responded affirmatively. Shocked, I reacted in anger on their behalf. Their professors could not talk to them that way! They should go to the department chairs and report it! They chuckled at me, mostly kindly, but were otherwise unmoved.

I see this moment now, more than a decade later, as one of many in which my privileged position as a white instructor distanced me from my students. Brené Brown states that "we're at our most dangerous when we think we've learned everything we need to know about [privilege]. That's when you stop paying attention to injustice. And make no mistake, not paying attention because you're not the one getting harassed or fired or pulled over or underpaid is the definition of privilege" (2015, track 56, 3:17–3:34). Brown's point about the danger of how we choose what to pay attention to helps me understand how we shape our classrooms.

My position as a fan studies scholar has primarily been concerned with higher education pedagogy, primarily in the United States in the literature and composition fields. My 2018 collection, *Fandom as Classroom Practice: A Teaching Guide*, had international input but focused primarily on English-speaking classrooms. When I write about fandom pedagogy, my main concern is the question of how fannish practices, broadly interpreted, affect the classroom. The key question I seek to understand has been how students respond to canonical knowledge, and I have explored this with literature both from the traditional canon, such as *Jane Eyre*, and from pop culture artifacts, such as *The Hunger Games* books and sketch comedy. Part of my focus in answering this pedagogical question has been centering the student voice, which is a key feature of this chapter and of my previous work. The students in this chapter, while coming from different backgrounds, participated in private higher education in Washington, D.C.

In the classroom, for the white teacher the definition of privilege follows the same pattern Brown describes: not paying attention when our students of color are not able to or are choosing not to talk about race in the classroom is privilege. (This applies to cisgender, heterosexual, or abled teachers also. This volume focuses on race, but exclusion happens in the classroom in a variety of ways that teachers do not necessarily pay attention to.) Dismissing those students when they do talk about race is also privilege. Both are dangerous—they risk derailing learning for the students, and for the fan studies classroom they risk derailing the pedagogical experiment altogether. I have been, as Helen Fox says of many white instructors, "well intentioned but 'naïve'"; I have not "fully recognize[d] the barriers [I] need to cross to really begin to hear" (2006, 253).

White teachers may struggle with recognizing these barriers in part because of a lack of self-reflection that Dianna Shank identifies. Considering the resistance of her students to a writing prompt asking them to engage in racial reflection, Shank suggests that liberal white ideologies allow white professors to excuse themselves "from continuing an active exploration of race—and whiteness. Since I was the teacher, I considered my own exploration into complex issues like race 'complete.'" This sense of completion—that professors hold finished knowledge and impart it to students—may or may not apply to every teacher; however, a failure to recognize the "unexplored gaps in an ongoing dialogue with race" means that we do not serve all our students as well as we might otherwise (2006, 129). Helle Rytkønen furthers this idea, reminding us that the professor "picks the material we discuss in class. And . . . the very selection of texts obviously sets the parameters of the discussion—for good and for bad" (2006, 50). Unexplored gaps may mean that the selection of texts sets the parameters for bad or at least for absence. And when white professors construct the classroom, they should view that as a place where, like fandom, they need to consider "how [their] other identities converge with the one[s they] portray when entering new communities" (Stedman 2012, 111).

Paul Booth argues that the fan studies professor guides students in the "critical skills of fandom," including enthusiasm and responsible media citizenship. This pedagogy encourages students to become critical fans who "demonstrate listening skills by interacting with other fans in thoughtful ways. Critical fans encourage discussion through individual contribution and empathetic conversation. Critical fans encourage civil discourse, even if it's a disagreement." These actions stand in contrast to the "neoliberal turn in fandom, which places cultural value on so-called right and wrong ways to be a fan, extols the individual over the community," and, Booth implies, mirrors the neoliberal turn in education, which situates students as consumers rather than members of learning communities. Fan studies often positions fan practices as "resistant, transformative, or critical of media practices." However, as this chapter aims to consider, fan practices are much like fan pedagogies: "in an always liminal state between resistant and complicit in institutional contexts" (Booth 2015a, 1.1, 1.3, 1.9, 2.3).

Urmitapa Dutta echoes the anxiety of this liminal state. While coauthoring her work with students, she "had unwittingly engaged in normative practices that would grant us legitimacy from gatekeeping institutions—the very institutional practices I was trying to contest." Inside the classroom she held power and privilege, but outside it, as "an untenured, female, non-American faculty of color," she lacked it. In order to create the text that questioned and invited engagement in the way she and her students wanted, Dutta had to embrace "vulnerabilities in teaching and learning, which acknowledged the limits of knowing." This acknowledgment allowed the critical text to emerge by working with discomfort instead of ignoring it and challenging neoliberal ideas that want teaching to be "static, content-based, cognitive transmission of information" (2016, 350, 351).

This chapter does not, ultimately, provide a challenge to the neoliberal corporate university model. Others have done so much more elegantly than I can. However, when we talk about race in the classroom, and when we talk about discomfort, particularly in the context of an expensive private university in the capitol of the United States like the one where I taught the classes I will discuss, we talk in the shadow of neoliberal and corporate educational ideas.

Within this shadow, we teach students who may or may not objectify or identify with fans. Students may see fans as extreme or weird; fans, to students unfamiliar with fandom cultures, might view fan activities as silly or strange or even deviant. On the other hand, students might identify as fans, have deeply internalized the norms of certain fandoms, and be resistant to even the gentlest analysis of fan activity. Both sets of these students may be suspicious of the academic work on fandom and may choose not to engage with it. It makes them uncomfortable; much like when they encounter someone new on campus, they are "sometimes cautious as to how to interact" (Geraghty 2012, 163). Fan identities may be far easier to overcome than the barriers created by racial ones. To the mainstream, fans have been racialized as white, regardless of their actual ethnicity. Mel Stanfill argues that this racialization both others and privileges fans: "Ultimately, this articulation of white bodies, fandom, and nonheteronormativity in the mainstream media constructs fandom as a nonheteronormative variety of whiteness, positioning the supposed inadequacy of fans as the result of substandard—but standardizable—self-control. This works both to reinforce the cultural commonsense that privilege is a natural property of white, heterosexual masculinity and to produce fandom as white" (2011, 1.2).

Racing fans as white creates a blind spot for fan studies, which as Rukmini Pande and Swati Moitra point out, favors analyses that "ignore or erase the role that race plays in these fan communities and their production. Because they do not speak to or of nonwhite fans, their analyses of subversion, resistance, and co-option do not have the weight they might have with a less parochial, more intersectional approach" (2017, 1.3). A mainstream media approach to fans as white (either normatively so or not) and a fan studies approach that eagerly examines gender, sexuality, and class turn attention away from race. Thus fan studies has not fully embraced a critical antiracist pedagogy; in this, we do not necessarily follow fans' examples. Pande and Moitra remind us that "the absence of attention to race in fan studies is ironic, because these debates have never been more hotly discussed and contested in fandom spaces than they have been in recent years" (2017, 1.4). I do not exempt myself from this absence.

I offer myself here as a primary object of study—I will use this chapter to reflect on two sections of two separate courses that I taught closely in time using fandom-based pedagogical philosophies at the same university. I taught each in the University Writing Program, where instructors can choose their own theme and use it to meet their course's learning objectives. The two courses were [Expletive Written]: Cursing and Culture, taught in the summer of 2015, and Remixing *Jane Eyre*, taught the following fall. The first class engaged in active and difficult conversations about race and many students wrote about race. The other did not.

My reflection relies on the generosity of two students in particular, Aminah Farmer and Christiana Miller. These two young Black women took

my courses and allowed me to guide them through vulnerable and risky writing. When I was writing this chapter, they were each willing to answer my
questions with frankness and honesty. I also rely here on Helen Fox's idea
that I, as a white teacher, have failed to recognize barriers. I aim to reveal
those and to offer in that revelation practical ways for other white teachers to
engage in antiracist fandom pedagogy.

Let me here acknowledge some things I did not pay attention to. In
the expletive class, I immediately introduced race as a topic. I showed clips
of Key and Peele's skits about Luther, Obama's Anger Translator, specifically
"Meet Luther," "Obama Shutdown," and "I Sunk Your Battleship, Bitch," and
I offered essays discussing the n-word, including Emily Bernard's "Teaching the N-Word." We had a class discussion about how I should handle the
n-word when reading texts aloud in class. I told the class, a mix of Black, white,
Latina, and Asian students studying in America, that it meant "something"
for a white woman to stand in front of a classroom as the teacher and say
racial slurs, even if she was reading or quoting from a text. I took it for granted
that they filled in the blank space of "something" with what I intended—to
do so would be a misuse of power and a potentially abusive one. This was
a blind spot. I should have defined "something" and had a discussion about
whether my "something" and their "something" were the same. I told them
that they could decide how they wanted me to approach this: skip the word,
use a euphemism, or say the word. They chose for me to say the word aloud. I
struggled to do it, but I paid attention to and respected their choice.

Students in my *Jane Eyre* course often wrote about disability, gender,
and sexuality. But despite the colonialism inscribed into the text, race did not
figure into their explorations. I taught in two ways that I thought were precise and true to the text but revealed blind spots. First, I used language like
"missionary" instead of "colonizer" when discussing St. John, Jane's long-lost
cousin and would-be husband, who coldly insists that she marry him and
travel to India to save souls. Students understood the historical context of
colonialism, and we discussed the issue in class, but we focused on Jane and
the novel, not on the racial consequences of the characters' actions.

Second, our conversations about Bertha proved more complicated.
I pushed my students to think about the term "Creole" in historical and
nuanced terms. "Creole," as a complicated term with multiple meanings, often
could be used incorrectly or out of context in our discussions of Bertha, and
so I pushed students to recognize the usage in context. Students could have
perceived this as shutting down racially oriented conversations. Our conversations generally focused on Bertha as the madwoman; we focused on her
disability rather than on her heritage or the complex scholarly discussion of it.

Looking back, I wonder, How can these two teaching selves emerge from the same person? Esther Ohito raises the point that "cocooned in the familiarity of comfort, we are often either unable or unwilling to jeopardize our sense of equilibrium by tackling emotional risks" (2016, 455). Student discomfort is important, maybe even necessary, for learning. But the noted contrast suggests that, for white professors, discomfort is also necessary, and not dealing openly with race, power, and privilege in the classroom preserves that "familiarity of comfort." Chris Zawaodniak reminds us that professors "who ignore lines of power within the class often reinforce them" (1997, 25).

I included a cover letter with the syllabus for [Expletive Written]: Cursing and Culture that served as both warning and course contract. It informed students that the material they would be studying could be offensive, troubling to their values, and possibly upsetting to them personally. It also stated that expletives, including slurs, would be used in readings and discussed in the class. It stated a clear boundary of the class: at no point could anyone use an expletive or slur against a classmate or the professor. It asked them to sign and date the contract if they decided to continue in the course. Modeled after fan content warnings, this allowed students to understand up front what the course would contain. All eight of my summer 2015 students did so in the first week of class. The actual content of the syllabus opened with an abridged version of the *Oxford English Dictionary's* definition of "fuck" as a noun. The syllabus continued:

> The myriad possible uses and meanings of the word reveal a great
> deal about how American culture deals with expletives, which the
> OED defines as adjectives "[s]erving to fill out; introduced merely
> to occupy space, or to make up a required quantity or number"
> ("expletive"). Other definitions of expletive include, an adjective that
> "serv[es] merely to fill out a sentence, help out a metrical line, etc.,"
> and a noun that is "a profane oath or other meaningless exclamation"
> ("expletive"). In this class, we will read personal essays about language by David Sedaris, Anne Lamott, and others. We'll also explore
> expletives in popular culture. We'll use these examples to explore the
> political implications of cursing. This political exploration will continue in manifestos like "BITCH Manifesto" and "QUEERS Read This."

Defining the terms and defending the course theme made it clear that expletives are cultural, that they have meaning, and that they are political. Looking back, I see that whiteness is present here as well, but Blackness is absent, and I list Sedaris and Lamott but not Bernard, a required reading for the course. According to Helle Rytkønen's setting of parameters, I set them for bad initially, even if I later corrected. My attention failed here.

On the first day of class, I asked students to share their favorite curse word. I went first, expounding on my love of the word "fuck," made plain by the syllabus at that point. This served as an icebreaker, and Aminah confirmed its effectiveness. In our discussion, she shared that my swearing made me feel approachable. It felt "weird" and yet comfortable to curse in class, she said. And that comfort level ultimately made it possible for her to write the kind of work she wrote.

Race, Aminah shared, is hard to talk about, particularly with a person of another race. Aminah is Black, and I am white. In our informal conversation, I wanted to know, Did I open the classroom, or did I push? She responded that she never felt unsafe in our class. She did, however, feel uncomfortable; that is always going to be part of how she responds emotionally when she discusses race with a nonminority. However, when I made it clear that I considered the n-word an expletive and, therefore, fair game for exploration in our classroom, she got excited about the course material. She chose to write about the n-word in rap lyrics and put in enthusiastic effort, looking critically at the music and musicians she was a fan of, how they connected with her personal life, and how all this resonated with a larger cultural story. While in class I may have used the full word with the permission of my students, I choked on it. During our conversation, Aminah used the phrase "the n-word," and I choose to honor that here by repeating that phrasing. When I quote her work, I will use the words she uses.

I asked Aminah about the experience of my first asking the class about using the n-word, then my using their permission to speak the word in discussion. "Deep down," she said, "I wanted you to say it. But deeper down, I didn't want you to say it." This was an important moment of vulnerability. Two years later, she remembers that discussion and her internal conflict. Aminah had attended Catholic secondary schools, where she was in the racial minority. She felt reluctant to discuss race or racial history because as a minority she felt singled out. Her larger educational experience followed this trend. When she was a senior, her class on race and sociology had a Black teaching assistant and the highest number of Black students she had ever had in one course at this university, two milestones. As a basketball player, she and her teammates had wanted to wear "I Can't Breathe" T-shirts to warm up before games in solidarity with Eric Garner's family. Their white coach told them that he thought they would be safer going to a protest than wearing the T-shirts at a warm-up.

These educational experiences and the ambivalence that Aminah expressed about wanting me to both say and not say the n-word in class clearly relate. For a student whose experiences have again and again included erasure, granting the white professor the acknowledgment that yes, it does mean "something" when she says the n-word, and yes, she should say it in this narrow context of quoting, reading, and discussing must certainly feel risky. I must take a moment to honor the trust Aminah and her classmates put in me by taking that risk. How vulnerable and brave they were in that moment.

Aminah's ambivalence toward the n-word extends beyond just our classroom and my use, however. In her personal narrative, "The N-Word," quoted here with permission, she writes of her experiences growing up in Philadelphia among white friends:

> For a few of them, I was probably their first black friend, so maybe they were expecting something different because of how Hip-Hop portrays the use of "Nigga" frequently in music. Deep down I knew that it was not in my personality to say that word, even if it was considered the "neighborhood slang." Let a black student constantly say "Nigga" in a predominantly white school and they will get expelled. No exceptions!

No exceptions for the Black student in the predominantly white school. For Aminah, the scrutiny she felt as a minority and the power of the n-word were reinforced by a locker room experience. During a pregame hype ritual, she played Drake's "Headlines." She describes the experiences of looking around at her primarily white teammates during the song:

> My head was pounding, my heart was racing and my mood did a complete 180. I wanted to see who was rapping the lyrics, most importantly who had the guts to say "Nigga" with me in the room. My teammates were rapping the lyrics but skipped over the word "Nigga." It was not until then when I realized the power of the word "Nigga." Before it was just a word to me, a word I would rap to myself, but at the moment the word "Nigga" coming out of a white person's mouth meant much more to me than a simple word. Honestly, if I had heard one of my teammates say "Nigga," and I'm glad I did not, I probably would have gone off right before the game, with no care in the world. Forget the game, the game would not have mattered to me.

The fact that a white person said the word "Nigga" would have mattered most to me.

This is extraordinarily vulnerable writing. This writing aims toward empathetic discussion. In large part because she felt safe in her discomfort, because she thought I was approachable, and because the course contract set the tone for respect, Aminah writes a deeply personal work that implicated me, a white person who said the n-word, in her pain. This is the kind of risk we should want our students to take and the kind of discomfort all teachers, particularly white teachers, should be willing to embrace for the sake of antiracist pedagogy.

The course justification for Remixing *Jane Eyre* was far less fun yet set exactly the tone I expected for the course:

> Chantal Zabus describes *Jane Eyre* as "an interpellative dream-text" (2001, 191) that writers have rewritten in order to interrogate and correct problems in the text. This act of re-writing, or as Zabus offers, "re-righting" (ibid.), has a long history of transforming canonical texts into new work. This act of transformation is akin to how scholars transform and produce ideas in their own work. Fan writing, or remix composition (Stedman 2012, 119), also mirrors how scholars approach writing and research.

The front cover of this syllabus included a frequently asked questions page, and the most memorable thing from it, according to Christiana, was that when my office door had a "Do Not Disturb" sign on it, students should take it seriously because I would be pumping breast milk in my office. The first day of class was ordinary; I made a low-key joke, and we went over the syllabus and talked about the skills needed in the transition to college writing. I emphasized getting the text and beginning the reading, as well making sure the class was the right fit—for example, if students did not want to spend sixteen weeks writing about a Victorian gothic romance, they should check with the registrar during the add and drop period.

For the first assignment of the course, a lens essay designed to teach students how to break out of old high school formats (in the US, a five-paragraph format is commonly used), and begin to think about using methodologies to conduct analyses, I assigned essays from which they could glean lens concepts. All the essays focused on gender with a twist, like class, friendship, or authorship. Christiana's comments show the impact:

Race was not a topic of much discussion within the Remix classroom. The only time race was mentioned was while discussing Bertha's upbringing. We briefly discussed her mixed-race background and referenced Jean Rhys's *Wide Sargasso Sea*. However, the discussion quickly turned from race to sexuality and freedom. The class began to reason that the main cause for her quarantine was her fierce sexuality which Rochester could not handle.

Christiana ultimately chose to explore fierce sexuality and ethics in her final project, examining BDSM relationships as a way of explaining what might have drawn Jane and Rochester together as well as what might have torn Rochester and Bertha apart. For the final assignment, students created a remix—a fanwork—of *Jane Eyre* and defended it using scholarly research. They explored the ideas that they perceived as being outside the traditional realm of the classroom. I call these wild ideas, and fandom pedagogy and the use of fanwork as models demonstrate to students that their ideas, which at first seem wild, are actually creative, thoughtful, and able to be presented ethically. In Christiana's remix, titled "Jane the Submissive" and quoted here with permission, she positions Edward Rochester as a regretful dominant trying to reconnect with his submissive Jane:

> I knew I needed to listen. Edward was lying before me pouring out his heart. He needed this, it was cathartic.
> Edward's face hardened and he spoke curtly, "Punishment." "I was a young dom back then and that's all I knew. I punished [Bertha] thinking that it would make her submit, when all it did was drive her further and further away. So much so that I think we both lost ourselves in the process. I wasn't a good dom to her. That yoke weighs heavy on my shoulders everyday."

While some may squirm at the idea of working with sexual material in a first-year writing course or in a course about *Jane Eyre*, I was enthusiastic. I love students' risky writing. It is, after all, how they learn what the academy has to offer them as well as its limits. In her scholarly defense, Christiana set the following as her agenda: "Though Jane's physical return to Rochester is one thing, her *need* or *desire* to return to Rochester is another. Her need or desire is something mental—psychological—and is deeply rooted within her inner thoughts and expressed in her physical actions. I aim to address the unique romance between Rochester and Jane, and try to place where this particular *desire* stems from, in 'Jane the Submissive,' through the use of a BDSM relationship." Such an ambitious goal set a high bar for the work of revision and research and indicated the level of trust that needed to be established between student and teacher in order to write such difficult material. Christiana and I established trust in an unfortunate manner.

I should note that what I am about to report is upsetting but that I have Christiana's permission to do so. It is the only significant way in which discussion of race entered our classroom. Early in the semester, after the grades were returned on the lens essay, Christiana stayed after class to apologize for what she saw as the poor quality of her work (it was not poor by any sense). She explained that her roommates were racially harassing her and that she was stressed because of it. A colleague of mine was faculty in residence in her dorm, and I was able to put Christiana in touch with her. I was also able to have a phone call with the director of the Multicultural Student Services Center that evening. Among the three of us, we advocated for the roommates to be moved. When I asked Christiana why she felt able to trust me with this disclosure, she responded:

> I felt comfortable doing so because of the way in which you made yourself accessible to students in the class and the unconventional nature of class texts. You encouraged students to participate in your office hours and even scheduled small group meetings to discuss our work. You got to know us individually and learned our personalities. In addition, Google Docs helped a great deal. I felt that we were able to receive direct feedback from you and the comment threads were akin to little dialogues. Also, I've never met a professor more responsive via email than you.

Christiana points here to key teaching practices that allow professors to connect with and work with students outside of classroom spaces. The classroom space might not be accessible for all students. Allowing for different types of participation builds opportunities for vulnerability and trust. Still I wonder, If we had discussed race in our classroom, what kind of work might have emerged? Christiana has considered the possibility as well, expressing a wish that we had discussed race more with regard to Bertha and perhaps had even read some of *Wide Sargasso Sea*.

I present these two student experiences as paths to key learnings to show what white professors can do to seek out discomfort and become practitioners of critical, antiracist fandom pedagogy (B. Brown 2015). In

[Expletive Written], race was an important and urgent factor, figuring into student conversation, student writing, and class engagement. In Remixing *Jane Eyre*, race was absent, even though the students were challenged in other ways.

The first key learning I offer regards the presentation of materials. The materials I presented to students in the course told them what held my attention. The students paid attention to me. In the first course, I presented sources on a diversity of topics, we moved through these topics in a way that functioned more like units, and I offered a mix of media. In the *Jane Eyre* course, I focused on meeting the course needs—the students had to read the novel before any writing or research could begin. I also focused on making sure that the students had time to do intensive research, so I reduced the number of required readings in the course. Finally, I committed to presenting female scholars to students, and so all but one of the required readings were by women. The voices we elevate are the voices that our students will listen to. Neither of these courses was about race, but one included texts that directly addressed racial issues, and that made a huge impact on the type of work the students did.

The second key learning I offer looks at unexplored gaps. The clear statement that I considered racial slurs expletives created an opening for Aminah and her classmates to write about them. The gap left unexplored in *Jane Eyre*, which both Christiana and I identified, was that of Bertha's racial heritage. I did not push to explore that space, and so neither did my students. I did not know the limits of my knowing, and so I closed myself to discovering the limits. In many other respects, however, I am open to my lack of knowledge; I will ask for help. I should have done so here. In developing an antiracist pedagogy, in creating a classroom that aims to teach critical fans with empathy, white professors should pay attention to the work and the needs of their colleagues of color both at their institution and in their field. I do not mean here to use them as unpaid and unseen professional development resources. Instead, if you want to support students of color, you also need to support colleagues of color (who, after all, were once students). What and how do they teach and research? What is happening with their course evaluations? Are they supported institutionally, or are they, like Dutta, scrutinized and marginalized? I developed a reputation in my program as the rabble-rousing adjunct; if a problem or a question arose about the union contract, the office, or the pay, people would email me or approach me for help and guidance. One way to find out the limits of your knowledge is to use your privilege to make a little trouble.

The third key learning I offer regards barriers to cross. In both courses, I saw that the key barrier was one of trust. My students came into the classroom with experiences of pain deeply connected to race and caused by whiteness. My willingness to be vulnerable, to allow Aminah the space to tell a complex and ambivalent truth, and to advocate for Christiana despite my own precarious status as an adjunct made it possible for these students to trust my classroom and my teaching. To implement this in our classrooms, the first step is to create a collaborative space by setting ground rules for class discussion. In the expletive course, these ground rules were set from the start with the contract in the syllabus: students could not use expletives against each other. The words were for analysis, not for weaponry. In both classes, group workshops had explicit instructions regarding the focus of the workshop, things like "Restate the main point of this essay in 1 sentence" or "How original is the claim? Have you come across anything similar in your reading? If so, provide the source to the author. How interesting is the claim? Is there a 'so what' element? Do you want to read more? Be honest—the author should know if the paper is boring so there is still time to revise."

I framed the first instance of peer review in the class with the reminder that students came from different backgrounds and, therefore, groups should focus on improving one another's content, not grammar. I made sure that they understood that grammatical instruction was my job, not theirs, and that editing each other's papers was out of bounds in class. Setting them up to talk about content made the classroom a place where, as Christiana emphasized, the students' voices were elevated. Aminah echoed this as well; in small groups, because of the focus on content and because everyone wrote about the theme, people engaged with each other. (After the expletive class ended, a white student challenged her grade. One of the reasons she gave was that she had seen the work of another student and had judged it to be bad. Based on her small group, I inferred that the student was a nonnative speaker of English with imperfect grammar. That student's success or failure in the course was irrelevant to the grade the white student received and was in fact protected not only by professional ethics but by US privacy laws. In the case of my grade challenger, she did not inflict her racism on her fellow student in the classroom, because the ground rules did not give her an opening to do so.)

Finally, all professors, including white professors, need to trust their students. They need to redefine risk taking or fannish student work not just as student work that talks back to the canon but come to understand themselves to be part of the canon. Students of color may admire white professors and may believe wholeheartedly that they do antiracist work, but these students should still be able to resist them in productive and incisive ways. Christiana, in the process of revising her paper, would push back against my suggestions, committed to her own ideas. Because I trusted her, she says that she "felt free to talk to you without being judged or worse—silenced."

When white professors begin to do the work of becoming *critical* academic fan teachers, our classroom spaces will become more resistant. They will also become more uncomfortable. Grading Christiana's explicitly sexual paper certainly was, and bearing witness to Aminah's pain was as well. But the results tell the truth: our field, our teaching, and our students are better off when we all take on some discomfort.

TWO. OTHERNESS

4. Raceplay

Whiteness and Erasure in Cross-Racial Cosplay

JOAN MILLER

AS BOTH A POP CULTURE FAN AND AN ACAFAN—a term coined by Henry Jenkins to describe an academic fan who takes both fandom and scholar roles in concert and with equal levity—I have been embedded in pop culture fandom as long as I can remember, but it was not until 2014 that I had the occasion to attempt my first real cosplay. In October of that year, my partner and I, New York Comic Con tickets in hand, decided to dress up as Batman's the Joker and Harley Quinn. Not only was this my first public cosplay, it was also my first cross-racial cosplay. Harley Quinn is typically portrayed as white-skinned, blond-haired, and blue-eyed, the exact opposite of my brown-skinned, brown-haired, and brown-eyed body. Even though the costume showed minimal skin and I'd seen cross-racial cosplayers before, I felt a certain anxiety. Would people recognize the character? Would I be harassed, as other cross-racial cosplayers have been?

Thankfully or not, my cosplay flew mostly under the radar. Those who recognized me were able to do so because I walked alongside my partner and the association became clear. The worst reactions I encountered were quizzical looks as con-goers tried to put the pieces together and figure me out. The same was not true for another cross-racial cosplay I discovered later that month.

Just a few weeks after New York Comic Con, a Tumblr post went viral throughout the cosplay community. Kira Markeljc, a white German cosplayer, posted a makeup test that revealed her in blackface in an attempt to cosplay a popular Black character named Michonne from the US-based television show *The Walking Dead*. The images caused a stir in social media scenes with various geek culture news outlets featuring the cosplay and seeking responses from readers. Reactions varied from outrage to support. Articles reporting on the topic generated a certain notoriety and broad knowledge of the performance within the cosplay community.

The synchronicity of these two events, as well as the buzz around Markeljc's post, piqued my interest. What was it about her post that was so objectionable? Why did my cross-racial cosplay circulate so differently? What kinds of ethical issues arise when people cosplay characters of a different race? Is it right for white people to cosplay Black characters? Does the performance of T'Challa, the Black Panther, become something different when the person playing him is white? It seemed like the obvious answers, at least in my case, lay in the identity of the performers.

As I will demonstrate in this chapter, my careful study and contemplation over the years since my cosplay suggest that something very important happens politically in the performance of cross-racial cosplay, especially when it comes to the function of whiteness. Black cosplayers performing white characters—because of the history of Black oppression by whites and the relative absence of Black characters in pop culture media—are doing something inherently different from white actors performing Black characters. In my analysis of specific performances, it became clear that Black cosplayers as white characters are, often intentionally, participating in a dialogue about the invisibility of Black characters in popular media. In this sense Black cosplayers, with varying degrees of intentionality, use their cosplay to take political action. According to Jacques Rancière, who defines politics as a moment in which uncounted or invisible subjects make themselves visible, Black cosplay is inherently political (1999). As my colleague Ante Ursic once put it, a moment is political when "there is a double role played by the ones who are uncounted. *A moment where they pretend to be something they are not in order to display that they aren't*" (my emphasis). We will see how this appears in cosplays by Chaka Cumberbatch and Vishavjit Singh, who use them to ask provocative questions about who can be considered a hero.

Thus, I ask, How can cross-racial cosplay make the invisible subject visible? How has the history of Black oppression and popular media produced the conditions for political cross-racial cosplay? Where, when, how, and by whom is cross-racial cosplay most effective as a political tool? How do whiteness and white privilege operate and perform in the realm of cosplay? In this chapter, I will address these questions by illuminating a brief history of cross-racial performance as it applies to the world of fandom and examining the performativity of those cross-racial appearances. Specifically, I analyze three cases of cross-racial cosplay, including white cosplayers in blackface, white cosplayers as Black characters without blackface, and Black cosplayers as white characters. Through these examples I engage with literature on Black performance and participatory culture with particular focus on the work of Jacques Rancière, Henry Jenkins, Michel de Certeau, Leslie Carr, and Tavia Nyong'o. I argue that cross-racial cosplay at its strongest functions as a Ranciéran moment of politics, prompting a change in the dialogue surrounding race and serving to break the silence of colorblind racism. A Ranciéran moment of politics in cosplay is achieved only when the invisible and nonspeaking subject makes itself visible by pretending to be something it is not. In this case, the moment of politics occurs when pop culture media producers and fans are forced to see characters and people who were previously invisible.

Early critiques of this piece resisted my impetus to unearth the racial politics of cosplay—an activity that, after all, includes play in its name. However, the work of cosplay should be taken seriously, as many cosplay artists and activists have already implied. Fan artworks must still be understood to be artworks, and while they are infused with passion, joy, and playfulness, they cannot be separated from their performance in the world. For this reason, I intend to make a strong claim about ethics in cosplay and the circulation of race and racial stereotypes within that realm. Fandom is not isolated from the world and therefore should not be immune to the same ethical and moral scrutiny applied to all other aspects of daily life. To borrow a phrase, "my conscience never takes a day off," and fandom should not function as an excuse for it to do so (Gervais 2011).

—What Makes Good Cosplay?

While a great deal of the art form consists of the costume itself, performance—or play—is usually a component. Often cosplayers strive to embody the values or personalities of their character while in costume. For example, Deadpool—a Marvel superhero who is known for his motor mouth and genre savviness—is an extremely popular subject for cosplayers. Deadpool cosplayers' performances emphasize their character's irreverent, self-aggrandizing, sarcastic, and oddball comedic style. Because he is well known for breaking the fourth wall, Deadpool offers cosplayers a plethora of options for combining characters and self-reflexive jokes. On the other hand, audiences might expect a Captain America cosplayer to be straightforward, polite, and gentlemanly when approached for pictures. Not all cosplays require such deep investment, however. While some cosplayers perform their characters as if they were onstage, imitating their vocal patterns, dialogue, image, and body language, others are content simply to wear the costume and occasionally pose for photos while otherwise attending the convention as themselves.

Regardless of the degree to which cosplayers embody the personality of their characters, many consider the performance an act of homage. A cosplayer's choice of character often comes from a place of love for or self-identification with that character. Though these are not the only reasons for choosing a cosplay, they tend to be some of the most popular ones. In some respects, a cosplayer can be seen as an individual proclaiming affection for a character or a story to anyone who will listen.

Probably the most prolific nondigital site of public cosplay is the pop culture convention, seen in various iterations but known colloquially as a comic con. In the United States, the two most popular cons in terms of attendance and media prevalence are the San Diego Comic Con (or Comic-Con International) and the New York Comic Con. The con itself is something of a cross-pollination between a typical academic conference and a more commercial meeting such as a car show. Inside, an attendee has access to a number of panels on topics as wide ranging as the premiere of a new show or the discussion of feminist characters in the golden age of comics. Additionally, the con is rife with opportunities to buy merchandise, both licensed and crafted by fans. Within the convention center—Jacob K. Javits for the New York con and the San Diego Convention Center for the California con—cosplayers make up large percentages of the one hundred and fifty thousand plus attendees regardless of the officially designated activities assigned to each space.

Cosplayers travel the areas of the con as frequently and as widely as any casual con-goer, often willing to pose for photos regardless of their location—partly because this desire for a photograph conveys acknowledgment and appreciation of the cosplay. For example, during New York Comic Con 2014, I witnessed a parade of cosplayers as the aforementioned Deadpool. The Deadpool parade included cosplayers portraying the superhero in numerous iterations, including Deadpool as Captain America, Deadpool as Stormtrooper, Deadpool as a French maid, Deadpool as a detective, ninja Deadpool, fem!Deadpool, and a self-proclaimed Hollywood Deadpool, among numerous others. The Deadpool cosplayers paraded through the aisles chanting "We are awesome!" and percussively striking their props.

In addition to conventions, cosplay images are widely circulated in fan communities online. Many cosplayers maintain social media pages for sharing their cosplays and their ideas about the identity of the genre. Similarly, groups of cosplayers organize in communities and use social media to engage discussions around certain themes within cosplay, such as the

Facebook group Minority Cosplayers, which focuses on sharing the struggles that minority cosplayers encounter when dealing with harassment and issues of representation.

— Cosplay in Blackface

It was through her Facebook page, "Purple Candy Cosplay," that Kira Markeljc first shared her cosplay of Michonne, a *Walking Dead* character played on television by Zimbabwean American actor Danai Gurira. The controversial images showed a portrait of a made-up Markeljc in a side-by-side comparison with a screenshot of Gurira's Michonne. Markeljc's test image included skin-darkening makeup that instantly evokes blackface minstrelsy, as well as a prosthetic nose enhancement and artificial dreadlocks. Naturally, in an American society where blackface is almost as culturally abjected as the swastika, the immediate response to Markeljc's cosplay was a heated argument surrounding the question of whether she was a racist.

In the case of the systemic racism that accounts for the lack of representation of Black bodies in popular media, however, the usefulness of labeling Markeljc as a racist is limited. As Stephanie Wildman explains, "Calling someone a racist individualizes the behavior and veils the fact that racism can occur only where it is culturally, socially and legally supported" (1996, 11). Certainly, Markeljc's actions were supported by her fans, who went to great efforts to defend her. Some—including Markeljc—suggested that the cosplay was not blackface but did not give any further explanation why a distinction should be made. The implication echoes another argument: because cosplay is usually intended as homage (and Markeljc did cite this as a rationale when challenged), the gesture should be seen as appreciative instead of violent. Others posited that Markeljc, as a German woman, had no context for the history of minstrelsy and blackface in American culture. While this is not true—Germany has a history of blackface that continues to this day—Markeljc's relative ignorance or lack thereof with regard to the history of blackface does not change how the image was received (Stonington 2014). Additionally, because I am not interested in labeling Markeljc as a racist, her intent is secondary to the cosplay's performative nature.

Markeljc's makeup cannot be divorced from its social and historical context. "We might say that blackface artists . . . stag[e] a sort of unintended play . . . a play that point[s] up rather than paper[s] over cracks in the historical bloc of mid-century America" (Lott 1993, 106). Like the minstrel artists Eric Lott refers to, Markeljc reenacts the appropriation of Blackness by

whites as personal entertainment, participating in the historical and ongoing violence extolled by Frederick Douglass describing blackface performers
as "the filthy scum of white society, who have stolen from us a complexion
denied to them by nature, in which to make money, and pander to the corrupt taste of their white fellow-citizens" (quoted in Lott 1993, 123). While
Tavia Nyong'o notes that Douglass takes an essentialist view of race in order
to make his point, he also suggests that we might consider Blackness as property if we agree with Pierre-Joseph Proudhon that there is no true owner of
Blackness but, rather, that it is constituted as property specifically when it is
being stolen (Nyong'o 2009).

We can generously assume that Markeljc did not intend theft, and
while she is unlikely to earn any income from her performance, she nonetheless profits affectively, much like the Deadpool cosplayers. Her privilege
as a white woman allows her to put on Blackness when it is happy and convenient and take it off when such an image is no longer pleasant. In fact, that
is exactly what happened. Confronted with numerous articles and the many
comments they prompted, Markeljc removed all images of her makeup test
from her page (also breaking embedded links to the images) and has yet to
return to Michonne or any other character of color (excluding nonhumans).

Considering the racial discourse or lack thereof surrounding Markeljc's
cosplay, we can ask whether it constitutes a political moment. Working with
Jacques Rancière, we can understand politics as a function of the democratic miscount. This miscount is the product of a process that performs
a balancing act between freedom and equality. In order to attempt equality among individuals in a heterogeneous group, certain freedoms must be
restricted; the democratic miscount obfuscates these contradictions. In this
case, Markeljc's freedom to cosplay whomever she likes is challenged by reference to a violent practice in direct conflict with Black and Brown equality.
Here the Black individual is miscounted and replaced with a white performance of Blackness. For Rancière, the political moment happens when that
miscounted subject is no longer covered up or ignored but is recognized as
a speaking subject. In his words, "Politics exist because those who have no
right to be counted as speaking beings make themselves of some account,
setting up a community by the fact of placing in common a wrong" (1999,
27). Ideally, the moment of politics—while inherently unstable—alters the
discourse and enables a redistribution of the sensible, an opportunity for the
miscounted subject to be counted. Keeping these criteria in mind, we can
point to the reasons that Markeljc's cosplay fails.

Markeljc's failure to engage in discourse—removing images, dismissing racial concerns, and refusing discussion—represents a rejection

of responsibility for her racialization of both herself and the character. As a result, she traffics in painful cultural memories and reasserts her own privilege. Further, the discourse surrounding her cosplay was ultimately truncated by the rhetoric of postracial ideology—supporters argued that the real racists were those who brought up race in the first place. Because the conversation ultimately devolved into a virtual shouting match between people for or against Markeljc and her cosplay, and because the event seemed to fly mostly under the radar of larger fan communities, it ultimately fails to be a critical or productive political moment.

Finally, the crux of Rancière's definition of politics revolves around the opportunity for the invisible subject to appear. In this case, the subject of the cosplay is Markeljc and, as a young white German woman, Markeljc is already a highly visible and easily speaking subject. Within popular media, I would argue, the invisible subject is the Black and Brown body, and this cosplay does nothing to make those bodies visible. Rather, it works to silence Black and Brown concerns about the appropriation of their skin for white pleasure. Ultimately, Markeljc's cosplay and others like it fail because of their inability to spark meaningful discourse surrounding racism and popular media.

—White Katara and the Erasure of Brown Bodies

While blackface cosplay may seem like an obvious pitfall to many, the question of white cosplayers performing characters of color sans makeup is more complex. Because sci-fi and fantasy culture—two of the genres most heavily populated by fan artists—are predominantly white, it is unsurprising that this mode is the most prevalent form of cross-racial cosplay. To illustrate, I choose to focus on a particular character, Katara, from the popular Nickelodeon cartoon *Avatar: The Last Airbender*. Katara is a popular subject for cosplay due to her exciting potential as a strong female leader in a world dominated by men. In *The Last Airbender*, she is the only principal female character for the first of the four-season series and thus one with whom many female fans identified. Within the context of the source material, the authors never explicitly state Katara's race, but cultural and social practices within her family and community suggest Inuit or Inuit-esque descent. Certainly, by comparison with other characters, she can accurately be described as brown-skinned.

It was thus disappointing, if not surprising, when I conducted a Google search for "katara cosplay" and discovered that roughly 80 percent of the images featured Katara as a white woman. Like Markeljc, these Katara cosplayers appropriate the character for their own affective purposes, but, in a further act of violence, the white cosplays serve to subordinate the Brown body of the character and replace her with a white-bodied character in their own image. At a convention filled with such cosplayers, a new fan could be forgiven for thinking that the character was white. The white Katara cosplay cannot serve as a site of political dialogue because it circulates in a society besieged by postracial ideology.

Unfortunately, there is nothing radical or surprising about the disappearance of yet another Brown body. When a dissenting voice—or the invisible subject made invisible again by the cosplay—attempts to introduce a discussion of race in relation to the white cosplayer, it is silenced through the same ideology that allows white Katara to exist in the first place. To mention the racializing qualities of white Katara is to be labeled as a racist for calling attention to race. Supporters argue that race should not matter in all things, especially not in cosplay. However, as Stephanie Wildman states in *Privilege Revealed*:

> The race-and-sex are irrelevant argument is attractive because its proponents advance it as if it were not an ideal, but a reality. We are asked to believe that the discrimination-free society is here and that to pay attention to race or sex would turn back the clock to the days before racism and sexism were eliminated. A moment's reflection makes it clear that we do not live in such a world. The argument is based on a false premise, that the nondiscriminatory future is now and that except for the occasional aberrant bigot or sexist, we live in a race- and sex-neutral society. (1996, 125)

In order for white cosplayers to protect their perceived freedoms and avoid being labeled with the aberrant term "racist," it is necessary to advance this postracial ideology and behave as if the race-free future is now. This ideal (for some) future does not yet exist. Systemic and institutionalized racism is still very much part of our society. It is only in the recent context of continued systemic violence against Black bodies—as seen in the deaths of Freddie Gray, Trayvon Martin, Michael Brown, Eric Garner, Ahmaud Arberry, George Floyd, Breonna Taylor, and numerous others—that the ideology of postracial racism is beginning to dissolve as Americans are confronted with endlessly repeating scenes of state-sanctioned violence against Black individuals.

Nonetheless, white Katara cosplayers are able to take their race for granted while subordinating the race of the character they profess to admire and respect. This erasure of Brown bodies is particularly troublesome in the context of a story like *Avatar* that includes themes of colonialism, cultural genocide, and racial supremacy.

Returning to Jacques Rancière, we can easily deduce why the white-Black or white-Brown cross-racial cosplay—such as white Katara—fails as a moment of politics. Because most dialogue around the cosplay is shouted down under the banner of postracial ideology, any racial discourse is preemptively foreclosed. This was my experience in speaking out about one such Katara cosplay in a public Facebook group. My comment was immediately buried under an onslaught of replies accusing me of racism and attacking me with personal insults. Any attempt at further discussion was lost in the virtual equivalent of screaming and stone throwing. This response, instead of allowing the invisible and miscounted subject to rise up and be noticed, works to punish the invisible subject for daring to appear.

—Chaka Cumberbatch, Vishavjit Singh, and Disidentification

Black and Brown cosplayers embodying white characters do not perform the same way, largely due to previously discussed structures of systemic and postracial racism. Chaka Cumberbatch is a Black cosplay artist who often chooses to cosplay characters outside her race. She also writes on Black cosplay through her blog and more formally on the feminist news site xoJane. Cumberbatch gained recognition in the cosplay community after a photo of her as Sailor Venus from the manga and anime series *Sailor Moon* went viral. Her cosplay features a highly accurate reconstruction of the costume, body type, and attitude of the character she portrays. The detail forestalling the belief that she is literally Sailor Venus come to life is Cumberbatch's skin color. Her own Blackness serves as the self-expressive aspect of her cosplay.

If the aforementioned white Katara cosplayers are whitewashing the characters they cosplay, Cumberbatch's work might be called blackwashing. In this case, the cosplayer makes the Black body visible by disregarding the idea of the white body as default. In confronting fans with images of Black bodies inhabiting white characters, Cumberbatch manages to create a moment similar to that seen with the white cosplayer in blackface. Much like Markeljc, Cumberbatch experienced an immediate onslaught of comments on race. She was called Nigger Venus and Sailor Venus Williams and told to stick to characters in her range (Cumberbatch 2013b). Unlike Markeljc, however, Cumberbatch chose to engage directly with her audience by using her cosplay and her newfound fame in concert to discuss issues of Black representation in pop culture through her online journalism:

> I'm tired of not seeing faces like mine in my comics. I have had it with people telling me to "stick to my range" when I cosplay my favorite characters, knowing all the while that my "range" is maybe in the double digits on a good day while their "range" is almost endless. I'm sick of the notion that a black female character is a rare treat, a special occasion—a sparingly awarded privilege, but not a right. Why shouldn't it be a right? (Cumberbatch 2013a)

Cumberbatch's demand for better representation highlights the Black and Brown body as the uncounted or invisible subject in terms of pop culture media representation. Her lament echoes the sentiments of Marlon Riggs in his 1989 video *Tongues Untied*, which documents his experiences coming out as homosexual and moving to San Francisco. Quoted in José Muñoz's *Disidentifications*, he says that "in this great gay mecca I was an invisible man; still I had no shadow, no substance. No history, no place. No reflection. I was alien, unseen, and seen, unwanted. Here, as in Hepzibah, I was a nigga, still" (1999, 9).

Muñoz understands Riggs as disidentifying with a certain type of white homosexuality, and we might understand Cumberbatch's cosplay as working in a similar mode. Within *Disidentifications*, the eponymous term is described as one of three potential ways to react to dominant ideologies. The first mode, identification, produces a "Good Subject" who easily fits in, who conforms to and answers the Althusserian call of the dominant discursive form. The second mode, counteridentification, produces a "Bad Subject" who acts in opposition to the dominant ideology by rebelling and turning against the system. Yet this counteridentification, by making itself the exception to the rule, reinforces and validates the dominant position. Muñoz locates disidentification as an alternative to these two modes, in which the subject,

> ... instead of buckling under the pressures of dominant ideology (identification, assimilation) or attempting to break free of its inescapable sphere (counteridentification, utopianism) ... tries to transform a cultural logic from within, always laboring to enact permanent structural change while at the same time valuing the importance of local or everyday struggles of resistance. ... To disidentify is to read

oneself and one's own life narrative in a moment, object or subject that is not culturally coded to "connect" with the disidentifying subject. (1999, 11–12)

Cumberbatch's cosplay, previously a negotiation between the source text and her own creativity, now becomes a way of negotiating between the dominant ideology and her identity as a Black woman. By reasserting the possibility of a popular white-appearing character to be Black—or simply asserting that a Black woman can have all the power and agency of a white female superhero—her performance contests "the hegemonic supremacy of the majoritarian public sphere" (Muñoz 1999, 1). In other words, Cumberbatch contests preconceived notions about what kinds of bodies should and can appear in popular media.

Vishavjit Singh, who cosplays a Sikh Captain America on the streets of New York City, makes a move similar to Cumberbatch's. The character of Captain America, originated by Jack Kirby and Joe Simon in "Captain America Comics #1," arrived on the scene in March 1941. Created during the midst of the American effort in World War II, the character's initial modus operandi was to gather support for the Allies and literally beat up the Nazis. In post-9/11 America, the character has regained popularity as he came to symbolize a nostalgic patriotism that burgeoned in the American psyche in response to a resurgence of terrorist attacks and the wars in Afghanistan and Iraq. That said, while Cap is American to his core, he has always been more good than lawful and not necessarily on the side of the government or popular opinion. One of the things about Captain America that tends to win over fans—including myself—is his enduring commitment to always do what is right by everyone, regardless of how difficult it will be or how much trouble it may cause him. This is especially courageous in light of the fact that Steve Rogers—Captain America's alter ego—practiced this ideology long before he had any superpowers. When Steve Rogers was just a skinny, homeless war orphan from Brooklyn, he was still sticking up for what was right, and that is what made him worthy of becoming a superhero.

Thus, it may not be surprising that Vishavjit Singh as a physically slight man from a religious minority would identify with a character as morally and ethically upstanding as Captain America. While Cap's alter ego Steve Rogers is typically portrayed as blond-haired and blue-eyed, his appeal speaks to a myriad of demographics and, much like Deadpool, he is a popular choice for cosplayers. By cosplaying Captain America with the added "accessories" of a long natural beard and a turban, Singh asserts his own Americanness and the possibility of any minority to disidentify with Captain America by rejecting the homogeneous whiteness of the character while embracing his principles of kindness, equality, self-sacrifice, and sticking up for one's beliefs. Singh describes his motivations as such:

> It started with an illustration I did for the New York Comic Con a couple years ago. A picture with a little catchy caption basically saying "Chill, it's just a turban, now let's kick some intolerant ass." A year later Milwaukee happens, the massacre at a [Sikh] temple in Milwaukee. There I was in June, walking the streets as Captain America. . . . [He's] the most patriotic of super heroes. He started in 1941 fighting the Axis powers, now, Captain America comes back, fights hate crimes. (quoted in Kondabolu 2013)

Singh's portrayal of Captain America has been both popular and controversial, spawning several news articles and a documentary called *Red, White, and Beard*. Within each of Singh's travels throughout the city, his goal seems to be focused on altering the perceptions of New Yorkers about what kinds of people can be superheroes. In a Salon article titled "Captain America in a Turban," Singh discusses an encounter with a young boy in Central Park. Initially the boy insists that Singh cannot be Captain America, that "Captain America does not have a turban or a beard." But Singh persists. "Why not?" he asks, "I was born here. We could have a new Captain America who is Sikh or black or hispanic." After some thought, the boy concedes that maybe such a thing would be okay. Singh reflects, "That's exactly what brought me to this park on a beautiful summer day. To make fresh neural connections in our collective consciousness. To leave a new image on the hard drive of that boy's mind" (Singh, 2013).

Both Cumberbatch's and Singh's disidentifications force their respective audiences to ask questions and think critically. Their cosplays challenge dominant ideologies about what kinds of bodies get marked as superheroes and what kinds of bodies are visible in pop culture media. Because they spark this dialogue among other cosplayers and viewers of these cosplays and because their cosplays are taken up on news sites such as xoJane and Salon, Singh and Cumberbatch start new discourses of pop culture representation. Ultimately this sparking of conversation indicates that both Singh's and Cumberbatch's cosplays manifest as successful political moments working on the redistribution of the sensible. Cumberbatch takes this political moment a step further by instituting the hashtag movement #28DaysOfBlackCosplay, which brings further attention and dialogue to the work of Black cosplayers throughout the month of February.

While it is difficult to determine the efficacy of artistic labor, there is an undeniable shift toward greater representation in pop culture media, as evidenced by the inclusion of feature-length films about Marvel superheroes such as Black Panther (with an African male superhero) and Captain Marvel (with a popular female superhero). In print, Marvel Comics has initiated a female Thor title that has rivaled the original Thor in terms of financial success, as well as the runaway hit series *Ms. Marvel*, starring a female, Muslim, Pakistani American teenager named Kamala Khan. I highlight Marvel because of its ownership of the characters Captain America and Deadpool, but it is not the only media producer to take notice. One can only hope that this trend will continue and that we will see more Black bodies through character creation, creative casting choices, or their own forms of blackwashing and brownwashing (such as Tessa Thompson in the 2017 *Thor: Ragnarok*).

—Freedom vs. Equality

Featured are only a few examples of endless opportunities to analyze modes of cross-racial cosplay in terms of theories of representation, identity, and critical race studies. Every cosplay performs differently, both in the fandom community and within the world at large. While a white cosplayer in blackface can serve as a disruptive and productive moment of visibility for racial issues—as seen in Kira Markeljc's Michonne cosplay—the performance utterly fails as politics if the cosplayer refuses to acknowledge the need for such a dialogue or abstains from participating in the conversation around it. In such a case, blackface in cosplay does little more than reactivate the age-old crime of cross-racial appropriation that reasserts and renormalizes the hegemonic attitude of white supremacy. Similarly, white cosplayers as characters of color—sometimes unknowingly—perpetrate and participate in the violent appropriation of Black bodies. Because white cosplay of characters of color contributes to the erasure of Black and Brown bodies, it is ultimately just as problematic, if not more so, than images of cosplayers in blackface. In every case, the cross-racial cosplay is most effective as political speech when it offers an opportunity for dialogue and when both the cosplayer and the community encourage and support that dialogue. Through disidentification and the embodiment of value sets from the characters themselves in the form of certain principles of particular characters, Black and Brown cosplayers can create an opportunity for the reappearance of their bodies in defiance of a culture where those bodies are constantly in danger of disappearing.

Some might read this as an ultimatum to white cosplayers, much like the epithets that Cumberbatch was confronted with in her Sailor Venus cosplay: stick to your range. However, the major difference between the two instances exists in the reality of systems of white supremacy throughout history. Because white cosplayers have such a vast range and because the appropriation of Black and Brown bodies for their own affective pleasure damages or erases those bodies, white cosplayers must deal with these ethical issues. Often white privilege exists in the ability to ignore or disregard issues of race and ethnicity, whether the activity is professional or playful. Politically, however, willful ignorance is not enough. In terms of the here and now, in the moment when politics happens, the white cosplayer is faced with the dilemma of the democratic miscount. The white cosplayer's personal freedom is in direct conflict with the equality of Black and Brown people— including their fellow cosplayers. White cosplayers must decide in every case whether it is more important to them to maintain their freedom to cosplay whomever they may choose or whether to yield that small amount of freedom in the interest of a much greater equality.

5. "But I'm a Foreigner Too"

Otherness, Racial Oversimplification, and Historical Amnesia in Japan's K-pop Scene

MIRANDA RUTH LARSEN

BY FOCUSING ON K-POP FANDOM, in this chapter I will attempt to unpack the implications of "Korean" in K-prefixed cultural products in the reception site of Tokyo. Given the turbulent history between Japan and both Koreas, the boom in South Korean cultural products—the Korean Wave—that began in the early 2000s remains an interesting example of transnational fandom. I will explore the anti–Korean Wave and generalized anti-Korean sentiments in Japan for context, which points to the conflation of race and nationality within the country, where "a racialistic myth of 'the Japanese' is widely shared by its citizenry" (Murphy-Shigemitsu 2008, 284). I will then offer some examples from my fieldwork with South Korean male idol groups in Tokyo and their Japanese fans, where my presence as a female multiracial academic from the United States served as a disruptive factor, and then outline how South Korean idols themselves are often treated within Japan. In doing so, I hope to draw attention to the frequent pattern where race is oversimplified within fandom in Japan—rather than being completely erased, fans or idols are reduced to one thing as if they are the same exportable product as music or television.

Academic and popular attention to the Korean Wave has frequently grappled with the implications of national product, often within the framework of soft power and cultural exportability. (The Korean Wave is also referred to as Hallyu, Hanryu, and Kanryu. I have left other terms, when quoted, in their original form.) The prefix attached to K-drama, K-pop, K-beauty, and so on promotes a sense of exportability and importability, a cultural togetherness ready for consumption and enjoyment; for example, a booth at KCON 2017 in Los Angeles invited convention visitors to assemble a scene with a variety of props and clothes for their K-life. Despite the fact that many hit K-pop songs are written and engineered by non-Korean talent and the hypnotizing dance routines of idol groups are taught by non-Korean talent, K-pop is currently at the forefront of the Korean Wave as we know it, and it is considered a representative facet of South Korean culture. This is compounded by South Korea's endorsement of K-pop in government discourse and funding, which further associates the prefix with a particular national brand. This so-called national brand's impact on a neighboring country, Japan, offers a site to examine the complications when the national is collapsed into the racial.

—The Korean Wave and K-pop in Japan

Japan is one of many sites in East Asia where the Korean Wave found an early footing and made a lasting impression. The beginning of the Korean Wave in this case was focused on South Korean dramas, particularly the immensely popular *Winter Sonata* in the early 2000s; the show was "the first Korean television (TV) drama broadcast by NHK and only the second in the entire history of Japanese TV broadcasting" (Hayashi and Lee 2007, 198). Dal Yong Jin explains that "while K-pop was part of the early growth in Hallyu, Korea did not achieve impressive popularity in the global music markets until recent years," leading him to make a demarcation between Hallyu 1.0 and 2.0 as distinct eras, where "K-pop has become a driver of Hallyu 2.0 as Korea exported $80.9 million worth of music in 2010, a 159 percent increase from 2009" (2015, 59). As Japan remains the second-largest market for physical CD sales, behind the United States, K-pop there is a lucrative investment for idols and their managing companies. K-pop fans in Japan often buy multiple copies of CDs in order to collect benefits tickets entitling them to exclusive concerts or autographs, pictures, and handshakes with their idols (Larsen 2018).

Japan's own pop culture found resonance abroad before the Korean Wave boom, and the Japanese government attempted to capitalize on this by beginning the Cool Japan initiative, generally recognized around 2005. Various case studies have compared the two nations in their deployment of soft power and pop culture abroad, especially the failure of J-pop in relation to K-pop (Brasor 2011; Lindvall 2013; Parc and Kawashima 2018). For over twenty years, South Korea banned Japanese cultural exports, and at the same time "Japan did not impose any ban on Korean popular culture; however, it mostly remained indifferent to its former colony, which was seen as inferior both racially and economically" (Jin 2016, 60). In principle, Japanese pop culture was forbidden as an import in South Korea from 1978 to 1999 (Meagan Morris cited in Creighton 2016). Since the lifting of the ban on Japanese cultural products, however, the Korean Wave has created a global flow.

While explanations for the different success rates are plentiful, one reason is South Korea's use of technological development side by side with cultural products. Specifically, Dal Yong Jin argues that "while Japanese popular culture did not have the benefit of digital and social media in its heyday, Korean popular culture has benefited from digital technologies, in particular locally developed digital media" (2016, 162). Ultimately, the situation still reflects the fact that "Japan and South Korea have been unable to come to grips with each other's rising cultural influence" (Hayashi and Lee 2007, 198).

While many pop culture phenomena tend to shift focus away from fans and fandom practices, K-pop as an overarching industry depends on and consistently engages (for better or for worse) with fans. This is particularly obvious—critically—outside South Korea. As JungBong Choi cogently argues:

> Here, the *elsewhereness* intrinsic to Hallyu cannot be overemphasized. For it foregrounds the question of governance in the Hallyu phenomenon and, more directly, the significance of non-Korean nationals as one of the main engines of Hallyu. Put differently, not only does Hallyu imply two geographic sites—Korea and elsewhere—but it also alludes to two autonomous agencies in content production on the one hand and cultural production on the other. (2015, 40)

In other words, markets outside South Korea are valued not only financially but as sites where fans and their practices further refine the media in question. These fans influence Korean Wave content, thereby affecting the situation in South Korea. The climate in Japan becomes much more complicated when race is brought into the discussion.

—The Anti–Korean Wave, *Zainichi* Koreans, and Gender

Japan is an essential site of the Korean Wave, yet it is also a historically antagonistic receptor—in certain circumstances—of racial, ethnic, and cultural differences. K-pop circulates regularly, and Korean dramas are constantly available on multiple TV networks and streaming services. Despite this, Japan in many ways remains as described in 2008: "the obsession with maintaining an illusion of oneness—of being a homogeneous nation that has evolved naturally since ancient times—makes it difficult for these Japanese to embrace the multiethnic newcomers who are now descending upon the country" (Murphy-Shigemitsu 2008, 284). In terms of migration, immigration, temporary residence, and refugee status, Japan has a track record of denial and reluctance (Japan Association for Refugees 2014).

The Korean Wave, in its various forms, therefore continues to create controversy. In Japan's case, the popularity of South Korean cultural products and the shift in attention toward South Korea since the airing of *Winter Sonata* have stirred up a "patriarchal xenophobic backlash" against South Koreans and their fans in Japan (Seung Cheung 2015, 196). Much of this response goes hand in hand with general xenophobia. As Kaori Mori Want puts it, "Japaneseness is the marker of racial sameness and non-Japaneseness constitutes racial difference" within Japanese society, which differs considerably from conceptions of race in South Korea or the United States (2016, 86). In other cases, the response is tied to more specific anti-Korean sentiments and prejudice against *zainichi* Koreans—"descendants of those who were forcibly moved to Japan from the Korean peninsula as slave labor during the Japanese occupation from 1910 to 1945" (Han et al. 2007, 156). *Zainichi* Koreans of later generations face prejudice in official contexts as well. They are still legally treated as foreign residents; in fact, "Japan is currently the only advanced nation with a fourth-generation immigrant problem derived from exclusivist policies in dealing with foreign residents, particularly colonial subjects" (S. I. Lee 2012, 1). *Zainichi* are required to pay Japanese taxes, yet they "are not granted the right to participate in civil society and vote in the most important elections" despite being born and raised in Japan (S. I. Lee 2012, 12).

In areas like Shin-Okubo in Tokyo, *zainichi* Koreans' "bodies have now become 'tokens' to represent the Hanryu culture, allowing for a public identification of their physical bodies and culture" that is inherently problematic given the history of *zainichi* Koreans and Japan (Han et al. 2007, 166–167). This goes hand in hand with the area becoming a destination for all things Korean Wave. The streets are lined with shops selling K-pop and K-drama merchandise, cosmetics stores, and trendy restaurants playing K-pop music videos, creating an image of an imagined South Korea within the confines of Tokyo—one of a handful of what Millie Creighton calls Koreascapes in Japan, "areas that present, visually highlight, and represent elements of Koreanness" (2016, 10). Therefore, even fans of the Korean Wave are occasionally guilty of conflating current South Korean pop culture with their own neighbors, who have been discriminated against formally and informally since before the partition of Korea.

Even from the beginning of the Korean Wave, "bookstores were flooded with publications claiming to be sick of Hanryu" (Creighton 2016, 5).

Political tensions, including the ongoing issues of textbook revisionism, the Dokdo-Takeshima island dispute, and Japan's stance on "comfort women," continue to make headlines. The increasingly volatile nature of North Korea and ballistic missile tests over Japanese waters and the Japanese mainland also contribute to a greater discourse pitting Japan against the Korean Peninsula in one way or another. (See "Tokyo's Textbook Rules Spark Protest from South Korea" 2018; McCurry 2010; and Nyshka 2018.) Identifying oneself as a fan of the Korean Wave in any iteration, therefore, can often come off as a political statement indicating more open views on any of those issues or, at least, an awareness of Japan–South Korea relations.

The initial boom of the Korean Wave in Japan left a deep impression on Japanese society regarding what a Korean Wave fan looked like—typically the *obasan*, the middle-aged housewife trailing after some attractive South Korean actor. Scholarship tends to focus on the gendered relations only, using fixed archetypes such as the *obasan* or the hyperactive male *otaku* obsessed with fan culture in discussions of K-pop fandom in Japan. Despite studies examining how these audiences were constructed in the first place (see Hayashi and Lee 2007), more recent scholarship continues to perpetuate this trend problematically. While John Lie makes the claim that Korean Wave fandom in Japan is almost exclusively female and therefore a point of "gender divergence," he pushes the argument further: he lists a series of convergences that such women encounter once they become "entrapped" in the fandom and the fantasy of falling in love with an idol, which is logical in his eyes given their actual reality, which he dismissively characterizes as "childrearing, housework, and so on and so on" (2016, 130). Not only does Lie emphasize the sexual magnetism of South Korean idols as somehow irresistible, he also characterizes Japanese fans as foolish for being drawn to that magnetism. This harks back to popular discourse viewing fandom—as examined in fan and audience studies—as inherently effeminate, emotional, and escapist (T. Anderson 2012; Bennett and Booth 2016). Therefore, Korean Wave fandom in Japan faces particular stereotypes from the get-go in academic circles and popular media, which use the gender discussion to both dismiss fans and diminish idols.

Critically, Korean Wave fandom in Japan is primarily female, as evidenced by a visit at any time to Shin-Okubo in Tokyo (Larsen 2018). K-pop girl groups have large numbers of male fans in Japan, however, which is also ignored by Lie. Similarly, BIGBANG's fandom in Japan is dominated by women but also visibly full of men. Millie Creighton makes an argument similar to John Lie's without the patronizing tone: she recognizes that the initial push of the Korean Wave into Japan does offer a space that, in some cases, "reflects women's discontent with hegemonic gender relations in Japan" (2016, 1). Creighton also argues that in Japan the Korean Wave "has often involved constructs of what is 'sexy,' is utilized to project gender images for both men and women, and to voice ideas about gender relations" (2016, 6). My research and writing contend that in addition to the paradigms of attractiveness and gender, the Korean Wave also opens up a space to talk about nationality and race—for better or for worse.

—Oversimplified Otherness and the Politics of "What Are You?" in Japan

Race in Japan is a complex issue frequently reduced to alarmingly simple categories. The distinctions between Japanese and outsiders as being based on blood feed structures that reinforce categorization and discrimination, often without respect to the actual heritage of the outsiders in question. While the recognition of Others exists both informally and formally, "the people of Japan are commonly depicted as forming a single ethnic group and therefore the mixture of diverse original constituents is dismissed as irrelevant" (Murphy-Shigemitsu 2008, 299). The same framework of dismissive essentialism, I argue, is applied to domestic Others like *zainichi* Koreans and newly arrived Others like visiting South Korean idols or even myself. Discussing the case of *zainichi* Koreans, Min Wa Han et alia note that "the breakthrough of Korean popular culture in Japan has made them more visible, but through this visibility they have to negotiate the stronger dose of 'amnesia' among the Japanese about the history of occupation, oppression, and discrimination" (2007, 169). Considering this difficulty with long-term residents who may appear ethnically, culturally, and linguistically Japanese, it is unsurprising that my own experiences in Japan have also been, at times, frustrating.

I am an American woman who identifies as multiracial. I'm also a doctoral candidate at one of Japan's most prestigious universities. My dissertation research focuses on male South Korean idol groups in Tokyo, primarily the K-pop scene in Shin-Okubo. In other words, I am dealing with many layers. Part of my research includes ethnography and participant-observation, which frequently require me to speak Japanese (my third language). I will now share some incidents from my fieldwork while researching the K-pop scene in Tokyo. I obtained written permission to reproduce quotes from idols and staff, and quotes from fans are from notes taken within the gathering space of concert venues. In both cases, I've anonymized any identifying information aside from that fact that these interactions happened in Shin-Okubo and involved male idols and female staff and fans. In sharing these incidents, I hope to outline some of the issues explicitly bound to the conflation of nationality and race in Japan as well as the oversimplification of fandom.

More than once, when I told an idol or a staff member that I was American, I was immediately met with the response, "I love America!" This response of course ignores the possibility that I may have mixed or negative feelings about my country of nationality. Some of these people had actually lived in America, some had great vacation stories to share, and others were enamored with American pop culture. As Colin Marshall notes in his study of Seoul and Los Angeles's famous Koreatown, "the California dream burns particularly bright, it seems, within those who've never come near the state"—something I encountered frequently after mentioning my time at UCLA (2015, 16). However, I often found myself in a tricky position when idols told me how much they loved Black music but, in many cases, could not name individual artists when I asked which ones they followed. I have had to dispel myths that all Americans are Christians and that we consume fried chicken at Christmas (a KFC marketing ploy in Japan). Most commonly, I find myself needing to emphasize geography, particularly the fact that my birthplace in the Finger Lakes region of central New York state is closer to Canada than New York City. I include this list not as a litany of complaints but as evidence of the pervasive oversimplification encountered on a daily basis in Japan.

At one point during my fieldwork, I was waiting in line for autographs from a male South Korean idol group. The woman in front of me struck up a conversation about what languages I use to speak to the members. The fact that I, along with the members, have to code-switch frequently is often a point of interest for fans and also a subject of my own research. Our conversation went as follows:

Fan: I notice that [idol] gives you a lot of attention during the concerts.
Me: Oh, I guess that's because I've been a fan of the group for awhile now.
Fan: I've also been a fan for awhile now.
Me: Oh . . . well, maybe because I'm a *gaikokujin*? [foreigner; politically correct word]
Fan: But I'm a *gaijin* too!! [outsider; contentious word]

First of all, the debate about the words *gaikokujin* and *gaijin* is a matter that must be dealt with. *Gaikokujin* is used in all official Japanese documents and is the polite way of saying "outside-country person," whereas the system of writing for *gaijin* signifies "outside person" or "outsider" in general. While some foreigners do not consider *gaijin* to be a slur, its usage to ostracize and discriminate can't be ignored. I do not use the word as a personal choice, and if my friends use it, I ask them what they mean to imply by designating someone as an outsider in that manner.

The conversation shows that in this situation a commonality of East Asian features or the interconnected history, culture, and physical proximity of Japan and South Korea didn't matter to the fan speaking to me. Because Japan and the United States were both *not* South Korea, she and I were supposed to be of equal exotic status to the group members. In other words, we were both oversimplified as outsiders in relation to the South Korean idols and therefore deserved the same amount of attention from the group members. What intrigues me about this incident in particular is that the identification I felt with the idols—that *we* were foreigners in the eyes of the Japanese—was completely disregarded. This makes sense when considering that Korea is essentially "the neighboring country that Japan has always regarded as 'other'" (Hayashi and Lee 2007, 199). Because the line shifted and we were unable to continue our conversation, I'm still honestly unsure how I would have responded.

At another event, immediately after I finished an autograph session with an idol group, a fan walked up to me before I could return to my seat, and the following exchange occurred:

Fan: Miranda, are you *haafu*?
Me: What? You mean part Japanese? No, I'm not.
Fan: See, I told you! [She yells loudly to a friend in the back.]
  She isn't *haafu*!

I was surprised to be asked this question, because my complexion is quite dark by Japanese standards, and "dark-skinned *haafu* are discriminated against in Japanese society" (Want 2016, 90). When pressed by the fan's friend to explain what I "was," I quickly earned irritation as I attempted to explain my heritage as I often do: my mother is Caucasian, with family coming from Denmark (hence my last name, which also indicates that I was born out of wedlock, another source of puzzlement), and my father is half Puerto Rican and half African American. I usually end my self-explanation by emphasizing that I consider my heritage to be Danish, Puerto Rican, and African American. When I did so in this case, the fan's friend was confused: "What? But you can't be three things. That's too complicated."

The flat denial of my self-identification in this instance was both upsetting and educational. After some reflection, I was less surprised by this reaction. The most popular way to identify any racial diversity is to call oneself *haafu*. However, identifying oneself as *haafu* indicates one Japanese and one non-Japanese parent. The term specifically conflates blood, race, and nationality, assuming Japanese citizenship and foreign features. As Penny Kinnear describes the label:

> . . . in social practice, an individual must 'look Japanese' racially and possess pure 'Japanese blood' to be considered 'Japanese'. The children of these [mixed] marriages are subsequently seen socially not as Japanese-Korean or Japanese-American, Japanese-French etc. but as non-Japanese. They are often labeled *haafu*, from the English 'half'. The non-scientific concept of Japanese blood is assumed to give exclusive ownership to cultural and linguistic knowledge. (2001, 47)

Haafu are immensely popular in Japanese advertising, as Kaori Mori Want notes, and those advertisements "inadvertently contribute to the creation of stereotypes of *haafu* as good-looking, multilingual, friendly, rich, cosmopolitan, and part-Japanese" (2016, 83). For approximately half a year, a major train station on my commute displayed a billboard for a Japanese cosmetics company entreating women to alter their Japanese features and "get the *haafu* look" by using their products. *Haafu* tend to embody a kind of achievable whiteness; an attitude persists that "while it is impossible for Japanese women to have Anglicized facial features, it seems possible to emulate the *haafu* face, which has both Western and Japanese facial features" (Want 2016, 87). The saturation of Japanese media with *haafu* leads to misunderstandings like the conversation where my explanation of my own heritage was met with puzzlement and disbelief. Again, the expectation was an oversimplified racial answer fitting neatly into the circulated categories within Japan.

Like *zainichi* Koreans, *haafu* have been subjected to discriminatory policies through official structures in Japan. The Japanese Nationality Law was revised in 1985 in an attempt to address gender inequality; "until then, Japanese women marrying non-Japanese men could not legally pass down Japanese citizenship to their children" (Want 2016, 93). Statistically speaking, the majority of *haafu* in Japan have a mixture of Japanese and Korean ancestry, yet their ability to pass as Japanese due to a lack of Western features is another area of racial oversimplification in Japan. In many cases they may identify completely as Japanese yet still face barriers reinforcing the fact that this identification is misplaced. After all, "no matter how popular *haafu* are in the media, they are still reduced to the status of Other because of their racial difference" (Want 2016, 89). Minority groups are rendered invisible most of the time unless desired (as idols or advertising ploys) or discriminated against.

At benefits sessions for idol groups, the hour and a half after a concert when the idols sign autographs and take photos with fans, fans usually purchase one or two items for the members to sign: for example, a photo for one member to sign and a CD that the entire group signs. At a session for an idol group that I attended, one woman bought a stack of twelve CDs. The idols had to open them and write their name and a message in each one, which was obviously very time-consuming. The usual flow of autographs allows fans to talk to an idol briefly, overseen by a staff member, and then promptly shift to the next member to repeat the process.

In this case, because of one fan's decision to have the group sign so many CDs at once, two younger Japanese fans and I were left waiting on the stage for a long time. We slowly moved from member to member as each idol finished with the stack of CDs. Eventually the three of us were waiting for the last member's signature, and we were all so tired that we finally gave in and sat down on the stage—in *seiza*. While traditionally *seiza* posture is used for formal occasions such as the tea ceremony, it is also a default sitting position in Japan. In my case, it was also a natural way to sit after a stint teaching at a children's English-language school in Japan, which required copious amounts of time on the floor. Almost immediately, there was an outcry from the audience: "Look, Mira is sitting like one of us!"

This was accompanied by commentary, pointing, and laughter. Perhaps it was the physical orientation of actually being in the middle of the stage, but this incident was extremely intense and uncomfortable for me. In that moment I was the focal point, and my otherness had literally taken center stage. I was grateful that the idols who were no longer busy with autographs attempted to smooth the situation over by telling the commentators not to talk so loud. They then spoke to me since I was visibly upset; however, I managed to suppress my first instinct, which was to get up and leave the stage. In retrospect, I wonder if the idols at that moment understood what I was feeling, given their own day-to-day status as onstage Others. The comments from the audience made it clear that there was something amusing in my seeming mimicry of Japaneseness, my attempt to be "like one of them" in that moment.

—Idols as Others

This brings us to the idols themselves and how their status as Others is a large part of their appeal within Japan. Simultaneously, this Other status is also a source of daily stress for the idols, complicated further by their professionally required to-be-looked-at-ness. The *seiza* incident stands out in my mind as an odd episode where despite sharing the stage with South Korean idols—the usual focus of otherness in Japan—I was momentarily turned into the main attraction for many fans because of my physical position.

Male South Korean idols, the fandom object in this case, are subject to compulsory military service in their home country. This greatly affects their schedules; for at least eighteen months, they are absent from the K-pop scene. Idols especially are expected to complete the service, because they represent globally marketable Koreanness to the world (Yeo 2017). Simultaneously, they run the risk of danger even in supplementary service positions because of the situation between North and South Korea. This contrasts sharply with the Japan Self-Defense Forces, essentially toothless military forces made up of volunteers (Kurashina 2005). Since entry into and discharge from the service period affect whether the idols can appear in Japan, their otherness is constantly used as a framework for accessibility. Some fans choose the youngest member of a K-pop group as their favorite simply because his age means more time with him before his military service.

Another area where idols continuously deal with their Other status is language. At all levels—rookies, mid-tier, and major—idols often have their Japanese corrected not only by an offstage translator but also by members of the audience. Sometimes major mistakes in grammar or vocabulary can create alarming sentences in Japanese, such as mistaking the word *kirai* (hate) for *kirei* (pretty), as I've witnessed more than once. Nevertheless, the continuous corrections often place immense pressure on the idols, with some of the most gregarious characters soon becoming silent due to fear of making a mistake. While Japanese and Korean share similar grammar, the use of three alphabets for Japanese often makes the language a daunting challenge for idols. The language difficulties form one of many sites where the divide between insider and outsider is clearly marked, where idols also become "affected by the meta-narrative of ethnic purity of the Japanese that clearly excludes them" (Murphy-Shigemitsu 2008, 289). While this is often laughed off or explained as something that can't be helped, the amount of forgiveness for poor proficiency decreases over time.

Many Japanese fans are able to speak, read, or write Korean, and the Korean male idols have varying proficiency levels in Japanese and English. Some idols simply feel more comfortable with English, which makes my research and my fandom participation easier. Yet English is another mark of otherness and is often regarded with suspicion by fans, whereas a South Korean idol speaking or writing Korean is considered situationally appropriate, and it is part of their appeal. Some of the Japanese fans are also proficient in English, though with a focus on reading comprehension and writing rather than speaking and listening. When the male idols cover songs in English by American or British artists, for example, I'm often asked about the content of the lyrics. Here we can circle back to JungBong Choi's argument about the vital importance of elsewhereness in K-pop. Choi also points out that "hallyu as a transnational cultural phenomenon is profoundly dependent on the cultural masonry carried out by a legion of underrecognized 'craftsmen,' namely, overseas fans" (2015, 41). When idols battle the native language of fans, this emphasizes their elsewhereness and the elsewhereness of the fan and the reception site. Nevertheless, the situation in Japan tends to shift the neutral elsewhereness into the oversimplified otherness.

All these incidents outline an issue with oversimplified racial categories in Japan, made more evident in transcultural fandom spaces. Given the Korean Wave and an increase in foreign workers and students, Japan is facing a convergence of circumstances that require a reassessment of these oversimplicities. While much of this must happen at the institutional level to alter the structures of power perpetuating these frameworks, sites like Shin-Okubo where Japanese fans gather to hear South Korean idols create an excellent opportunity for expanding horizons. In fact, many K-pop fans understand that they are making a potentially political statement in their music tastes, free time, and fan labor; pinning badges in Korean to their backpacks with the names of their favorite groups remains a risky choice in certain parts of the country. K-pop fandom in Japan and elsewhere reminds us that "identity resolutions and assertions vary among different individuals and are also situationally determined" (Murphy-Shigemitsu 2008, 300). What I have detailed is limited by my own experiences, the testimonies of idols and fans, and the physical location of Tokyo.

The Korean Wave remains a fruitful topic of study in various fields, especially fan studies, and deserves more attention as a global phenomenon. Nevertheless, the focus on nationality—prompted by the ever-present K prefix—often elides discussions about race in fandom. In Japan this becomes more clear, given its citizenship policies, treatment of *haafu* as exploitable

Others in media, and history of formal and informal discrimination against *zainichi* Koreans. The undulations of the Korean Wave have created a space for changing attitudes, cultural awareness, and transnational connections, yet heralding the movement within Japan as inherently negative or positive underestimates the intricacy of the situation.

In Japan's case, race is often collapsed with nationality and consequently oversimplified, which ignores the complexity of racial, ethnic, and national identity of individuals—including Japanese citizens themselves. Undoubtedly my own experiences have been and will continue to be profoundly affected by my multiracial identity, my American nationality, my use of languages, and my status as a doctoral candidate at a Japanese university. Nevertheless, I hope this chapter emphasizes the day-to-day situations experienced by many in Japan and the complex nature of transcultural flows like the Korean Wave. More importantly, I hope it opens a space where "difference is a form of disjuncture, interruption, and fracture, as well as celebration," within fandom (Murphy-Shigemitsu 2008, 300) that creates more conversations in this globally produced media space.

THREE. AFFIRMATIVE/TRANSFORMATIVE

6. Alpha/Beta/Omega

Racialized Narratives and Fandom's Investment in Whiteness

ANGIE FAZEKAS

IN 2017, IN AN ARTICLE in the *New Yorker* titled "The Promise and Potential of Fan Fiction," Stephanie Burt argued that fan fiction had the potential to "give its creators a powerful sense of participatory equality." Many fans celebrated this take on fan fiction, particularly since it came from a mainstream press typically more interested in stigmatizing fandom as a weird and potentially dangerous hobby. Indicative of the mainstreaming of nerd culture, the *New Yorker* article also gave voice to sentiments long held by many fans—sentiments that extol the progressive potential of transformative fandom, particularly when it comes to exploring diverse representations of gender and sexuality. While I too welcome the turn away from stigmatization, the article also mirrors another side of fan attitudes in that it ignores the biggest reason why transformative fandom is not the diverse utopia it often claims to be: fandom has an ongoing and overwhelming problem with race. Accordingly, in this chapter, I argue that despite claims of progressiveness, there is a significant tension in transformative fandom between its unmet potential to be a space of gender subversion and radical sexual politics and the way it often ends up falling short and falling back on racist narratives.

One popular fan fiction genre in transformative media fandom, alpha/beta/omega fan fiction—or the omegaverse—provides an evocative illustration of this tension and a poignant example of the centrality of whiteness to fandom. While the omegaverse opens up possibilities of playing with gender and sexuality in new and interesting ways, the stories overwhelmingly focus on pairings between two white men, effectively foreclosing their progressive potential and recentering whiteness. Further, omegaverse stories often exist as a subset of another popular fan fiction genre: slavery alternate universes. Populating stories that explicitly draw on the horrors of transatlantic slavery with white bodies effectively decenters the lived experiences of Black people, trivializes historical and intergenerational trauma, and foregrounds white feelings and experiences within a specifically racialized narrative.

To make this argument, I first outline how the omegaverse came to be a popular fan fiction genre. I focus primarily on the trope as it plays out in fandom centered around male-male slash pairings. Female-female or femslash versions of this trope do exist in smaller quantities, but as my argument centers on a critique of the ubiquity of white masculinity in transformative fandom spaces, they are not my focus in this chapter. Female characters are largely absent from male-male slash fan fiction. When women do appear, they tend to be persistently devalued or outright villainized to prop up the male slash pairing, particularly when these characters are women of color (see Scodari 2003, 2012). Then, using the results of an informal fandom survey of omegaverse authors and readers conducted by a fan using the pseudonym songlin, the results of which were made publicly available, I consider fan investment in gender and sexual progressiveness. Finally, drawing on specific examples from fan fiction, I detail how these stories remain part of a larger racial structure—one that prioritizes whiteness. This chapter deals specifically with English-language, transformative media fandom based predominantly in Canada, the United States, and the United Kingdom and is centered around media sources from these countries. Because other fandom spaces have their own particular dynamics when it comes to race, sexuality, and gender, the same tropes interface differently with them. For instance, anime and K-pop fandoms have their own particular communities and racial dynamics that do not revolve around whiteness and the white body (see Chin and Morimoto 2013; Jung 2011). Therefore, the argument I make here is not universal and cannot simply be extended to those other spheres.

—The Rise of the Omegaverse

Omegaverse fan fiction originated in the *Supernatural* (2005–present) fandom between the summers of 2010 and 2011. *Supernatural*, a television show about two brothers hunting supernatural creatures, first aired on the Warner Brothers network in the fall of 2005. In 2007, at the same moment as the height of the *Supernatural* fandom's popularity, fans on LiveJournal began participating in a new kind of anonymous writing challenge, the kink meme. Essentially, kink memes are spaces where one fan will anonymously post a prompt outlining a kinky scenario, and another fan will reply by writing out a story. The conceptualization of what constitutes a kink in these spaces is exceptionally broad and ranges from someone requesting a story where two characters hold hands to requests for more extreme stories about bestiality, bloodplay, and necrophilia (along with everything in between). In the *Supernatural* fandom, the two most significant kink memes were blind-fold_spn and spnkink_meme. The principal rules for these memes, as well as for many other kink memes, were mandatory anonymity and a policy of "your kink is not my kink and that's okay!" Essentially, kink memes are part of a permissive culture that discourages censorship or kink shaming and encourages privacy.

In 2010, on both blindfold_spn and spnkink_meme, anonymous authors wrote several stories in which the main characters, Sam and Dean Winchester—or Jared Padalecki and Jensen Ackles, the actors who play them—were transformed into werewolves. The characterization and plot in these stories drew heavily on animalistic traits, specifically those of wolves. It was in the context of this growing popularity of fan fiction involving werewolves and drawing on animalistic traits that the anonymous prompt that would bring about the omegaverse appeared on spnkink_meme:

> Their world is just like ours . . . except . . . in their world there are two types of men. One is the alpha male, the other is the bitch male. Alpha males are like any ordinary guy with the exception of their cocks, they work just like dog cocks (the knot, tons of cum etc). The bitch male is just an ordinary guy without the special cock. ("Alpha/Beta/Omega" n.d.)

Based on this prompt, one fan wrote the story "I Ain't No Lady, but You'd Be the Tramp" on July 24, 2010. The prompt—and the story based on it—set up several elements that have since become staples of fan fiction in the omegaverse. Most importantly, it introduced the idea of a fictional alternative universe in which, alongside gender as we experience it in our reality, there is another layering of biological differentiation wherein people are either alphas, betas, or omegas. As fan scholar Kristina Busse describes it:

> Many A/B/O stories posit societies where biological imperatives divide people based on wolf pack hierarchies into sexual dominants (alphas), sexual submissives (omegas), and everyone else (betas). Beyond the biologically determined hierarchy, these wolf-like humans often have other wolf-like traits: they may scent their partners or imprint on first sight, and often mate for life. Sometimes alphas and omegas are rare, sometimes they are only males, sometimes they have altered sex organs. Often omegas go into heat and release pheromones that drive alphas wild. . . . A/B/O stories also

seem to draw from other tropes, including mating and heat cycles, breeding and male pregnancy (mpreg), as well as imprinting and soul bonds. (2013, 317–318)

Based on alpha/beta/omega, A/B/O is another term for the omegaverse; some fans prefer it because of the similarity of A/B/O to a racial slur for Aboriginal Australians. Mpreg, typically shorthand for cisgender men becoming pregnant, is differentiated from transgender men becoming pregnant. The focus in mpreg stories is often on magic or other supernatural influences on biology that allow cisgender men to carry children. At the top of the societal hierarchy are alphas, generally dominant and able to impregnate omegas. Alphas are typically larger and more aggressive and command societal respect. On the other end of the spectrum are omegas, often smaller, submissive, and able to be impregnated. Omegas with penises, in fact, often have self-lubricating anuses to make penetration and impregnation easier. Set in the middle of the two are betas, who may have a mix of alpha and omega traits or their own unique set of traits, depending on the story.

One fan going by the pseudonym netweight has chronicled a comprehensive history of the omegaverse on Archive of Our Own that describes how this first story set the tone for the universe as "a whole dystopian 50'esque society based on this gender division . . . at the same time it reflected on its sexism/gender-based prejudice and referred to the existence of more liberal movements that were pushing for equality. Women's Lib turned Betas' Lib" (2013). Essentially what the prompt and the corresponding story did was take the trends and concepts floating around the *Supernatural* fandom and fan fiction at the time and distill them into one unified world—a world based on a prominent, rigorous gender hierarchy. Right from its inception, the omegaverse was a metaphor for gender oppression and gender equality movements.

Over the next several months, anonymous authors published several stories on the *Supernatural* kink memes with the same use of animalistic traits and societal hierarchies. On November 9, 2010, another anonymous user posted a prompt for a story involving "three types of men, alpha males, beta males, and omega males"—the first use of the full alpha/beta/omega triad that would become the standard in the omegaverse. Eventually, three pieces of fan fiction were written based on this prompt, including the story "Not," wherein social hierarchies were based on racial, rather than gender, metaphors and to which I will return later in this chapter. Beyond this, it is difficult to track the precise spread of the trope because authors did not always use any sort of common tag or identifier, but spread it did. By May and June 2011, the terms "alpha/beta/omega dynamics" and "omegaverse" were in common circulation. July 2011 saw the posting of the first femslash story written in the omegaverse, as well as the first use of the trope outside the *Supernatural* fandom. Most likely via fans who were active in multiple fandoms, the genre jumped from the *Supernatural* fandom to the fandoms of *Sherlock* (2010–present) and *X-Men: First Class* (2011). From there, the trope spread like wildfire and soon became a staple of such diverse fandoms as *Glee* (2009–2015), *Teen Wolf* (2011–2017), the *Avengers* (2012), and *Doctor Who* (1963–present).

The exact chronology of the spread of the omegaverse trope is difficult to follow, both because its fandom, while nominally clustered around a few online platforms, is still quite dispersed and because many of these stories were written on anonymous kink memes where comments have subsequently been deleted or edited. Yet, as of July 2018, there were over 39,000 stories written in the omegaverse on just one fan fiction platform, Archive of Our Own. Considering the existence of multiple online fan fiction websites, the actual number is almost certainly much higher. As fan netweight says, "any fan can just come up with her or his variation, keep to known combinations and recreate worldbuilding structures, or radically reinterpret them and introduce new alternatives, make it full of filthy porn or well thought-out social commentary, or both" (2013). It is within this possibility for radical reinterpretation and social commentary that the omegaverse ironically becomes a poignant example of fandom's limited view of who can be part of new and radical queer narratives and who is left out.

—Claims of Progressiveness

While the omegaverse, set as it is in a "dystopian 50'esque society," is founded on a fixed gender hierarchy and problematic gender stereotypes, from the very first story, "I Ain't No Lady, but You'd Be the Tramp," fans were writing allegories reimagining sexual and gender narratives. Subsequent stories have continued along these lines, playing with ideas of gender fluidity and queer sexuality that unsettle conventional male-female and hetero-homosexual binaries.

In 2015, a fan going by the pseudonym songlin conducted an informal survey that reveals something of the way that fans interact with gender and sexuality in the omegaverse. Although by her own admission the survey was not meant to be any kind of objective measure and thus the statistics are anecdotal at best, it contains a comment section that provides productive insight into why this trope has gained such popularity. Alongside the fact that most fans appreciate the "crazy hot sex" and "dirtybadwrong" nature of the explicit sexuality in the omegaverse, there is a repeated reference to the ability of the trope to question, consider, and subvert gender and sexual hierarchies and oppressions. For example, respondents comment that the appeal of the omegaverse lies in "having a different set of gender and social dynamics to explore within an already familiar framework"; "the heck-up of gender roles"; "fluidity of gender and attraction"; "exploration of gender and power dynamics within a variety of social hierarchies and constructed universes"; and "frank discussions of (secondary) gender stereotypes, how they are harmful, and steeped in bias." The sentiment that the omegaverse can play with traditional gender and sexual roles and stereotypes recurs multiple times in the comments of songlin's survey. Clearly many fans, particularly queer ones, experience reading omegaverse fan fiction as a space of queer possibility.

Because the term "queer" is used in a myriad of different ways, some productive and some so expansive as to become meaningless, I pause to offer a brief definition of how I employ it in my analysis. My use of "queer" means to interrogate "the social processes that not only produced and recognized but also normalized and sustained identity . . . the political promise of the term reside[s] specifically in its broad critique of multiple social antagonisms, including race, gender, class, nationality, and religion, in addition to sexuality" (Morris and Rawson 2013, 75). I also follow José Muñoz's conceptualization that "queerness is a structuring and educated mode of desiring that allows us to see and feel beyond the quagmire of the present." By attending to the temporal dimensions of the term, he offers a "theory of queer futurity that is attentive to the past for the purposes of critiquing a present." Put differently, he suggests that by being attentive to traces of desire that exist in the gaps and fissures of the past or the "no-longer-conscious," we can activate glimpses of queer desires for the future, the "not-yet-conscious." As he argues, "if queerness is to have any value whatsoever, it must be viewed as being visible only in the horizon" (2009, 1, 18, 11).

From this understanding of queer temporality and hope for the future, Muñoz introduces his concept of queer utopianism. He differentiates between abstract utopias that are void of historical consciousness and offer only a type of "bland optimism" and concrete utopias that are historically situated and offer "educated hope" (2009, 3). In this way, he does not offer a utopian orientation that seeks a perfect future but, rather, one that is based in hope as an anticipatory affect, one that sees the potentiality in the quotidian. Queer utopianism is thus not about following a blueprint to a specific futurity but is "a temporal arrangement in which the past is a field of possibility in which subjects can act in the present in the service of a new futurity" (Muñoz 2009, 16). It is through sentiments echoing queer utopian ideals that the fans in songlin's survey place the potential of the omegaverse, and it is in these same ideals that the utopian vision ultimately fails.

In the omegaverse, fans use traditional tropes of gender and sexuality to imagine a universe where queer sexuality is the norm and normative gender roles are often skewed and upended. A narrative that looks on the surface to be unproblematically reproducing gender stratification is subverting views of a future void of queerness to imagine a different kind of futurity.

To provide a concrete example, consider a 2011 story written in the *Supernatural* fandom titled "Show Me How You Do That Trick," in which characters could shift at will among the designations of alpha, beta, and omega. The story is set in a school, known simply as the Academy, that teaches young people how to control the shift. Students are required to remain in beta form, as it is considered neutral and most "normal," but as the story progresses it becomes clear that many characters identify more strongly with either the alpha or the omega designation, while others shift fluidly among two or three, depending on their current sense of self.

Through the experiences of main character Jared, who cannot seem to control his ability to shift, the story uses the alpha/beta/omega positions as a metaphor for gender fluidity and gender queerness in a way that draws on conventional notions of normal and excessive gender while unsettling fixed gender roles. Setting the story in a school meant to teach people how to appropriately perform their gender denaturalizes gender roles and highlights the part that societal education plays in teaching normative ideologies of gender and sexuality. In so doing, it draws on oppressive narratives from the past with the goal of unsettling the present for the chance at a more hopeful future. As with Muñoz's queer utopianism, the story does not offer any sort of definitive resolution or idealized optimism for a future void of gender and sexual oppression, merely a glimpse of the potential for a different and more hopeful way of living with gender and sexuality beyond the binary. Yet in spite of this potential for queer possibility, it is here, I argue, that the omegaverse ultimately fails in the project of queer futurity.

—Two White Guys

To return to a definition of "queer" in which "the political promise . . . reside[s] specifically in its broad critique of multiple social antagonisms, including race, gender, class, nationality, and religion, in addition to sexuality," clearly any promise or potential of queer futurity cannot be upheld in a narrative that includes only the lives and experiences of white people (Morris and Rawson 2013, 75). This is where the omegaverse, as with slash fan fiction more broadly, continually fails to live up to the progressiveness that its fandom bestows upon it. White supremacy permeates fandom and fan fiction, including that written in the omegaverse. When I looked at the "Alpha/Beta/Omega Dynamics" tag on Archive of Our Own, as of July 2018 nine out of the top ten pairings involved a relationship between two white men, and all the top ten characters were white men. The overwhelming focus on relationships between white men in fan fiction is ubiquitous enough that it has garnered a title: the Two White Guys trope. The Two White Guys trope describes the process by which fan fiction authors repeatedly foreground the experiences of conventionally attractive white cisgender men even, perhaps especially, when racialized characters are present in the source material.

Fandom's tendency to claim gender and sexuality progressiveness while continuing to center whiteness in fan fiction mirrors many mainstream gay rights movements, particularly those that center the push for marriage equality. Mainstream LGBT identity and activism are infused with queer liberal ideologies that replicate white heterosexual life scripts and remain focused on heteronormative institutions like marriage (Eng 2010). Representations of queer lives, including fictional ones, are often similarly built on queer liberal ideologies that emulate what Audre Lorde calls the "mythical norm"—people in society who are "white, thin, male, young, heterosexual, Christian, financially secure" (1984, 116). Gay rights movements and fictional representations of queerness center the lives of people who most closely emulate the mythical norm while attributing oppression only to a departure from heterosexuality. Any intersectional view of queer lives that accounts for other aspects of oppression is foreclosed and the white gay subject remains central to representations of queerness.

It is important to note that the centrality of the white male subject is a phenomenon particular to the sphere of fandom that is my focus here: anglophone transformative media fandom located primarily in North America and the United Kingdom. Race in the North American context tends to be built on a white-Black binary. This binary becomes central to my discussion of slavery alternate universes in the omegaverse as these are built on histories and dynamics that conceptualize race along a white-Black divide. The omegaverse trope plays out quite differently within fandom spheres outside this context, and these remain an important avenue of future research.

To return to the Two White Guys, when considering a trope like the omegaverse as imbued with the potential for queer futurity, we must attend to José Muñoz's warning:

> The future is only the stuff of some kids. Racialized kids, queer kids, are not the sovereign princes of futurity. . . . It is important not to hand over futurity to normative white reproductive futurity. That dominant mode of futurity is indeed "winning," but that is all the more reason to call on a utopian political imagination that will enable us to glimpse another time and place: a "not-yet" where queer youths of color actually get to grow up. (2009, 95)

If queer characters of color do not even get to exist in many stories set in the omegaverse, any potential for a queer imagining of the future is essentially foreclosed. The omegaverse simply becomes yet another narrative where white reproductive futurity is normalized and white supremacy remains firmly intact.

One of the earliest stories written in the omegaverse, "Not," illustrates how the Two White Guys trope functions to center whiteness even in stories built around a racial metaphor. Specifically drawing on discourses surrounding segregation and antimiscegenation laws, "Not" is set in a world where alphas, known as Nots, are legally barred from dating, marrying, having sex with, or procreating with betas. In the story, when Jensen, a beta and the star of a popular television series, is assigned to work with Jared, a Not, he immediately thinks:

> Will there be segregated catering? Separate trailers? How much time is he going to have to spend with the Not? What's it going to do to his reputation—is he going to be known as the guy that works with Nots for the rest of his career? . . . It's not as if he's never spoken to a Not. He prides himself on his liberal views. . . . But—

Here the racial metaphor is made clear through parallels to the ideology of segregation, seen specifically in Jensen's concerns about sharing space and the impact on his reputation as well as in the reference to his "liberal views." Given that the two main characters are white, this story begs the question of whether a narrative centered on white men could possibly say anything about race that does not reaffirm the invisible norm of whiteness. Even in a story that is supposed to interrogate and condemn racial hierarchies, by positioning two white men as its main characters the narrative still serves the project of white reproductive futurity. Racialized characters are not offered a future—indeed, they do not even get to exist.

—The Case of Slavery Alternate Universes

Alongside the minimization and often outright erasure of racialized characters, stories set in the omegaverse often cross over, in whole or in part, to another genre of fan fiction: the slavery alternate universe or slavery AU. Because of the power imbalances among alphas, betas, and omegas in omegaverse narratives, many of these stories are set in worlds where some people can legally be owned by others; often it is alphas who own omegas, but there are stories in which this is reversed.

Exploring themes of power exchange and power differentials is not unique to omegaverse or slavery AU stories—a significant amount of fan fiction deals in some way with power differentials and the complicated plea-sure of reading them. Pairings involving unequal power relationships (e.g., boss-employee, teacher-student) and/or based in power exchange dynam-ics are common narratives in fan fiction. In her analysis of "The Story of Obi," a piece of fan fiction exploring themes of BDSM and ostensibly con-sensual sexual slavery, Anne Kustritz discusses the appeal of masochistic power differentials:

> Readers may gravitate towards [the main character's] journey to
> experience taboo titillation, increased sexual intensity, novelty, intra-
> psychic or interpersonal extremes, or any number of roles or fetishes
> they find attractive either conceptually or in practice.... The unique
> conjunction of same-sex erotics and the richly contextual lives of
> previously published characters combine in BDSM slash fan fiction
> to produce a new language for thinking about erotic power exchange.
> (2008, 4.2)

Slavery AUs fall into the category of fan fiction that explores power differentials and can appeal to the same kind of masochistic sexual pleasure. Yet the pleasure of reading slavery AUs is more complicated than that of a lot of other power differential fan fiction because it is built upon a narrative that appropriates the historical experiences and intergenerational trauma of Black people to further a romantic or sexual narrative between white characters. Unlike other power exchange scenarios, the position of slave (and the intergenerational trauma that follows from it) cannot be experienced by white authors and readers. Slavery AUs thus constitute a form of historical appropriation and rely on a worldview that negates Blackness and equates only whiteness with humanity.

To explain the historical and historically present workings of equating whiteness with humanity, I draw on Sylvia Wynter's compelling account of the "conception of the human, Man," and the history of modernity. Wynter proposes that "our present ethnoclass (i.e., Western bourgeois) conception of the human, Man . . . overrepresents itself as if it were the human itself." In other words, she argues that modernity is organized by a Western European understanding of humanity built on the subordination of racialized Others understood to be other than human or subhuman. Following from a worldview that posits rationality as the solution to the "significant ills" of society, she argues that "the invention of race" was predicated on the creation of a "projected Chain of Being, comprised of differential/hierarchical degrees of rationality" (2003, 260, 300). Modernity, in sum, is built on the following principles: to be truly human is to be rational; only white Western Europeans have the full capacity for rationality; therefore, only white Western Europeans, "our present ethnoclass," are fully human.

Not only is modernity built on the premise of equating whiteness with humanity but, as Frantz Fanon argues in his 1967 *Black Skin, White Masks*, it is built specifically on the negation of the category of Blackness—one-half of a binary that developed to justify and sustain the transatlantic slave trade. In contrast with white rationality, cultural representations of Blackness tend to be animalistic in nature and depict Black people as undifferentiated bodies rather than as people with individual personalities, minds, and emotions. Black people become associated merely with their bodily capacity (productive or reproductive) and disassociated from humanity. As such, the binary of Blackness associated with irrationality and whiteness associated with rationality seeks to justify the possession and enslavement of Black people as a purportedly natural consequence of Sylvia Wynter's "Chain of Being."

By foregrounding the stories of white characters, omegaverse fan fiction set in slavery alternate universes takes the historical horror and trauma of slavery and divorces it from Black people and their experiences. Given that most of these stories are not meditations on the societal and historical implications of slavery but, rather, sexual or romantic narratives, the relationship between master and slave itself becomes romanticized and sexualized and often ends with the enslaved character being set free. Slavery becomes a plot device—one that is available only to white characters who can move in and out of the position of slave because of the historical association between whiteness and humanity and, hence, whiteness and freedom. Unlike fictional meditations on the historical horrors of slavery in books like Toni Morrison's *Beloved* and Octavia Butler's *Kindred*, these fan fiction stories do not center the lived experiences of Black people. Rather, they serve to co-opt and trivialize slavery while absolving white readers of any need to acknowledge the horrors perpetrated by white people.

As a more concrete example, the *Supernatural* fan fiction "Kind Alpha" demonstrates how stories set in slavery AUs appropriate the history of slavery in the service of telling stories about white people. The story's summary reads:

> Castiel had pretty much been owned his whole life. Omegas were not treated well so when Castiel comes home with the Alpha who bought him he wasn't pleased. . . . Nobody wanted Castiel's spitfire attitude or his ability to fight back so well. Except Dean. Dean was one of the few who saw Omegas were something to be protected.
>
> Dean wanted somebody to want to be with him. Somebody who questioned him and had his own opinion . . . in his eyes Castiel was perfect. Now Dean just had to earn the Omega's trust.

The story begins just after an auction where Dean purchases Castiel—a setting that clearly evokes images of chattel slavery. Yet as with the majority of omegaverse fan fiction, both of the main characters in this story, Dean and Castiel, are white men. In removing Blackness from the narrative, "Kind Alpha" reduces the historical trauma of slavery to a plot device used to jump-start a sexual relationship between white men. Without the presence of Black lives in the story, it cannot serve as a meditation on the meaning and experiences of slavery and freedom but, instead, is used as an angsty set piece to provide convenient drama for a romance. Populated only with white bodies, "Kind Alpha" is emblematic of many slavery AUs that disassociate slavery from its historical and racialized context, reaffirming the belief that the only stories worthy of being told are those about white people.

Simultaneously, the story vacates responsibility from whiteness—if white people are both the masters and the slaves in this universe, then slavery becomes unrelated to race and white readers do not have to confront any of their own discomfort in reading about the actual workings of slavery.

Christina Sharpe, in explaining the reaction of white audiences to art by Kara Walker that depicts scenes of slavery in silhouettes, argues that white people "locate [the] signifying effect [of slavery] almost exclusively on Black people" by seeing only the *black* Black silhouettes and not acknowledging those that represent the ominous presence of white slaveholders (2010, 174). White audiences thus see slavery as a history experienced only by Black people and safely ignore the presence of white slaveholders.

I argue that slavery AUs do something similar in removing the ominous presence from whiteness by flattening it—whiteness is oppressor and oppressed, master and slave, and thus not explicitly tied to either. White subjects are therefore not complicit in slavery, and slave narratives can safely be consumed as sites of pleasure without any attendant guilt or acknowledgment of responsibility on behalf of white readers. "Kind Alpha," by treating Dean as "one of the few" alphas who do not see omegas as objects to be owned, positions him as an example of an exceptional white character—one who can be sympathetic, romantic, and even heroic despite being a slaveholder. The story absolves him of any real responsibility for perpetuating slavery. Many omegaverse stories follow a similar pattern wherein white slaveholders are characterized as different or exceptional in their reluctance to support slavery or their active opposition to it. These stories sidestep an examination of white responsibility and safely protect white readers from discomfort. Whiteness and the white slaveholder remain uninterrogated.

It could be tempting to consider omegaverse stories that play with gender and sexuality as potential sites of a breaking down of neoliberal heteronormativity—spaces of enacting moments of queer futurity in the visceral, carnal celebration of sex of all sorts. The omegaverse offers a tantalizing glimpse of how fan fiction brings together gender, sexuality, and pop culture in a way that is messy, ambiguous, and full of possibility. Yet to return to José Muñoz's words, this possibility is "only the stuff of some kids." The transformative *potential* of fan fiction is not enough. The omegaverse, like so many other fandom tropes, overwhelmingly becomes a place for white fans to write white narratives about white characters—a place to feign discussing race without ever actually discussing race.

Tropes like the omegaverse reveal the foundational white supremacist underpinnings of so many fan fiction narratives. Until white fans begin to acknowledge this fact and actively work to disrupt white supremacy, white authors will continue to write stories that reproduce a fictional world in which only whiteness is allowed to have the full experience of humanity. In the current state of fandom, where fans of color who do the work of fighting racism are continually shouted down, demeaned, and harassed, the structures of white supremacy remain firmly intact. The world of "participatory equality" envisioned in the *New Yorker* article with which I began this chapter is not the one in which we live, and tropes like the omegaverse show us why.

7. Fill in the Blank
Customizable Player Characters and Video Game Fandom Practice

INDIRA NEILL HOCH

"WAIT, I THOUGHT we hated [user name]?"

I took a breath, reading through the full comment thread in front of me a second time, just to make sure that I understood what exactly had been written by this anonymous user and the users with whom they were in conversation. Already having committed myself to feeling terrible for the rest of the day, I let the comment sink in. That was my user name. What else could I hope to feel but bad, having voluntarily gone to one of the (at the time) many fandom wank comms on Dreamwidth and scanned for posts containing my user name? I had allowed myself to visit a community well known for saying terrible things about notable fandom participants and their creative output, and now I was paying the emotional price. Yep, someone was saying something awful about me. Except that it wasn't quite what I expected.

The comment was on a thread of fan fiction recommendations. A particular story that I had written was being recommended—it was considered good, but in fact it was I who was hated. Yet there was still more nuance to it. It wasn't even really that I was hated—after all, I was capable of writing stories that were worth recommending, and these users didn't really know me at all—instead they were discussing how my original characters were bad. They were abusive and abrasive and I'm sure a host of other terrible adjectives that I cannot recall and, since the community has since been deleted, cannot recover now. Lingering behind the thin explanations of why they "hated [user name]" was an accusation that wasn't written down but that, having been a participant in Western fandom since my childhood, I was well acquainted with. I was writing, by these anonymous users' assessments, Mary Sues.

In this chapter, I trace how original female characters (OFCs) in subcultural fandom practice always constitute a potential threat, particularly in the writing of fan fiction, and how avoiding any physical description of the OFC serves to mitigate this threat. I use "threat" to invoke two ideas. The first is to reference the use of threats in persuasive communication, often overlapping conceptually with fear appeals. A source (here, the OFC) presents a potential negative outcome (fear, anxiety, cognitive dissonance) if one does not undertake a specific contingent behavior (Donovan and Henley 1997). However, I also wish to invoke the notion of a threat as posed in Jasbir Puar's 2005 assemblage framework and discussion of the suicide bomber, who articulates the perceived threat formulated by combinations of the organic and inorganic materials that make up human bodies. Importantly, the original female character of color is always less stable than her white counterpart and more prone to becoming a violent, chaotic threat in both meanings. She generates potential negative outcomes in fan fiction readers while also invoking real-life bodies aligned with dangerous potential in a world where terrorist threats in particular are racialized.

These threats are mitigated by the relative prominence of underdefined OFCs with few, if any, described physical characteristics in the most prominent fan fics on Archive of Our Own, even within a fandom and a character pairing that require an OFC in order to exist. The OFC is always on the verge of destroying herself, of exploding, in the narrative. And, perhaps paradoxically, the more descriptive detail assigned to her, the less stable she becomes. Nonwhite racial indicators in an otherwise structurally and culturally white fantasy world increase the threat associated with the OFC's peaceful existence within Western fan fiction practice (see Young 2016). She is a representational threat precisely because she is specific and detailed.

For a case study, I consider fan fiction depictions of the female Trevelyan in BioWare's *Dragon Age* fandom. In the *Dragon Age* games, the playable protagonist is a canonical placeholder for an original character. The game begins with a character-creation screen where the player can select the gender, fantasy race, and physical attributes (including skin, eye, and hair color but also facial shape, eyebrows, and scars) of the game's protagonist. In fan fiction practice, authors then use the protagonist that they created in their works. Yet even in a fandom where an original character is all but required for the fan fiction narrative to function, the OFC, particularly the OFC of color, poses a threat that must repeatedly be neutralized.

—Whiteness, Assemblage, and the Threat of Having a Body

Whiteness in media is assumed to be the default by which other characters are set in relation (Dyer 1997). Western fantasy settings in particular largely operate in accordance with norms and themes established by white male British and American authors at the turn of the twentieth century (Young 2016). Similarly, fandom studies conceptualizes the public face of fandom as a failure of heterosexual white masculinity, from which other fans diverge (Stanfill 2011). Even if fandom is about a failure to live up to the expectations of heterosexual white masculinity, using such a designation as the focal point of comparison reinforces the importance of the ideal to structure the experiences of others.

Jasbir Puar notes that this difference from the white norm has continually plagued intersectional feminisms, never fully managing to recalibrate to concepts that do not place whiteness at the center (2005). Intersectionality may strive to account for the structures of oppression that inhibit the lives of, say, a lesbian Black woman and a disabled transgender Latina, but their position is legible only in how they are encumbered differently from white cisgender women. Puar instead turns to Gilles Deleuze and Felix Guattari's formulation of assemblage as a means of understanding particular queer embodiments that are less stable than intersectional identities. Based on "enunciation and dissolution, causality and effect," the Deleuzian assemblage claims a greater stake in the passage of time and the incoherency that mark the body as it encounters multiple life performances (2005, 127). The assemblage fails to be static and easily defined despite having specific expressed characteristics.

Rather than standing in opposition to intersectional frameworks, Puar sees the concepts of intersectionality and assemblage as allowing for productive frictions (2012, 50–51). Using the turbaned Sikh man in Anglo North America as an example, she traces how oil, fabric, hair, religion, sexuality, and gender interact to produce a set of embodied expectations. The turbaned Sikh is then conflated with the suicide bomber, a mixture of destructive technologies and the body that is also racialized, sexualized, and gendered. The suicide bomber is unstable, threatening to explode in all directions, indiscriminate in its risk. These formulations extend the concept of queer from a stable subject identity to a temporal and embodied performance encompassing threat and risk.

Comparing the original female character to the racialized disorder mangled together with the suicide bomber is, admittedly, a conceptual leap. But these representational trends occur in English-language fandom, a landscape dominated by native English speakers and thus by American, British, Canadian, and Australian fans. The mainstream culture that surrounds fan production is bound by the same social and ideological controls put into place in Puar's argument. Citing Achille Mbembe's 2003 construction of

US nationalism as necropolitics, a regulation of who lives and who dies in the War on Terror, Puar reframes the project of queerness as one that must consider the shifting and unstable formulations of who is and who is not a threat. The least-threatening OFC is, potentially, the one that cannot be pinned down at all, a character without a physical referent, even if acts of carnal desire, heightened emotion, and physical violence are depicted in fan fiction. The least-threatening OFC is one that has no specific characterization at all, that is, by extension, assumed to be white.

—The Mary Sue and the Specter of Imminent Failure

The Mary Sue herself haunts the halls of English-language fan fiction, from her earliest incarnation in predominantly American convention halls and printed *Star Trek* zines passed from fan to fan (Bacon-Smith 1992). She stretches her feminine hand into places she does not belong in, grabbing up bits of plot, twisting them to her own ends. She takes canonical men between her teeth, grinding them up and swallowing them down. Choking on their bones, she's never satisfied. More, she yells, more. More plot, more men, more action, more charisma, more competence, more attention! She has always been a threat, invoking anger, fear, and anxiety in both readers and authors attempting desperately not to conjure her into being.

A. Rodgers defines the Mary Sue as "an original character who overshadows the canonical cast" (2003). Julia Beck and Frauke Herrling clarify this point further, arguing that "the Sue's defining feature is her habit of distorting other characters and warping the fictional world around her" (2009). Camille Bacon-Smith takes the time to more precisely differentiate between very young, hypercompetent Mary Sues and the older, matriarchal original female characters deployed in lay-Spock fan fiction of the 1970s and 1980s (1992). Largely in the intervening years, however, this distinction has broken down. Virtually all female characters integrated into canonical worlds risk being labeled Mary Sues, regardless of age. She is too much of an interruption, merely by existing, and always carries the potential of leading to a negative outcome. Bacon-Smith documents a mentorship system in pre-internet fan cultures that included instruction on how to avoid writing a Mary Sue that has largely fallen by the wayside as fandom has become more widespread and less tightly controlled (Bury et al. 2013; Jenkins 2006). But even now young authors are still largely socialized away from overt Mary Sues as they develop as writers (Willis 2006).

Kristina Busse and Karen Hellekson directly equate the Mary Sue (and her male counterpart, the Marty Stu, though I have always heard the reference as Gary Stu) with bad fic, characterized by deliberate parody. They connect the Mary Sue with all original characters in unflattering terms, writing that she is "all too often an avatar of the author herself, . . . presented as the beautiful, smart heroine who saves the day and then gets the guy, all to the exclusion of the canonical characters" (2006, 11). Ika Willis is somewhat more sympathetic; her own writing includes deliberate Mary Sue characters in order to enact new spaces for discussion and representation within the canon (2006). Similarly, Anupam Chander and Madhavi Sunder deploy the Mary Sue as a metonym for a multitude of transformative procedures carried out in fandom, understanding the significance of the Mary Sue vis-à-vis underrepresented and marginalized populations (2007).

Mainstream media franchises fail to be inclusive of all identities. Female-led superhero movies increasingly depict white women in power positions formerly occupied by white men; see *Mad Max: Fury Road*, 2015; *Star Wars: The Force Awakens*, 2015; and *Wonder Woman*, 2017. While the bodies in the background might be quite diverse, the lead role is still assigned to a white hero. Recent releases from the *Star Wars* franchise led by white female protagonists include a number of nonwhite male actors in important roles. These films visually reinforce Kimberlé Crenshaw's framing of the impossibility of being at once Black and female in relation to structural and social powers (1991). Chander and Sunder importantly note that "the official Mary Sue may still leave much to be desired in the characterization of the newly represented group" (2007, 623). Canonical characters will never be one-size-fits-all. They may be deliberately designed to be one-size-fits-many. But never all.

Yet for all her faults, chief among them tending to be her implausibility and other popular characters' devotion to her, the Mary Sue has the potential to make the fandom universe more diverse. However, as we shall see in practice, she is at least physically often no one at all. But she is a potential that authors continue to be socialized away from, despite her possible positive contributions to representational diversity.

—Customizable Character Role-Playing Games and Dress-Up Identity

While primarily written off as an unwanted addition in multiple television and film fandoms, the one place where the Mary Sue—or, more accurately, the original female character—has found solace is in video game fandoms, particularly games that require the player to customize an avatar that serves as the narrative's protagonist. Games such as the *Dragon Age* series have amassed relatively large fandoms for video game properties. *Dragon Age* is arguably the largest video game fandom by fan fiction production. Tags related to the series make up three of the top five video game fandoms on Archive of Our Own, and it only misses the top honor because of the inclusion of the very general "Star Wars—All Media Types" tag. While much smaller than some blockbuster television and film fandoms—see the tags "Marvel Cinematic Universe," "Harry Potter," "Sherlock Holmes & Related Fandoms," etc.—the prominence of *Dragon Age* within the subset of video game fandom practice is notable.

Video game fandom practice—as opposed to studies that address video game players or gamers—has received relatively little academic attention compared with larger television, book, and movie properties. Mark Chen has written on expert player groups that participate in high-level, high-cooperation raids in Blizzard Entertainment's *World of Warcraft* (2009, 2012). Highly involved with the core media and adapting the game through modifications, these fans made digital add-ons that adjust the core game. *WoW* players expend a great deal of unpaid labor to create these mods. And often publishers benefit from this labor by being able to sell additional copies of the game or extend subscription periods. Ryan Milner focuses on fan labor more explicitly, documenting and critiquing publisher Bethesda Softworks' interactions with fans of the *Fallout* franchise when the publisher purchased the intellectual property and Bethesda Game Studios developed *Fallout 3* in 2008 (2009).

Heidi McDonald specifically tackles romances with nonplayable characters (NPCs) in BioWare games, analyzing survey data of players across the *Dragon Age* series, the *Mass Effect* series, and *Star Wars: Knights of the Old Republic* (2012). In each *Dragon Age* (and most other BioWare) game, the player can choose to engage in a number of plotlines with these nonplayable characters. Both same- and other-gender NPCs are available for romance, though not always in equal numbers. McDonald finds that some players use the customizable protagonists and variety of available romances to experiment with gender and sexuality in ways that recall Lisa Nakamura's 1995 concept of identity tourism. However, since the games are largely single-player, this experimentation occurs in a controlled environment that does not require players to misrepresent themselves to other humans.

Notwithstanding the potential to be an identity tourist through playing games and writing fiction, video game fandom practice, particularly that of romantically oriented fan fiction and fan art production and consumption, has resulted in online behaviors that promote and encourage the creation of female (and male and nonbinary) original characters to a level almost unheard of in other fandoms. Rather than being seen as superfluous, these OFCs are necessary to move the story forward.

But none of this canonical framework for originality in characters guarantees fandom success or acceptance, however that may be measured. The OFC can still be labeled a self-insert, a Mary Sue, and pose a threat. Conditions for being accepted as a legitimate OFC are nebulous at best. Accounting for taste and popularity is difficult and may vary among online platforms. Authors may post their fan fiction to Archive of Our Own, write descriptive meta on Tumblr, commission artwork, produce artwork, or engage in role playing on applications such as Discord. Each of these platforms may invoke a different response in both authors and other users contributing to or consuming content about that OFC.

Rather than focus here on the particularities of how OFCs gain prominence, I would like to argue that all OFCs, even so-called successful ones, are in fact threats waiting to happen if their authors insist on defining them too concretely. This is particularly true of an OFC that represents nonwhite identities, because in order to be recognized as being a character of color in a cultural setting where whiteness is assumed, she must be described.

—She Is Everyone and No One and Waiting to Become

For the sake of privacy of other fans, in the following section I most often draw specific examples of my own OFC from the *Dragon Age* fandom, Sabina Trevelyan. Sabina is a bisexual, half-Rivani (dark-skinned people from the north whose homeland has never appeared in the game) human rogue who takes on the mantle of the Inquisitor in the third *Dragon Age* game, *Dragon Age: Inquisition*. Sabina engages in a romance with the NPC Cullen Rutherford, a heterosexual, blond-haired, brown-eyed human male from Ferelden, the primary setting of the first game and a secondary location in the third game.

I compare Sabina's construction to that of the character of the female Trevelyan in seventeen of the top twenty most kudo'd stories in the "Cullen Rutherford/Female Trevelyan" pairing tag on Archive of Our Own. (I excluded three stories because "Cullen Rutherford/Female Trevelyan" did not constitute the main pairing of the story, being instead ancillary to a different relationship.) At the time of my analysis, October 2017, this was the third most populated pairing tag in the *Dragon Age* fandom on the archive, following the more general "Female Inquisitor/Cullen Rutherford" and "Female Lavellan/Solas" pairing tags. The former pairing tag includes both female Trevelyans and female Inquisitors who are nonhuman (mostly elves but also dwarfs and gray-skinned horned giants called Qunari), and the latter pairing tag is a customizable "Elf OFC/Male Elf NPC" pairing. While the racialized narrative and representational history of elves in fantasy settings is well worth examining, doing so lies beyond the scope of the current essay (see Poor 2012; Rearick 2004; Yamazaki 2008). I have limited myself to looking at the portrayal of a "Human OFC/Human NPC" relationship. All stories, including my own, are rated either E (explicit) or M (mature) on Archive of Our Own, though only a small minority include sexual acts in the first chapter. All except one are multichaptered. My analysis considers only the first chapter of each story, when the original character is first introduced. Of course, my knowledge of Sabina is far more intimate.

> That has always been her childhood dream as well, that she could weave magic, little bursts of electricity from her fingertips. When she was quite young, maybe six or so, she had run to her mother exclaiming she was a mage indeed and miming the gestures she had made in the Fade, but no magic came flowing out. Her dark hair tied up in curly ringlets, she screamed and cried that she had magic, she was sure of it. While her mother sighed with relief she cried herself out until she was an exhausted heap on the floor. With magic being such a curse, she never could figure out why she was so upset.

In the first chapter of my story, *Both Matter*, the only physical descriptor of Sabina (besides a later comment that she is "not squishy") appears in the passage noted. When she was six, she had dark curly hair. Nothing about her current appearance is revealed; instead, the narration works to highlight the contrasts between the two leads.

Rather than describing the color of Sabina's skin, the narration of this first chapter, which is given from Sabina's perspective, continually comments on Cullen's appearance. Taking herself as the normalized human to which other people are compared, Sabina notes again and again how easily his skin "flushes" or "pinks" when he is embarrassed. This isn't to say that she is incapable of blushing, but she is continually drawn to how dramatically Cullen's face changes color when he is embarrassed, cold, or overexerted.

My strategies for describing Sabina, at least early in the story, rarely differ from the other depictions of female Trevelyans in the top seventeen stories. Only two of the seventeen stories make a direct reference to Trevelyan's skin color, describing her as "fair" or "pale." Hair color is the physical characteristic most often noted for the Inquisitor. Nine stories describe her hair color, and seven of those note that she has "dark hair." Not brown, not black, but "dark." One story gives her red hair, one "wheat colored." This still leaves eight stories where nothing is said about the color of her hair. Only two stories mention her eye color: one blue, one "slate." Overwhelmingly, Trevelyan is a name but not a concrete appearance.

In fact, in some cases she is not even a specific name. In four stories, she is given no first name, referred to only as Trevelyan, the unchangeable canonical last name for human Inquisitors, or by one of her titles (Inquisitor, Herald). Another three stories give her the first name Evelyn, the default first name for the female human Inquisitor. This can be changed in the game itself, but these three authors have chosen to retain the default name. Finally, another four stories have names other than Evelyn that still start with E (two of these are stories about the same Inquisitor by the same author). Only six of the seventeen have given names that do not start with E, and three of these are by the same author!

What do such remarkable consistencies across stories mean for the transformative potential of transformative works? As my primary interest in this essay is on issues of race in the construction of OFCs, I have said little about the personalities of these fourteen fictional women (one author/Inquisitor appears twice; another appears three times). And there is some degree of variation in their responses to the stresses of their office, their interactions with Cullen and other characters, their level of sexual experience, their personal confidence, and so on. But overwhelmingly, in their first introductions, their physical attributes are vague at best and entirely absent in some cases.

And my own narrative work, a story about a nonwhite Inquisitor by a nonwhite author, is not immune to these trends. I know there are other pieces of writing I have completed with Sabina that address issues of her biracial identity, the whitewashing of her appearance by court painters, and her discomfort around the NPC Dorian, who looks and acts remarkably like her in some cases, causing bouts of anxiety (am I/Sabina Brown *enough*?). But none of this work occurs in the first chapter of what was the narrative about Sabina most widely read by audiences. (*Both Matter* was at the time in the top twenty most kudo'd "Cullen Rutherford/Female Trevelyan" fics on Archive of Our Own, but it has long since fallen much further down the list.) My Brown Inquisitor is not presented to the audience in a way that differs significantly from the white Inquisitors of other stories. For the most part, I cannot even verify if these other Trevelyans are white based on the first chapter alone. Two are pale, two have blue eyes, two stories come with artwork of fair-skinned women embedded in the first chapter. But none of them announces her whiteness.

Trevelyan's canonical background places her in the privileged position of a child of a noble house, largely accepted unquestioningly as the Herald of Andraste (and thus also a religious figure) and later as the Inquisitor. This is in contrast to the other fantasy racial options available to players. Elves, dwarves, and especially Qunari are faced with prejudice and racist statements from NPCs regarding their suitability for the role. As is the case in many fantasy worlds, humans are the dominant and majority race, and those humans are majority white (Young 2016). Furthermore, humans are the only race allowed within the religious ranks of the Chantry, though any race may worship the Maker. Trevelyan's potentially malleable skin tone does not alter the prescripted game dialogue. As long as she is human, she is considered competent.

In her role as the Inquisitor, Trevelyan wields both the power to kill and the power to pardon, and her will is often absolute, a theme that is often more prominent in fanworks than her appearance. She is perfectly acceptable as a powerful, commanding agent of war and death. She kills hundreds with few consequences, all in the name of saving Thedas. While romance-centric works may focus less on the Inquisitor's involvement with mass-scale violence and war, there is often a direct reference to her combat prowess in the first chapter of the stories under analysis, whether it is a display of magical competence or a flash of steel. This focus on violent physical competence may be partially attributed to the game's mechanics, which require the player to kill hundreds of men and monsters over the dozens of hours it takes to complete the game. But in light of Achille Mbembe's understanding of US nationalism as centered around necropolitics, a regulation of who lives and who dies in the War on Terror, with Brown and Black people disproportionately being among those who die, Trevelyan's state- and church-sanctioned acts of violence within the game tie intimately to the legitimization of her strength of character enacted through her power as an executioner without trial (though she also oversees a number of trials). Her appearance and race are not important, but what is crucial to her character's power is her ability to kill and to spare.

Both Matter likewise begins with sparring practice between the dagger-wielding rogue Sabina and the sword-and-shield knight Cullen. She has the opportunity to slit his throat with her blade, warning him that she is always armed. Each Trevelyan is similarly armed, a collection of weapons, hair, and sparkling personality, or is she shy? Heaving breasts and short tempers, but sometimes she is patient and kind as well.

Why then is Sabina both Brown and, in the first chapter, just as easily assumed to be white as every other Trevelyan? I purposely kept her racial identity out of the first chapter. I want to say that I liked the idea of switching the readers' expectations later along the story line, proving to them that the (assumed) white default character was a Brown woman after all—in a sense exploding her identity and forcing a rereading of previous chapters in light of additional context. I make no claims to this execution being particularly well rendered. I'm bristling even now at how much my fiction writing has improved since the publication of *Both Matter*. But even then I had a sense of wrestling with the popular tropes swirling around Trevelyan, both in terms of her physical appearance and her personality, and I wanted desperately for people to like Sabina, despite some overwhelmingly negative aspects of her personality. Dark-haired confident women were in at the moment. And the construction of her occasional descriptors undoubtedly led to different visions in the minds of readers, before my decision to more deliberately introduce her as nonwhite.

Sabina's ambiguity—the fact that she is not initially marked as nonwhite yet later established much more clearly as having darker skin and possessing a racial identity that differs from the majority of NPCs in the game— complicates her position as being a powerful wielder of necropolitics as well as physically resembling some of the peoples most likely to be subjected to death under a regime bent on rooting out the terrorists external to the game. Because the Muslim, the Sikh, the Hindu, the Middle Eastern body, and the South Asian body are all read as belonging to a group of possible terrorist assemblages indistinguishable from one another, the South Asian– analogous Inquisitor becomes part of a politics of representation outside the fictional world in which she exists (see Puar 2005). She is a violent Brown woman who can literally cause explosions and manipulate tears in the fabric between Thedas and the Fade world with her body (specifically a piece of ancient elfin magic that has become grafted to her off-hand). White Trevelyans can simply be white Trevelyans. Sabina becomes a commentary, but one that can never convey a particular identity in a stable fashion. She shifts as information about her is added through the course of the narrative and the assumptions that readers pin onto her. With every description, she becomes someone else, someone new.

Similarly, for authors of color who perhaps specify earlier in their stories that their Trevelyans are not white, the presence of their characters within the narrative as other than white introduces quick accusations of being Mary Sues and a profound discomfort in some readers, as evidenced by aggressive comments left on Archive of Our Own, anonymous asks on Tumblr, or repeated harassment, both direct and indirect, stemming from wank comms. Indirectly, this discomfort might also be gauged from the lack of a visible Trevelyan of color in the top seventeen stories on Archive of Our Own (at least in the first chapter, when many readers decide whether to continue reading). Which is not to say that white authors of white OFCs do not also receive disturbing reactions from other fans, but as evidenced by the popularity of the relatively physically underdefined Trevelyans in fan fiction, the prominent fandom Trevelyan does not question basic assumptions regarding the character. She does not question the assumption of whiteness, despite the fact that she is designed to be physically customized. She generates no additional threat by being specifically embodied.

The fewer markers of difference provided by the author, the less friction arises between the narrative and the character, resulting in greater stability and reducing the threat that she poses. Her assemblage is unstable in part because of the possibility of reinterpretation of identities in context and in light of newly expressed performances. Rather than a stable identity, the interpretation and reinterpretation of bodies generate threat and anxiety. Subsequently, the lack of any bodily descriptors of the OFC stems this threat. A body cannot be interpreted if it is not present. And that body which is not defined is, particularly in fantasy, a white one. The mere act of attributing an other-than-white identity to a OFC wrenches her away from the safety of ambiguity and immediately deposits her into a position where she may be strenuously interpreted and blown apart. She is now a Mary Sue because she is something other than ambiguous.

—Damned If You Do, Damned If You Don't, Damn

When I consider again, years later and with a much more critical eye, why I spent so little time describing Sabina's appearance in the first chapter, I realize that my decision originated with an overt desire to avoid the basic tropes associated with the Mary Sue, including any overwrought description that highlighted her own uniqueness. So much for that, since she ended up being labeled a Mary Sue anyway.

In my estimation, introducing the physical attributes of an OFC in the early paragraphs of a fan fic signaled a lack of sophistication, a denial of the "show, don't tell" axiom. And yet what I had long considered to be a marker of good writing ultimately perpetuated my own obfuscation of Sabina's specificity as a character. Ebony Dark'ness Dementia Raven Way, from the infamous *Harry Potter* fan fic *My Immortal*, published between 2006 and 2007, has emerged as the ur–Mary Sue. An infinitely meme-able description introduces her to the audience in detail:

> Hi my name is Ebony Dark'ness Dementia Raven Way and I have long ebony black hair (that's how I got my name) with purple streaks and red tips that reaches my mid-back and icy blue eyes like limpid tears and a lot of people tell me I look like Amy Lee (author note: if u don't know who she is get da hell out of here!). (Gilesbie 2006)

It is possible that the other authors in the top seventeen stories were driven by similar concerns. Likely, even, given the long history of authors being either explicitly mentored away from writing Mary Sues or given more diffuse warnings to stay away. The author who writes well does not dwell on physical attributes, at least not early on in the narrative. The ridicule of Ebony taught us that much. But by extension all Trevelyans, at least in the sample of popular stories, are remarkably similar, despite the openness afforded to players of the game. The fandom reverts to an underdefined presence in the narrative, usually dark-haired, almost always skilled in combat, most likely with a name that starts with E, and a basic assumption of whiteness. While *Dragon Age* fandom opens up possibilities for representation with the inclusion of a canonical original character as the protagonist, in practice the most prominent fandom Trevelyans threaten—and represent—no one at all.

8. Waiting in the Wings
Inclusivity and the Limits of Racebending

SAMIRA NADKARNI AND DEEPA SIVARAJAN

THE INCREASE IN CONTEMPORARY CALLS for diversity in cultural production reflects a belief that such a shift in pop culture and global mediascapes (with regional variations) might more effectively represent social and ethnic realities. Racebending and a presumed nonacknowledgment of race have gained currency as a means to approach the issue of inclusivity in mainstream media as well as international fan spaces. Notably, "racebending" was a term originally used to protest the live-action film *The Last Airbender* (2010), which largely recast the Asian characters of the Nickelodeon television series *Avatar: The Last Airbender* (2005–2008) with white actors. However, racebending has since "become the code word for fan-casting characters of color into traditionally white franchises" (Gilliland 2016, 2.5). In fandom, racebending occurs in a variety of media: for example, through fan art that depicts the character's race differently but often retains some physical resemblance to the character as originally described or portrayed, fan fiction that textually explores the character's shifted identity, and fan vids and fan-casting photo sets that recast a specific actor of color into a traditionally white role.

Racebending in fan spaces exists parallel to the practice of deraced casting in theater, television, and film, in which actors are ostensibly cast without regard for the written or presumed race of the character. However, as Kristen Warner notes in *The Cultural Politics of Colorblind TV Casting*, this seemingly postracial landscape sees language used in casting contexts that is often contradictory in nature—it assumes a deliberate lack of awareness of racial identity while insisting on an awareness of nonwhite ethnicities to deviate from traditions of casting that privilege whiteness. This system of casting seeks to make race in/visible while suggesting that ethnicities are interchangeable; any specific identity or experience is not part of this process. As a result, whiteness (which is falsely seen as a nonraced and de facto identity) continues to underlie the context of racebent cultural production, reinforcing Warner's claim that casting that ignores ethnicity "obliterates cultural specificity because if race is not written into the script after an actor of color is hired, the script will inevitably result in a normalization vis-à-vis the whiteness of characters" (2015b, 155). In effect, a nonraced or postracial identity presumes a relation to whiteness, even when portrayed by characters of color, normalizing these identities under the purview of progressiveness and inclusion.

Both racebending and postracial casting appear to disrupt the concept of whiteness as the default, but racebending differs in its intentionality: postracial productions often do not address or acknowledge the specific change, which erases historical struggles, differences, and identities in favor of perpetuating an ideology wherein differences are erased in service of a shared human experience. Problematically, this concept of the human can itself be predicated on histories of colonialism, racism, and prejudice wherein nonwhite identities and cultures, particularly in the Global South, were seen as animalistic, less civilized, and backward. As a result, concepts of the human often function within invisibilized presumptions of these historical white European frameworks and are linked with an increased closeness to these established white identities rather than viewed on their own racial, national, or cultural merits. In effect, this may subversively propound racist ideologies under the guise of inclusion.

One example of this kind of casting is Andrea Arnold's 2011 adaptation of *Wuthering Heights*, where Heathcliff was played by James Howson, a Black actor. While this racebending does allow for representation of the Black community in the narrative, it fails to engage with the manner in which Heathcliff is written to have his passions overtake him, an assertion yet again of monstrous Black masculinity overwhelming and preying upon frail white femininity—all of which are racist colonial conceits. Notably, Arnold justified the casting through Brontë's descriptions of Heathcliff as a "dark-skinned gypsy in aspect" and "a little Lascar" (of possible Arab or Indian subcontinental descent), which suggests both a deliberate seeking of greater fidelity to Brontë's text as well as a disavowal of the knowledge that this would reproduce the novel's often noted racism. The same parameters applied to white masculinity cannot be transferred to Black masculinity without an understanding of the sociopolitical milieu created by racist colonial constructs that violently penalize the latter.

However, racebending can also exhibit these tendencies. Elizabeth Gilliland notes that racebent fan casts without further exploration of racial context can result in "an exoticization of these diversified characters as figures to be inserted into popular mediums at will, but without carrying any of the racial insight or history that would allow these fan art pieces to be truly futuristic in scope" (2016, 4.3). This surface engagement with racial difference echoes Edward Said's theory of orientalism, where these differences function to indicate more about the fan creator and the fandom than about the peoples or cultures being othered. Lori Kido Lopez notes similar issues around fan activism at the time of *The Last Airbender* protests, as the nonspecific conceptions of an Asian identity required during casting suggested a view that had orientalizing aspects to it. Lopez notes that as a result, "we can see the term 'racebending' as part of a long history of racial masquerade that can work both to destabilize the fixity of identity, as well as to shore up racialized hegemonic power structures" (2011, 432).

In terms of our own positionality, Deepa is Indian American, resides in the United States, and primarily engages in US anglophone fan spaces that focus on TV shows and films. Samira is Indian, currently resides in India although she spent several years in Scotland, and engages in anglophone and nonanglophone (Hindi or Hinglish) fan spaces that encompass primarily US- and UK-based anglophone films, TV shows, and books as well as Bollywood films. While we do not ignore the issues underlying a search for an "authentic" representation or the value in increased media presence for these communities, systems of racebending and nonacknowledgment of racial specificities do (perhaps inadvertently) participate in systems wherein racial liberalism—as defined by Charles Mills (2008) and Kimberlé Crenshaw (2017)—flourishes. That is, emphasis is placed on small reforms to an existing system of fundamentally unjust structures that work toward its continued existence. While both pop culture mediascapes and fandom have lauded the necessity and use of racebending and postracial identities, we suggest that these claims of inclusiveness require deeper consideration and critique. While racebending is viewed as an effort at inclusive and diverse representation for otherwise underrepresented cultures, the process of postracial and racebent casting may also inadvertently create or further systems of violence within racial and cultural hierarchies.

Diverse representation remains an important first step toward changing exclusionary structures of representation, but inclusion that lacks an understanding of racial specificity has its own pitfalls, further adding to a complex process wherein identity is both presented and abstracted on these raced bodies, creating them as interchangeable and nonspecific. These attempts at inclusion may also create scenarios wherein violence among and within various communities of color is ignored or abstracted. For example, the 2014 Bollywood film *Mary Kom* had North Indian actor Priyanka Chopra play Northeast Indian (Manipuri) boxer Kom's biographical role, despite complex inter- and intraracial hierarchies within India that often invisibilize Northeast Indian bodies while creating them as sites of sexual, economic, and physical violence (*Newsminute* 2014). Another example is Dominican American Zoë Saldaña's use of blackface in the 2016 biopic *Nina*, based on the life of African American singer and activist Nina Simone (France 2016).

This essay considers the 2015 theatrical production of *Hamilton: An American Musical*, created by Lin-Manuel Miranda and based on the 2004 biography *Alexander Hamilton* by Ron Chernow, as an example of racial inclusion through racebending and postracial casting and its consequent limitations. The musical saw widespread success predicated on its inclusion of people of color in a narrative that traditionally excludes them in favor of white men. The musical itself has been viewed by fans as a fanwork because Miranda uses Chernow's biography to rewrite the lives of historical figures, therefore functioning as historical real person fiction or RPF fanwork ("Hamilton" 2018). In doing so, the musical situates itself within systems of fandom discourses around racebending, suggesting itself as "a political act of resistance and a 'talking back' to powerful discourses that coercively dictate what kinds of narratives in Western popular cultural texts are *allowable* for non-white characters" (Pande 2016a, 173). This attempted interruption of white supremacy through music and lyric interventions, casting choices, and promotion offers representation to certain populations of nonwhite Americans, performing what Edward Said terms contrapuntal reading. Thus, the musical simultaneously intervenes in white supremacy while continuing to perform a narrative of American settler imperialism derived from these historical frameworks.

Hamilton has spawned numerous fanworks—a term that includes fan fiction, fan videos, fan art, fan mixes, etc.—memes, reaction GIFs, and more. However, despite this attempt to claim these historically white identities for people of color, fandom's response to *Hamilton* appears to echo Warner's concerns that a de/raced identity will remain linked to whiteness. Numerous fans have reappropriated *Hamilton*'s lyrics and themes for use with primarily white characters in their fanworks. Our analysis thus includes not only an examination of moments where the musical's racebending and postracial casting come into conflict with its historical sources but also the production of fan media that is complicated by this mix of free-floating racial signifiers. We have chosen to use media easily available on popular sites such as Fanlore and TV Tropes and metanarrative on Tumblr for our analysis since these are clearly intended for mass viewing, though fanworks themselves exist in a multiplicity of locales that are themselves private or public depending on the content creator's choice of audience.

—"The World Was Wide Enough": The Racebending of American History

The March 2015 Equity casting call for *Hamilton*'s run on Broadway specified that all principal characters were to be nonwhite except for King George, predicated on the narrative's reliance upon actors of color to bring to life both its forms of musical expression (hip-hop, rhythm and blues, and rap) and its key themes (Broadway World News Desk 2015). (The July 2014 casting notice for *Hamilton*'s initial run at the Public Theater stated that the production was "looking for people of all ages and ethnicities for these roles"; see L. V. Anderson 2016.) In this manner, modern American political themes and contexts are entwined with both history and historiography throughout the show, creating an ahistorical space within which to approach the narrative and its effects. Beginning with George Washington's refrains in "History Has Its Eyes on You," *Hamilton* returns often to the themes of stories and the people who craft them throughout history, most memorably with the line "you have no control / who lives, who dies, who tells your story." The implication that there are stories we never hear or find distorted because history is written by people with power could be applied not only to the specific circumstances of Alexander Hamilton and Aaron Burr but to the suppression of marginalized voices in a larger sense. By situating the musical simultaneously in the time period that it depicts and in the modern context in which it was written and performed, these themes take on additional affective meaning: to experience actors of color singing "rise up!" in the context of the political origins of the United States can be undeniably powerful.

Hamilton creates a referential connection between the history of the American Revolution and modern civil rights struggles in America. The musical uses racialized coding to identify the character of Alexander Hamilton as an outsider, leaning hard on his Caribbean origins, his immigrant status, and his allegiance to an urban metropolis. The show further develops the immigrant narrative with both Hamilton and Lafayette, most famously with the line "immigrants—we get the job done!" in the song "Yorktown/The World Turned Upside Down"; the line became the basis for the song "Immigrants (We Get the Job Done)" on *The Hamilton Mixtape*, which addresses the lived experience of immigrants in the United States as a response to rising anti-immigrant sentiment during and after the 2016 presidential election

(Feliciano et al. 2015). Casting King George as the sole white principal character further allows for the implication that the revolution is battling white supremacy, that the "freedom" invoked by the rebels is a freedom for all, including people of color. This comparison is made explicit through the character of John Laurens, who ties his abolitionist aims to the larger struggle for independence from the British, and who links the violence inflicted by redcoats with modern-day police brutality by identifying them as cops in the song "Aaron Burr, Sir." Notably, echoing a song about racism in the musical *South Pacific*, Aaron Burr himself invokes similar associations with the civil rights movement, in particular the Black Lives Matter movement, through his own cautionary words in the song "My Shot": "You've got to be carefully taught / If you talk, you're gonna get shot!" (Miranda and McCarter 2016).

Yet despite this positioning, *Hamilton*'s racially coded intervention is limited. Unlike conventionally racebent texts, the question that *Hamilton* seeks to ask is not, What if the founding fathers were people of color? This would require a more fundamental alternate history, one far beyond the scope of the musical. Rather, it seems to try to portray a kind of universality in its characters and themes, one expressed by casting people of color rather than transformed by that casting. In doing so, its erasure of racial specificity inadvertently reverts to an understanding of American history that centers whiteness as its default. Indeed, the mantra invoked by the creators that the musical is "a story about America then, told by America now," assumes that "America then" was a solely white space (Miranda and McCarter 2016, 33). Lyra Monteiro points out that this landscape of whiteness is not historically justified, that "during the Revolutionary era, around 14 percent of New York City's inhabitants were African American, the majority of whom were enslaved" (2006, 93). Additionally, while John Laurens's hope for an all-Black battalion was never achieved, between 5,000 and 8,000 Black people are estimated to have participated in the war on both sides, as soldiers or in noncombatant roles, and they had a significant impact on the war (Ayres n.d.; Kaplan and Kaplan 1989). Monteiro specifically calls out the erasure of Cato, a slave owned by Hercules Mulligan who was essential to Mulligan's espionage efforts, which are celebrated in the musical solely as Mulligan's achievements (2006, 95).

Intentional or not, this focus on rewriting and recasting white historical figures as nonwhite characters implies that the reality of nonwhite historical figures is less worthy of note. Problematically, the fact that this inadvertent erasure is lauded as inclusion shows *Hamilton* functioning within systems of racial liberalism. For example, the only time a specific person of color is mentioned is a cursory reference to Sally Hemings by Thomas Jefferson in the song "What'd I Miss?" when Jefferson returns from Paris after the end of the war. In the musical, Hemings is played by a member of the ensemble who has no lines; she dances in when Jefferson calls for her, opens a proffered letter, and twirls back out. Hemings's appearance is meant to contrast in sharp relief with Jefferson's subsequent lyric, "Looking at the rolling fields / I can't believe that we are free"—a lyric that attempts to invoke irony since these fields no doubt included plantation slaves. However, this attempt requires the show to reinforce Hemings's role as solely Jefferson's property, whom he kept as a concubine, fathered six children with, and never freed. The show gives no space at all to portraying Hemings as a person in her own right, a woman who experienced freedom and paid employment under Jefferson in Paris, who "with the aid of what she and Jefferson considered to be the power of French law, extracted promises from Jefferson" to free her children after her death, a condition for her return with him to Virginia (Gordon-Reed 2017). While Jefferson's position as a slave owner should indeed be fair game for criticism, *Hamilton* aims to address it by using Hemings as a tool, depriving her of agency, voice, or any humanity at all.

Jefferson's slave owning is addressed instead in "Cabinet Battle #1," where he connects the South's economic profits with slavery but never goes so far as to mention emancipation, despite the musical's often lauded outspokenness. (In 2016, Miranda released a demo version of "Cabinet Rap Battle #3," cut from the original score, in which Hamilton and Jefferson debate a petition from a Quaker delegation on the abolition of slavery. Miranda notes that while the song was "worthy for me to write, and cathartic for me to write," he could not justify including it in the staged musical because "you just get to a point where you look at all these flawed, human characters, and they didn't do anything. Nothing really happened on slavery until the Civil War a hundred years later." See Biedenharn 2016; Feliciano et al. 2015.)

The final version of the score includes more references to the antislavery bona fides of its principal characters than to enslaved people and no references at all to freed Black people (Monteiro 2016, 95). Annette Gordon-Reed notes that while slavery and antislavery are used specifically as tools to mark the morality of characters in the show, when the show attempts to wield the label of slave owner as a signifier of moral repugnance, only one of Hamilton's unequivocal antagonists, Thomas Jefferson, is painted with this brush. Meanwhile, slaveholder George Washington, Hamilton's hero and father figure, receives only the oblique insult of being labeled as one of the Virginians. Hamilton and his wife, Eliza Schuyler Hamilton, are lauded for their abolitionist views despite, as Monteiro points out, the "fact that members of [Eliza's] family were major slaveowners. While Hamilton himself may not have owned slaves, he certainly was linked to transactions involving them, including hiring them from their owners to do work for them" (2016, 95–96).

Writing in 2016 with regard to *Hamilton's* position in ostensibly including people omitted from the American narrative, Adrienne Keene addresses the musical's refusal to acknowledge the existence of Indigenous peoples and Native nations. She notes the complete omission of any mention of Native Americans in the show, which reinforces the message that white colonists were fighting for land that "belonged" to them rather than land that had been stolen through violent conquest. George Washington's lament over watching his soldiers massacred in "History Has Its Eyes on You" takes on a different meaning when understood alongside his own orders to destroy forty Haudenosaunee villages that sided with the British.

Hamilton further fails to highlight even a better-known figure in Crispus Attucks, the Wampanoag and Black man who is considered to have been "the first martyr of the American Revolution" (Kaplan and Kaplan 1989, 6). Nor does the musical acknowledge the larger effects that Indigenous people had on the founding of the United States: for one, Keene references the influence of Iroquois principles of governance on the US Constitution. Additionally, acknowledgment of Native presence further conflicts with the musical's careful positioning of "good" and "bad" identities framed through its construction of colonial Britain as white-led and colonial America as exclusively nonwhite. The existence of Black and Indigenous peoples who fought against the colonists disrupts the traditional framing of the colonists as heroic freedom fighters reclaiming their rightful territory. As Keene notes, Native people knew that the American Revolution was "a battle for Native land as much as a battle for freedom from British rule"; tribes such as the Cherokee, Mohawk, Cayuga, Onondaga, Seneca, and more joined the British in an effort to protect Native lands from colonial encroachment and theft (Calloway 2008; Keene 2016b). Many Black men, both free and enslaved, also fought with the British against the colonists in pursuit of their own liberation (Ayres n.d.; Kaplan and Kaplan 1989).

Perhaps these inaccuracies would hold less significance in a musical less focused on its own storytelling as a way to reinterpret history and its fandom's joyful acceptance of it on these terms. Indeed, the very premise of *Hamilton's* casting requires audience members to engage in a tricky balancing act between the aspects of their disbelief that they can reliably suspend and those that they cannot. Annette Gordon-Reed points out that viewers "*must* notice that the actors are Black, or the play's central conceit does not work. We are asked to be open to their blackness so that the play's touted message—that the founding era also 'belongs' to Black people—gets through. At the same time, we are presumably not to be so open to the actors' blackness that we feel discomfited seeing them dancing around during the sublime 'The Schuyler Sisters' proclaiming how 'lucky' they were 'to be alive' during a time of African chattel slavery" (2016). Additionally, the erasure of Native nations from this seeming reappropriation of the American founding myth suggests that in order for people of color—Black, Latino, and Asian—to locate themselves in this American identity, they must invisibilize and affirm their own participation in historical and contemporary settler colonialism. That is, reclaiming the American myth can occur only when these otherwise historically excluded nonwhite identities are allowed to acknowledge their participation in narratives of mythologized imperialism.

Moreover, the affective "benefits" of *Hamilton*'s deraced casting are in fact inaccessible to many, particularly Indigenous people. The creators of *Hamilton* frequently promote the positive reactions of people of color, including children and teenagers, viewing Black and Latino people "represented" in American history. Indeed, the perceived inspiration provided by the musical has led to a $1.5 million philanthropic grant to purchase tickets for 20,000 students (many of them students of color) in the New York public school system (Miranda and McCarter 2016). In contrast, Debbie Reese speaks to the particular pain of watching *Hamilton* as a Native woman, scholar, and critic, noting that while watching Hamilton and Burr sing about a "new nation" to their children in the song "Dear Theodosia," "it is crucial that I/we remember that Native parents were experiencing something far different at that moment in time, and since then, too. What of our nations? Our children?" (2017).

—"I Can't Apologize Because It's True": Fandom's Issues with Race

Given *Hamilton*'s own context as racially reparative and Miranda's fame and particular position as its feted Puerto Rican creator, fanworks of the musical often function within these charged contexts of American sociopolitical milieus and fandom's own issues with white supremacy (Pande 2016a). Additionally, fandom's embracing of *Hamilton* marks a significant moment because theater as a medium is rarely the site of a significantly sized fandom. While filmed musical productions such as *Les Misérables*

(2012) have seen large fandom engagement, nonfilmed stage productions rarely receive similar treatment, perhaps due to access and availability issues. Notably, *Hamilton*'s early fandom engagement has been constructed through both access and nonaccess to the staged musical itself, with several fans choosing to create fanworks around the soundtrack rather than the staging or, occasionally, gleaning information from GIFs or descriptions available online. The musical's position as a site of (seemingly reparative but limited) racial social justice is produced within theater audiences and fandom—sites traditionally dominated by white identities—and through complex economic conditions, as tickets are often expensive or unavailable (Monteiro 2016; Pande 2016a).

Numerous fans have made note of the problematic frameworks within which the work functions. A great deal of fandom metanarrative addresses the ahistorical frameworks wherein (largely rich) white male historical characters are made more palatable and seemingly stripped of racial privilege due to the casting; the use of historical research, such as Hamilton's letters to Laurens, by which to hypothesize Hamilton's bisexuality and further embrace his character; the same historical research not being extended to nonwhite historical figures despite their presence at the same events; and the manner in which race, so omnipresent in discussions of *Hamilton*, is largely absented from fanworks. Tumblr blogger afrosoka notes many of these points, concluding:

> . . . as a Black person, I appreciate *Hamilton* as a piece of art that has dynamic, multi-dimensional roles meant for people of color. as a writer and fangirl, I especially love thinking about its creation closely mirrors that of fic au: identifying with a character while reading the source material, going "but what if so and so?", and then putting one's own spin on it. . . . but art, fanfiction (which is famed for the research dedicated writers do about everything but people of color) and other types of transformative works included, do not exist in a vacuum. they're part of the real world. a world where antiblackness, American history, glorification of the Founding Fathers, the downplaying of slavery, the erasure of historical Black figures, and heteronormativity are real things that hurt real people. (2016)

Staging *Hamilton* as a racebent American musical suggests that white male privilege played a minor role in the events depicted onstage and opens the musical up to assumptions of a deraced and shared humanity representative of American identity. Thus, a reappropriation of its lyrics or ethos to white American identity fails to conflict with the source text. As a result, the musical has led to a rise in fanworks that recontextualize it with the original historical figures as well as memes that reappropriate its lyrics over images of the same. A notable example of this from TV Tropes is a portrait of Alexander Hamilton modified to show the historical figure wearing sunglasses with the quote "I'm not throwing away my shot" as overlaid text in the bottom third of the image. The meme thus transfers the adapted racial social justice parameters of the musical to the original historical figure, transferring sentiment previously directed away from white male identity within the founding fathers myth back to it. A post by Tumblr user quintessentialqueer archived on Fanlore points to a similar issue with the engagement of white fans with *Hamilton*, noting that many have taken the musical as means by which to romanticize the original historical figures:

> I love *Hamilton*, but something about the way white fans engage with the musical really bothers me: a lot of them are posting in the tag about the actual, historical revolutionaries and founding fathers in a way that makes them seem like funny, sweet, good people. They weren't. I don't just mean "Jefferson was a piece of shit": none of them were good. Every one of their asses saw black people as inferior, even if not all of them supported slavery. All of them participated in genocidal policy against Indigenous peoples. If you're watching/listening to *Hamilton* and then going out and romanticizing the real founding fathers/American revolutionaries, you're missing the entire point. (2015)

While we chose not to call out specific fanworks in our analysis, it's worth noting that the *Hamilton* fandom has a significant number of fan fics that use slavery as a trope or alternate universe setting. Certain characters in these fan fics are recast as slaves, with the term being used variously to denote sex slavery, chattel slavery, indentured servitude, and forcible prostitution in contemporary settings as "slave whores." These are frequently related to hurt-comfort fic, wherein a character suffers only to eventually receive comfort from the other character in a chosen romantic or nonromantic pairing, or dark fic, wherein characters are recast as evil, often with abuse (frequently sexual abuse) associated with the tag. This is in addition to fan fiction that uses racist descriptive imagery of genitalia for the musical's (racebent) Black characters.

Certain fan creators have chosen to code their works as being within the *Hamilton* fandom while not racebending the characters, exploring "white slavery" within their alternate universe scenarios while still tagging the works within the "Hamilton—Miranda" fandom. While many of these works have received criticism and pushback from fans, fan creators have chosen to argue that slavery would not have the same weighted context with white characters, that their headcanon—their imaginative world—includes a different world wherein slavery carries different cultural meanings, and/or that they will deal with slavery by having the character eventually freed or rescued. The use of slavery as a means for titillation within this specific fandom not only participates in systems where historical pain and trauma are appropriated as racial and sexual fantasy, but the proliferation of these works arguably points to fandom's own problems with and participation in systems of white supremacy.

Perhaps more complex are the fan fiction representations of *Hamilton* that do engage with race by keeping the 2015 cast's ethnicities present in descriptions of the characters, usually in modern political contexts. However, this racial awareness rarely extends beyond descriptions of a character's physical traits and/or brief descriptions of skin color. While an argument could be made that the fan writer has no responsibility or reason to engage specifically with race in these situations, this suggests that race is a context that *can* be discarded when inconvenient, a factor not afforded in reality to people of color. Its use in the alternate universe of modern American politics, itself a field notably dominated by white men, erases the violence within these spaces aimed at nonwhite identities. Repeating the musical's postracial assumption that whiteness is not integral to American political structures, these fics rarely expand on the play's own attempts to grapple with race. That is, while the musical opens (contested) spaces for engagement with racism, such as Hamilton's being on the receiving end of racist taunts or its problematic acknowledgment of American histories of slavery, its fan fiction rarely chooses to address race itself as a factor in lived experience. Little or no space is available for hierarchies or conflict among different racial groups outside of a white-nonwhite binary, flattening all nonwhite identities into a false equality with each other. And few, if any, fan fics appear to engage with Eliza's racebending (Phillipa Soo is Chinese American) since racial engagement is focused solely on characters cast as Black or Latino.

Writing for Vox, Aja Romano echoes the ethos that underlies these fics, stating that *Hamilton* is "simultaneously an alternate version of American history and a modern political AU in which none of the Founding

Fathers are white and everything happens in a blurred temporality that could be modern-day America" (2016). Yet Romano, while arguing for an acknowledgment of the musical's racebending and attempts at inclusion, equates the validity of *Hamilton*'s racebending with fan fiction of a white male character birthing were-kittens—an assertion that suggests that white queerness is somehow a subversive equivalent to racial representation in these narratives and disregards nonwhite queer identities in its false equation of race and queer sexuality. Romano's assertion displays the likely outcome of Kristen Warner's theory that whiteness underlying postracial casting contexts will lead to an assumption of a universalized whiteness as human, with race becoming a free-floating signifier of difference or transgression.

To clarify, this is to suggest not that all fan fiction must deal with racism or reduce nonwhite identities to suffering under racism but that race functions as more than simple outward appearance. While reviewing Sarah Gailey's *River of Teeth*, an alternate history novella set in the American South during the early twentieth century, acafan Zina Hutton argues that headcanons that deliberately choose to absent racism still need to engage with ethnicity and culture within these confines:

> I'm not referring simply to showing characters dealing with racism or rehashing the history of slavery in your world because, again, I'm pretty much the poster child for "we are more than that", but even just being in the South is a complicated experience for Black people in the U.S. and it always has been. . . . There's so much to consider when writing a Black person in the South at any time: culture, community, language, how class/gender/sexuality would intersect. These things all need to show up in the character you're writing because of the way Blackness in the U.S. has worked for generations. (2017)

Hutton's plea argues for an analysis of Black identities in particular, but this theorizing could be extended to the various racebent identities within the *Hamilton* fandom that would have individual cultural connotations.

Problematic in a different way are crossover fanworks that situate the musical alongside other fandoms to reappropriate its racebent ethos to bolster an underlying (white-coded) humanity. An example of this can be seen in the fanwork "*Hamilton* in Sunnydale," which has screenshots or GIFs from the TV series *Buffy the Vampire Slayer* (1997–2003) overlaid with quotes from *Hamilton*. For example, a screenshot of Joyce Summers's funeral in "Forever" is annotated with Aaron Burr's lyrics "death doesn't discriminate / between the sinners and the saints," suggesting that these two events—racebent Burr's own loss of his parents and the Buffy gang's loss of Joyce Summers—are essentially similar in nature. And a still from the episode "Amends" shows Angel and Buffy reconciled after his potential suicidal impulse walking the streets of Sunnydale annotated with the lyrics of the townspeople during Hamilton and Eliza's fraught reconciliation in the aftermath of Philip's death: "See them walking in the park / long after dark / taking in the sights of the city." Much like the previous post, these lyrics are also reappropriated to a seemingly universalized event—in this case, reconciliation—that remains coded to whiteness within fandom.

The use of *Hamilton*'s lyrics to annotate events within Sunnydale not only makes present this reappropriation to white bodies but fails to account for *Buffy the Vampire Slayer*'s own well-documented history of nonwhite erasure and the notable whiteness of Sunnydale as a fictional town in California (Edwards 2017; Salah 2014; Smith 2010; Strehlau 2017). As Jon Stratton notes, "the world of Sunnydale is implacably white, and not only white but Anglo-white in terms of the American everyday discourse of race" (2008, 225). Crucially, Miranda's claim that *Hamilton* represents America then as a more diverse America now coincides with the contemporaneity of Sunnydale in this framing. The effects of the musical's racebending are thus absented, suggesting that the crossover fandoms of *Hamilton* and *Buffy the Vampire Slayer*, both seen to be established narratives of American identity, are not necessarily required to acknowledge or engage with each other's historical interventions with regard to gender or race.

Hamilton's widespread cultural impact brings a heavier weight to its effects. Achieving near-universal acclaim, it has also had a voice in the public realm beyond Broadway, most famously (or infamously) in the spheres of education and American politics. While discussion of its effects in the public domain are beyond the scope of this essay, *Hamilton* does function as an intervention in discourses of US-centric racial identity. Fandom's engagement as validated by this racial interruption while insisting that race not function as a central component in its fanworks therefore produces a complicated space wherein racebending is employed to erase the importance of acknowledging raced identities and lived experiences, particularly in American contexts. As a microcosm of fandom inextricably linked to discussions of race, the manner in which race is disavowed indicates not only the problematic whiteness underlying these fandom spaces but also the fact that racebending and postracial casting are, by themselves, still not equal to the problem at hand.

9. Understanding Good and Evil

The Influence of Fandom on Overcoming Reductive Racial Representations in Dungeons and Dragons

CARINA LAPOINTE

ELVES, DWARFS, ORCS, AND GOBLINS are some of the races populating fantasy realms, each with its own culture and history. With increased
critical discussion in popular and academic circles, fantasy explores what it
means to be human and how people understand themselves. Kathryn Hume
argues that fantasy is expressive literature, presenting readers "with a new
interpretation of reality" that encourages the examination of how people
understand the world (1984, xii). By using fantasy as a metaphor for exploring
and redefining current realities, people can observe the subtle ways that racial
thinking continues to influence everyday life. *Dungeons and Dragons* (*D&D*)
is an example of how pop culture represents race in the fantasy genre, and this
chapter examines the implications of these representations as "signs and signifiers of our times" (Warnes 2005, 2).

It is necessary to examine racial interactions in fantasy settings to
facilitate understandings of identity and "its wider socio-cultural applicabil-
ity" because the thinking that occurs in game worlds has direct applications
for everyday life (Walden 2015, iii). Antero Garcia supports Corey Walden's
theory because "although [game] systems encourage iteration and systems
change over time, the ideological assumptions underneath them largely do
not," particularly racial ideologies (2017). Fans' passion for *D&D* prepares
them to experiment with how people think about fictional races. While different national and cultural contexts affect how particular individuals think
about racial differences, representations of different fantasy races provide
awareness into subconscious racial understandings. Racial understandings
are further complicated in fantasy due to the immense popularity and subsequent standardization of tropes from the works of influential authors like
J. R. R. Tolkien. Despite the efforts of postcolonial fantasy writers, many
writers engage in what Mark Hrisho calls "broad stroke depictions" of
"monotype culture" (2014). Simplified racial representations are problematic and encourage a continued acceptance of one standard racial identity,
which fans are challenging, especially in *D&D*.

Although game manuals dictate racial morality and encourage violent solutions through ludic elements, players can promote liberating experiences by challenging traditional definitions. Whether through playing campaigns or writing novels, as R. A. Salvatore has done by rewriting understandings of race through his subversion and complication of his drow characters, players reveal the cultural implications for how people can think about race and can properly challenge the structural racism people accept from their entertainment.

—*Dungeons and Dragons*, Tolkien, and Race

Created in 1974 by Gary Gygax and Dave Arneson, *Dungeons and Dragons* has been prominent in shaping Western pop culture. While gaming sessions may differ depending on the players and the Dungeon Masters (DMs), the core game remains the same: the players tell stories, and "D&D gives structure to the stories, a way of determining the consequences of the adventurers' action" (Mearls and Crawford 2014, 5). *D&D* also imports racially constructed ideologies; the worlds and creatures reflect the original authors' mindset about the world, which can cause racial undertones to emerge whether consciously or subconsciously. Although the game draws on many authors, mythologies, and histories, Tolkien's Middle-earth is its primary inspiration. Gary Gygax claims that Tolkien had a strong influence on his game and credits his work for popularizing the game (2000, 2004). This influence helped establish the game as a success but also brought concerns about representations of race (M. Hall 2005, 15).

Critics, including R. A. Salvatore, believe that fantasy is racist as a genre because of how it encourages simplistic racial representations since the success of *The Lord of the Rings* (Craddock 2014). John Rumsby argues that the "unfathomable popularity of his works made it so that his portrayal of race, racism and racial discrimination, heavily influenced by Tolkien's own Eurocentrism, helped some forms of old European racism to subtly re-enter social and literary imaginations across the globe, and, to a certain extent, endure" (2017, 42). Stephen Shapiro is one critic who claims Tolkien was racist because of how he physically represents good and evil: "Tolkien's good guys are white and the bad guys are black, slant-eyed, unattractive, inarticulate and a psychologically undeveloped horde" (2002).

This type of physical representation is problematic in how consistently it is applied, and it extends beyond Tolkien's work. Because much of the fantasy literature published after Tolkien was attempting to capture the popular Tolkienesque spirit, fantasy publishers were less willing to deviate too far from Tolkien's model, a guaranteed moneymaker. Racial hierarchy and thinking became so embedded within fantasy literature that it was increasingly difficult to craft a world without these racist constructions. Helen Young suggests that new writers and gamers have felt pressure to follow these expected racial identities either because that was the expectation or to enjoy continued commercial success, which discouraged differences in representation (2016). The popularity of *D&D* has established it as a model for other fantasy tabletop and online role-playing games, further spreading standard racial expectations into other aspects of pop culture. Thus, a more limited racial mindset flourished, which explains the limited racial identities in fantasy literature. However, many fans and scholars see potential in *D&D* for expanding these limitations. Philip Clements argues that examining *D&D* "as both a text and cultural practice ... shows the progress that has been made toward increasing sensitivity and equality," which leads to stronger interpersonal connections in the real world (2019, 4).

Race in fantasy helps to classify the differences among vastly different groups, usually distinctly enough that there is minimal confusion about what a creature is, and to permit the exploration of what it means to be human. Fantasy is subject to racial prejudices. Hierarchies suggest who is respected or despised based on race: gnomes are good and trolls are bad. Race is a metaphor of difference and is often used as a reductive identifier to determine friend or foe. All the races can be organized hierarchically regarding how humans relate to them. An elf, Tolkien's idealization of humankind, would be higher on this scale than a human because elves are considered to be superior to humans (Tolkien 1981). Contrarily a goblin, humans' antithesis, would be lower on this scale than humans because goblins represent traits that people should disassociate themselves from (Puls 2018). By understanding the races relative to humans, people can recognize human fears and desires.

D&D offers a troubling binary of good and evil because its presentation of the world suggests that "good and evil are so simplistic that an entire culture, race, or species can be *inherently* evil" (Sturtevant 2017). Many fantasy races fall under the classic categories of good and evil. These recognitions shape the interactions someone has with other races. The way people think about these races is problematic in its reductiveness. Some people will more likely struggle with associating good creatures with evil and find it even more difficult to accept evil creatures' actions as good. Strong prejudice is stacked against this type of character; a goblin hero is uncommon, and people can resist this representation. Through using Tolkien's archetypes, *D&D* solidifies certain expectations for racial identities, making it much more difficult to accept a personal identity—who or what individuals believe they are—that does not adhere to one's expected racial identity. People struggle to recognize these ingrained racial identifiers, and to overcome the subtle influences of racial thinking is a difficult task. Michael Omi argues that "concepts of race and racial images are both overt and implicit within popular culture.... Particular racial meanings, stereotypes, and myths can change, but in the presence of a *system* of racial meanings and stereotypes of racial ideology seems to be an enduring aspect of American popular culture" (1989, 121).

It is not enough to flip the expectations; having evil elves and heroic giants does not solve the problem that racial identities are their first characteristic rather than personal identities. While people have overcome some stereotypes, more remain because people often restrict creatures to the expected racial identities. This conditioned thinking is what Omi finds so troublesome and resistant to change. Understanding racial ideology stems from distinguishing what people actually believe from what they claim they believe. Because fantasy literature and pop culture are intertwined, "fantasy literature can represent or address the racial attitudes of its audience and reveal accurate understandings of how race is viewed in contemporary culture" (Lavender 2009, 190). These thoughts are often buried beneath fantastic metaphors that blur the difficult truths people are reluctant to acknowledge: people believe that they have surpassed racist thinking when they have not, and it is extremely difficult to change how people think. *D&D* provides opportunities to see how this mindset operates within a game setting and to let players explore possible solutions for overcoming the default method of thinking about racial differences within fantasy worlds.

—Fandom, *D&D*, and Racial Stereotyping

Fandom has become an acceptable, often embraced aspect of everyday life. Increasingly common in academia, fandom invites an exploration of popular thought. With this shift, the image of fans becomes "active, critically engaged, and creative" (Jenkins 2006, 1). Although some fans are passive consumers, others engage with a text and establish a personal connection with it. Fandom is the state not just of being a fan but of being part of a collective. Fans are people "*re-writing* the meaning behind the source text... *re-reading* these texts through the mutual collaboration of divergent parties, and ... *re-produc[ing]* ... this mutual collaboration in larger cultural contexts" (Booth 2009, ix). In *D&D*, this rewriting, rereading, and reproducing occur during play. One example of this play is Gygax and Salvatore's creation of the drow. The drow live underground in matriarchal societies, and most drow worship the chaotic evil goddess Lolth. Unlike the Tolkienesque elves, who are fair in appearance, the drow are black-skinned with white hair and red eyes, a choice that immediately raises questions about the association of skin color and evil. Gygax and Salvatore rewrite and reread the definition of the elf by introducing an evil elf, and they reproduce this type of elf in larger cultural contexts through the *D&D* game manuals and Salvatore's Legend of Drizzt series, which first popularized the drow. This reversal questions what it means to be an elf, which can challenge how people think about race and its current limitations.

One of the unique aspects of tabletop role-playing games is the potential fans have for influencing game production and play. *D&D* is designed to give Dungeon Masters control over their campaigns because the manuals are only suggestions (Heinsoo, Collins, and Wyatt 2008). Players are also active in their feedback and encourage the changes they want to see in the games, which can influence future editions. While not a reciprocal relationship, some influence is distributed between producer and consumer. Additionally, the fans who grew up reading Tolkien and playing *D&D* are now the ones producing the games, enabling them to make their desired changes. *D&D* is also a product of fandom, created by people interested in war games who seek a fantasy background.

Fans have already influenced how the game represents race. In the first to fourth editions, fans demanded more inclusive artwork in the manuals to incorporate nonwhite humanoids because this representation was low; either there were few nonwhite pictures of creatures or the manuals encouraged the development of the Western gaze on certain ethnic groups, as in *Oriental Adventures* (1985) and *Al-Quadim* (1992). In the fifth edition, the artists included greater visual representations of minority groups. Therefore, as John Rumsby argues, if people want to address racism in fantasy as a whole, "we must all take responsibility" to actively work on change to challenge the traditional default representation (2017, 181). Fans are embracing his call as they demand more from game designers to challenge racial thinking.

D&D relies on the players' agency to choose the influence the world has on character interactions and definitions of evil. Antero Garcia notes that "players extend and build from the tools of narrative construction they are provided in order to collaboratively extend problematic representations embedded within this system" (2017). This means that if players accept without question a conflict between elves and dwarfs, they are more likely to role-play their characters with this conflict in mind rather than move toward resolution. Fans must actively seek new options, and the game provides possibilities for playing different races that were at one time only evil, including half-orcs and drow. By being allowed to play these traditionally evil creatures, players are making them more familiar and can develop empathy with them. By providing a complete picture of who an orc is, these players can work to undermine the traditional one-dimensional racial standard. Ilan Mitchell-Smith attributes this development to "changing perceptions of racialized behavior among the consumers of the game" (2009, 220). Fans are questioning the once-clear binaries between good and evil, especially why someone is considered to be evil, to explore how evil is represented in fantasy.

The act of character creation is one way that *D&D* limits race, because the manuals tend to reinforce racial stereotyping. These editions "suggest a genetic determinism of what individuals can be and their capacity to excel at various aspects of D&D gameplay" (Garcia 2017). Dwarfs, for example, "share many qualities with the rocks they love. They are strong, hardy, and dependable . . . they believe in the importance of clan ties and ancestry . . . seek guidance and protection from the gods . . . [and] harbor a fierce hatred for orcs" (Heinsoo, Collins, and Wyatt 2008, 37). These are just a few phrases that outline what it means to be a dwarf, and most players role-playing a dwarf adopt these characteristics. The dwarfs' bonuses for their endurance create the expectation that they can succeed in acts requiring stamina. Different races and classes have predetermined bonuses that encourage players to match complementary race-class combinations to maximize their characters' abilities. This strategy is especially common among beginning players, who are learning how race defines attributes and skills. Some players, however, are eager to find unique race-class combinations. A halfling barbarian—a barbarian is a primal warrior who prefers to fight in melee combat, often focused on dealing maximum damage directly—for example, can become a powerful character in the fourth edition through careful manipulation of the game's mechanics. Usually, a halfling barbarian would not exist because this build works against the halfling's racial background, but players are free to explore this option. Although character creation is the players' responsibility, the resources provided for them tend to reinforce reductive racial identities through stereotypes.

Racial descriptions in fantasy RPG's do more than influence character creation, as Helen Young notes in the context of the video games released as part of the *Lord of The Rings* franchise, since "race determines not only appearance and ability but also moral capacity and purpose because of the ways the narratives of the games frame their actions; ludic and narrative elements combine to reinforce racial logics" (Young 2015). Each race has an assigned alignment that reinforces the understanding of different races. Alignment is "a character's dedication to a set of moral principles" (Heinsoo, Collins, and Wyatt 2008, 19). There are nine types of alignment: lawful good, chaotic good, neutral good, unaligned, neutral evil, lawful neutral, chaotic neutral, lawful evil, and chaotic evil. Alignment is not entirely restrictive—characters can change alignments over the course of a game—but serves as a guideline for how to play a character type.

The problem arises when alignment is assigned to races within the game: for example, an aboleth is lawful evil while a centaur is neutral good. (Aboleths are a race of eel-like creatures with psychic powers; lawful evil creatures use society's laws to benefit themselves at the expense of others; neutral good creatures do what they think is best while following their own moral code.) Corey Walden argues that alignment is "simply a game mechanic used to distinguish between friend and foe, rather than a granular system of meaning or an advanced ethical framework" (2015, 69). This mechanic generally guides how players interact with characters and limits the potential for these creatures to embrace an alignment not assigned to their race. The reductive nature of this system further limits racial possibilities and continues to reinforce stereotypical racial identities.

Racial representation helps determine the interactivity between characters and nonplayer characters, which affects narrative development. This reaction is based on culturally ingrained ideas rather than giving individuals of a particular race a chance to reveal their personal identity instead of their expected racial identity. Morality is a racial trait and a conforming feature throughout gameplay (Mitchell-Smith 2009). First impressions, based on what one race knows about another, shape interactivity and may result in biased conduct. Although expectations for different creatures' racial identities have been resistant to change, fandom can influence attitudes toward and understandings of race, racism, and racial differences within fantasy literature and D&D.

To progress through the game, players strive to maximize a character's level by completing quests and killing monsters, however they are defined. While lower levels tend to focus on beasts and other natural enemies, many early opponents also include goblins and orcs, creatures typically associated with evil in fantasy. Dungeon Masters (DMs) have options for what they place in front of players, but the abundance of certain creatures being evil is likely to lead them to continue these traditions and these traditional violent outcomes. In a situation where goblins are raiding a village, players may try a diplomatic solution, which may be successful or impossible depending on how the DM presents the goblins and how the players want to solve the problem. A common expectation would be to kill the goblins and, because of how the *D&D* manuals describe goblins' nature, diplomatic solutions are improbable and a fight is almost inevitable because that violent reaction is the expectation in most fantasy. Although it is possible depending on the players' mindset to have games where racial identities are questioned and can be transcended, it is difficult given the game's mechanics and may be less likely to occur.

Part of being a hero in these games involves a transformative experience from a level 1 nobody to a level 30 god-like figure. Corey Walden argues that "through these mythologies, narratives, and challenges, characters are transmuted from nameless individual to vanquisher of the shadow. The character's journey is a narrative of survival as they quest for power and wealth on the road to heroism" (2015, 66). These characters are defined as heroes, regardless of their alignment, because they are the player characters. If they are considered heroes in the making then, by default, anyone who stands in their way becomes the villain. Because of the typical reductive nature of games like *D&D*, many of the villains are simply monsters to be defeated, another test in the process of the players becoming heroes. A hero, after all, must have monsters to fight, and monsters are defined by what the hero is not, which in many cases includes racial differences (Bowman 2010).

One of the problems in *D&D* involves how racial differences encourage violent solutions to conflict. Antero Garcia argues that "D&D's role in shaping a history of symbolic violence in gaming culture is a legacy that is acknowledged but not empirically interrogated" (2017). Fans accept violence, but few realize the implications of why the violence occurs and the significance of whom it occurs to. One example of this type of fan is quinn, who compares expected racial identity in the *D&D* world and the real world. Because he recognizes the inherent problems of racial representation, he writes his *Thoughtcrime* blog and works to design tabletop games as he believes they should be. One problem that he sees lies in the representation of the kobolds and their struggles:

> The kobolds are evil from birth and when you see one, it is probably going to be attacking you and you are OK to slay it. It's a convenience, and it's a reason I grow more and more disenchanted with it. I'll be honest and say when I think of this I think about my own life as an African-American and how many times I am pre-judged to

be, be all these threatening things when I am really just a nerd trying to raise a kid and be a good employee, father, and husband . . . and all of a sudden I feel bad for the kobold. It's not that being a kobold has anything to do with being black; it's that in both of these cases we are told this is who we are by societies and people know nothing about us as individuals. (2014)

Like other traditionally evil races, kobolds—small, aggressive, reptilian humanoids with a lawful evil alignment—are prejudged by other races, which reinforces their expected racial identity. Other races rarely give kobolds a chance to grow beyond societal expectation or work on personal development. Instead, violence is the answer to these problems, comparable to the solutions in human history. Paul Sturtevant argues that the problematic alignment system, coupled with the stereotypical representations of dark-skinned evil creatures, "smacks with the worst sort of colonial racisms . . . worlds are loaded with the idea at the core of white supremacy: that having dark skin is bad" (2017). This connection is increasingly recognized, and fans must find ways to reconcile game interests with moral dilemmas.

D&D provides opportunities for telling new stories and exploring racial questions, but the game's structure—limited to what is written in the rulebooks and not what DMs may choose to do for campaigns—contains ludic elements reinforcing racial thinking. Helen Young argues that similar elements in the games she studied "reproduced and intensified" racial thinking because of how players progressed through them (2015). In *D&D* as well, killing is encouraged if players kill the right creatures. When dwarfs kill a nearby goblin clan, this action is celebrated because they have defended their homeland from the goblin threat posed just by proximity. These game mechanics tend to establish the expectations behind the races, but this is something that fans can change when they have more control over the gameplay. If players do not assert control over the game mechanics, *D&D*'s rules encourage simplistic understandings of good and evil. Thus "D&D encourages its players to use racial stereotypes as justification for genocide, and to profit from ethnic cleansing" (Clements 2015, 48). The characters progress as they eradicate various forms of evil, which is usually defined first by ethnicity.

Despite the game's intended structure, it does not eliminate the possibility of players having personal growth experiences regarding racial thinking, depending on how the DMs represent creatures and the kinds of interactions they permit or encourage. The way that players interact with the world is central to the game. The rulebooks, after all, are guidelines and do not have to be taken as absolute. There is great potential for personal growth experiences, but they are difficult to accomplish without deliberate action from the entire group. Most of the current research on this issue focuses on how skills learned from *D&D* lead to workplace success, especially in management roles, and how its value as an acceptable multicultural activity for prison inmates is a key for social rehabilitation (Mims 2014; Richie 2017). By encouraging teamwork and recognizing a need for diversity (mostly on abilities and classes), people can grow, but there remains a progress area for racial understandings beyond those from players' realizations with real-life applications. Philip Clements interviewed one player who noticed that playing *D&D* made him "way more open-minded" because the game encouraged him to see the world from his character's perspective (2019, 6). More research is needed on this topic, but it is clear that people are challenging the racial structures built into fantasy games, and increasing numbers of people are working toward overcoming these ways of thinking.

While most of the responsibility seems to rest on DMs and players, fans are challenging game designers to take more responsibility for embracing diversity and reducing the game's racial restrictions. Antero Garcia argues that "as a tool for creative, collaborative, and—ideally—*fun* storytelling and play, *D&D*'s system must both guide and provide liberating opportunities for innovation" (2017). Garcia stresses that the creators need to take more responsibility for how they continue to portray racial representations. *D&D*'s manuals guide new players, which encourages them to continue following reductive philosophies regarding racial identities. If game creators take control over these representations from the beginning of players' experiences, they will help shape more complex understandings of different races from individuals who may not adhere to the traditional mindset of their race and may combat racial prejudice.

—R. A. Salvatore and the Legend of Drizzt

Advanced online communication networks allow fans more opportunities to share their ideas with others, but fewer fans can influence large-scale conversations. R. A. Salvatore was hired by *D&D*'s publishing company, Wizards of the Coast, to write stories to fit within the Forgotten Realms, *D&D*'s world. Because of Salvatore's position as both a player of the game and a contributor to the game world, John Rumsby argues that he uses "D&D lore against itself [to] demonstrat[e] how familiar or overused tropes in Fantasy could communicate racism if handled poorly, all while addressing the racism inherent to D&D's foundational universe" (2017, 56). Salvatore is responsible for popularizing the drow created by Gary Gygax by taking a race used exclusively as a monster in dungeons and challenging its expected racial identity.

The Legend of Drizzt series has shaped player demand for the drow in *D&D*, which has contributed to Drizzt becoming a prominent character in the *D&D* canon. Credited as popularizing the drow through having a drow protagonist (and many other drow fan favorites), Salvatore has worked to increase materials available for fan consumption. With coauthoring manuals—including *The Drow of the Underdark* and *Menzoberranzan: The Famed City of the Drow, Revealed at Last!*—he provides players with the tools to build characters and campaigns. More importantly, he has been able to create an elf character who does not conform to the standard expectation of the fair-haired and light-skinned elf, yet the character is still held in high esteem by other characters and fans. The popularity of Drizzt has inspired the "dual-wielding drow elf ranger [and] has become a caricature" (LaSala 2018). The fan imitation of people trying to be Drizzt has led to some frustration—players are tired of seeing Drizzt copycats—yet Drizzt's popularity in *D&D* is undeniable (Douglas 2008). In the fifth edition's discussion on elves, it is Drizzt's picture that readers first see rather than a more traditional Tolkien-esque elf. AtomicKitKat describes how "Drizzt, Raistlin, Aragorn, Legolas, [and] Gandalf . . . are the names that you see in practically any fantasy setting," characters who are the archetypal representations of the elfin archer or the drow hero (2007). Drizzt's prominence within *D&D* has affected fan understandings of elf heroes, shifting the elf archetype regarding appearance and weapon choice and thus beginning to diversify racial expectations.

Salvatore recognizes that fantasy tends to reinforce reductive racial identities, but he challenges these traditions in his writing, influencing both the fans of his books and the fans of the *D&D* world. Paul Sturtevant credits Salvatore as being someone who has worked to improve racial ideas by recognizing how racism has permeated the fantasy genre, including Salvatore's own early stories, and worked to complicate how he displays race (2017). His work to dismantle this structured racial prejudice has inspired many fans and helped them reconcile their identities. One fan, MasqueofComus, mentions the racism he faced in childhood and how it was amplified after 9/11. Drizzt's journey especially was "a way for [him] to cope with racism . . . Funny enough, Drizzt helped [him] to not hate [himself] for [his] skin color" (2012). For A. A. George, Drizzt helped him recognize that "white wasn't the only color of value" for fantasy protagonists (2014).

As someone who has faced prejudice and has had to prove who he is, Drizzt is an inspiration to many fans like MasqueofComus and George because he is "a rare example of an heroic person of color" (Sturtevant 2017). Others have been inspired by Salvatore. Salvatore references fan letters in interviews where multiple fans from various minority groups thank him for inspiring them (Staggs 2015). By recognizing the familiar within such a popular character, Drizzt has become relatable and inspirational while challenging perceptions of what makes an elf an elf. As a successful author, Salvatore uses his stories to prompt further racial discussions in the genre as a whole; he has added to the fan movement for reducing the traditional structural racism. Although he is only one author, he offers valuable contributions through literary examples of challenging traditional racial conventions. This act is exactly what Sturtevant wants fans to do to overcome fantasy's racism: acknowledge its presence and "subvert and dismantle the racist structures" to ensure that new fantasy reflects current cultural values (2017).

Because race in fantasy is used as a metaphor for difference, fandom can challenge *D&D*'s representations and encourage further questioning of reductive racial ideologies. Within the realms of play, games reflect society, which is "so mired with racism, it is no wonder that our fantasy worlds, the ones we escape to, the ones we dream in, would maintain even stricter racial laws than are possible in real life" (Joanna 2013). Although Helen Young suggests that the racial systems built into fantasy may be too much to overcome, it is necessary to attempt to reshape the worlds and the characters' interactions within them (2016). This process, although slow, is becoming more successful because of fans' interventions. Despite *D&D*'s ludic elements shaping interactivity and reinforcing reductive racial identities, fans can encourage liberating experiences by challenging these traditional definitions and suggesting other alternatives to how different races interact. John Rumsby argues that "fantasy can be one of the single most accessible, most powerful weapons at our disposal in the battle against racism, as it is capable of both acknowledging the innumerable evils of racism's reality, and offering unimaginable escapes from them simultaneously" (2017, 19).

Through games, individuals have some control over how race affects characters. It is easier to understand the subtleties of racial thinking in a world removed from the real one. *D&D* can, therefore, "offer a unique space where the concept of race, often a difficult and uncomfortable topic of conversation, is questioned, criticized, and reshaped by the players" for the purpose of acknowledging this kind of thinking and finding ways to change it (Clements 2015, iii). Players can explore what it means to be an evil elf or a heroic goblin and recognize the consequences of traditional reductive identities. Through fans' intervention, people can work together to reinterpret contemporary understandings of fantasy races and the relations among them, as Salvatore's writing has encouraged. Antero Garcia argues that although people can interpret *D&D* as continuing bad racist history, it is a "promising reminder that people, cultural constructions, and systems *change*" (2017). When awareness of these issues is raised, change begins to follow: fans are not merely passive consumers but people who actively challenge and question current representations and suggest possible solutions. Asking these questions has led some players to restructure their own fantasy environments to encourage a more inclusive world and thus work to overcome the racism that has permeated the genre. By recognizing these problems in cultural thought and in realms of play, people can better grasp the subtle ways that racial thinking continues to shape everyday perceptions.

FOUR. IDENTITY/AUTHENTICITY

10. Whose Representation Is It Anyway?

Contemporary Debates in Femslash Fandoms

RUKMINI PANDE AND SWATI MOITRA

IN MANY SENSES, 2018 was a watershed year for queer visibility in English-language popular media texts produced in the US and UK media industries, with many viewers embracing singer Hayley Kiyoko's dubbing of it as "20-gay-teen" (2018). Indeed, as noted in the "Where We Are on TV" report issued by the GLAAD Media Institute, the 2017–18 season in the United States featured the most number of queer characters—433 over prime-time broadcast cable and streaming platforms—ever recorded over the fourteen years of the study. The report also underlines the fact that this was also a significant year for nonwhite queer characters, noting that it was "the first time there are more LGBTQ people of color on broadcast than white LGBTQ people" (2018, 16). This increase was also reflected on cable (46 percent) and on streaming platforms (48 percent). The expansion of visibility and central roles for queer characters, especially nonwhite characters, is certainly an encouraging sign and also raises key questions for fan scholars interested in the ways these characters are received by audiences, particularly those that engage in the production of fanwork or media fandom as it is broadly termed.

The particular lens that this chapter will consider is the interface of pop culture texts and media fandom communities, with the differential connotations of the idea of representation in media. While the catchphrase "representation matters" is frequently invoked regarding queer characters, not much attention has been paid to the fractures and fissures around what that representation looks like and what kinds of queer characters and relationships are elevated both in mainstream media and within fandom. Therefore, we argue that the evolving nature of pop culture texts and contemporary debates within fandom communities requires us to pay much more attention to these moments of conflict.

Our primary subjects here are the discussions of the politics of representation after the cultural and discursive turns, particularly around marginalized subjects, that have been taken up repeatedly in disciplines including feminist studies, postcolonial studies, and queer theory (Gates 1993; hooks 1984; Hull, Bell-Scott, and Smith 1982; Mohanty 1984; Morris 1994; Puar 2007; Trinh 1989). Although these theorizations cover a wide and complex range of ideas, a shared concern has coalesced around how these regimes of representation or how these signifying practices that structure how we see the world function continue to be troubled by issues of essentialism, racialization, and respectability politics.

This is especially true when fans employ this language with regard to pop culture texts since *which* representation is being discussed continues to prompt debate. Stuart Hall's examination of Black cultural representation in the United Kingdom is particularly pertinent here. In "New Ethnicities," he maps the ways in which the term was coined as "a way of referencing the common experience of racism and marginalization in Britain and came to provide the organizing category of a new politics of resistance, among groups and communities with, in fact, very different histories, traditions and ethnic identities." For Hall, this politics of resistance, initially formed around a double-pronged push for access to representational space for Black artists and a contestation of their marginal position, morphed into a new phase. He posits that this was a shift from "the relations of representation to a politics of representation itself," which signaled an "end to the innocent notion of the essential black subject" (1996, 442, 444).

This was in effect a call to end the claims of authenticity for any sort of cultural production—not as a sign of defeat but as an acknowledgment of the vast heterogeneity that makes up any racial or ethnic category as well as its inherent slipperiness. For Hall, to be involved in a politics of representation is to be "plunged headlong into the maelstrom of a continuously contingent, unguaranteed, political argument and debate: a critical politics, a politics of criticism" (1996, 445). When we look at the debates within fandom, this description—"a maelstrom of a continuously contingent, unguaranteed political argument and debate"—seems especially insightful.

We would also add here Kristen Warner's articulation of the concept of plastic representation. She argues that due to the emphasis on the mere presence of nonwhite bodies onscreen, "the degree of diversity became synonymous with the quantity of difference rather than with the dimensionality of those performances" (2017). To push the idea of dimensionality further here, while Warner's critique focuses on the logics of industrial production, if we follow traditional arguments within media fan studies, adding dimensionality to flat characters is exactly what fans are primarily engaged with when creating fanwork. If plastic representation offered by media houses is, in Warner's estimation, often depthless and inorganic, then how do those characters fare within fan communities? It is through this question that fan claims and concerns around representation must be examined further. In this chapter, we will approach these questions through a series of case studies focusing on the femslash fandoms formed around *The 100* (2014–present), *Black Lightning* (2018–present), and *Supergirl* (2015–present).

—The Curious Case of the Missing Fandoms

The first thread that we will examine, with regard to the question of adding dimensionality, concerns the effects of the growing primacy of non-white queer characters in pop culture texts on fandom communities, particularly with respect to their presence in fanwork. We will take up this question using the frame of the fandom algorithm, which denotes the structures that are seen to order the workings of media fandom, in terms of both communitarian etiquettes and technical strategies that involve fannish digital infrastructures, like archiving fanworks, and organizational strategies such as tagging on various digital platforms like Tumblr (Pande 2018b). These structures are seen to operate neutrally to promote fannish energy around certain characters. While these are seen to be neutral, characters of color often seem to make them glitch. The particular fandom algorithm referenced here is the axiom that queer fanwork exists to fulfill the need for representation for queer fans within heterosexist scripts. As Pande points out: "The interaction between fan text and media text has mostly been examined in terms of it being productive of an almost limitless multiplicity. However, an analysis of the effect (or lack thereof) on fan texts of the expanding canonical roles for non-white characters is key to bringing into focus the limits of those imaginative exchanges" (2018b, 131).

The idea of representation is once again implicated in these discussions because if characters of color are seen to be somehow outside of modes of fannish pleasure, empathy, and imaginative expansion, this prompts questions about the extent to which the logics of white supremacy continue to structure these interactions. The unequal distribution of fannish energy is seen not just in which texts gain traction within fandom in terms of the production of fanwork but also in physical spaces like conventions that are billed to be safe spaces for *all* queer fans.

Our first case study focuses on the CW show *The 100*. The show centered around a postapocalyptic scenario where humans had to flee Earth due to nuclear disaster and have been surviving on twelve international space stations for three generations. At the beginning of the show, a group of a hundred teenagers sent back to the surface must survive extremely hostile conditions. In fandom terms, the show gathered a lot of attention due to the centrality of the queer couple of Clarke Griffin (Eliza Taylor) and Lexa (Alycia Debnam-Carey), and the pairing, known as Clexa, gathered considerable amounts of excitement and fanwork. Just as an indication, there are over 10,000 fan fics listed with the pairing tag on Archive of Our Own. In episode 7 of season 3, however, Lexa was suddenly and brutally killed onscreen, prompting a very understandable backlash that has been well documented (Roth 2016). Fans expressed their hurt and anger through hashtag campaigns, such as #LexaDeservedBetter and #LGBTFansDeservedBetter, and also linked this incident to the historic issue of lesbian characters being killed in television narratives for shock value.

The position of fans invested in queer narratives on television—with regard to English-language pop culture texts produced in the US and UK media industries—has undergone quite a significant shift in the last ten years. A significant turning point came when fans of *Glee* (2009–2015) convinced showrunner Ryan Murphy to make their favorite character pairing of Santana Lopez (Naya Rivera) and Brittany Pierce (Heather Morris), also known as Brittana, an acutal canonical couple on the show (Berk 2011). These are certainly still niche audiences, but ones that have increased visibility and influence, especially in the age of social media. In this instance, fans not only made their displeasure felt online but also raised $11,000 to place messages on four billboards in Los Angeles. Notably, the campaign to raise money for the billboards was led by Mix, a fan in the Philippines (Murphy 2016). Some fans of the show have also campaigned to get a potential spin-off series—potentially called *Grounders*—which would focus on Lexa's origin story (LEXASPINOFF 2018).

In their essay on queer fan hashtag campaigns as production interventions, Annemarie Navar-Gill and Mel Stanfill track a series of such campaigns spanning controversies like the killing off of queer female characters such as Lexa in *The 100* and Poussey Washington (Samira Wiley) in *Orange Is the New Black*. In their analysis, they note that such campaigns are "strategic interventions meant to alter both representational and structural television production processes by leveraging the importance of audience feedback in a connected viewing environment" (2018, 85). However, as they also point out, the characters that get the most momentum or are seen as turning points in such campaigns are still governed by whiteness.

For instance one fan, when asked about the character death of Lexa, said that "episode 307 slapped me right back to reality, where LGBT people are killed for their sexuality, bullied, disowned by their parents. It reminded me of the Orlando Shooting, it reminded me of death. Death that I, a queer lady, deserve" (Karlan 2017). It is notable that the episode aired on March 3, 2016, and the Orlando shooting was on June 12, 2016, showing that the link was made explicitly between the violence onscreen and the real-life violence inflicted on queer bodies. What was not registered in this response was the fact that the Orlando attack was specifically against racialized queer bodies.

In the case of *The 100*, it is important to note that while the death of Lexa was indeed played for shock value and furthered the "bury your gays" trope, the show itself had major problems with regard to its portrayal of non-white characters right from its initial episodes. One example was the brutal onscreen death of Wells Jaha (Eli Goree) in the third episode of the first season. In the narrative, Wells was the son of Chancellor Thelonious Jaha (Isaiah Washington) and Clarke Griffin's childhood best friend. He got himself arrested when he found out that his father was sending the 100 to the ground, including Clarke, for whom he harbored feelings. Given some of the laws his father had enforced, Wells was not popular among the 100. He was portrayed as a capable and empathetic character who frequently advocated for making moral choices and privileging cooperation over conflict. However, he was murdered by a young white girl character called Charlotte (Izabela Vidovic) in the third episode, who wanted retribution for her parents' execution on the Ark by his father.

Wells's death then was coded in extremely problematic ways and functioned mainly to set the stakes of the show in terms of its brutality and the expendability of its characters. As the show's Wiki points out: "His death set the stage for Clarke and Bellamy to work together as co-leaders in an attempt to stop more senseless deaths" ("Wells Jaha" n.d.). A question that arises, given the language used by the fan referenced before, is how this scene might have functioned as a slap "right back to reality" for its Black viewers. Nonetheless, even after Wells's death, the show continued to be portrayed as a groundbreaking and diverse narrative, based almost solely on its representation of (white) queerness by its fans—until the death of Lexa. One nonwhite queer fan traced her unease with the sudden outrage, writing that the reaction felt markedly different from those around previous deaths that were also graphic and exploitative:

I kept thinking, "Sure, a lot of dead lesbians are on TV. And that sucks. But there are even more dead POC on TV. None of the Clexa stans I followed gave a shit about Wells. Or Anya. What makes Lexa different? What makes the death of a white queer woman on a show more bigoted than the repeated torture and death of POC characters?" (distressedcinnamonroll 2017)

It is crucial to note here that this fan also recounted that she had previously suppressed her unease with the treatment of nonwhite characters on the show because of the pervasive positive discourse around representation, particularly among those fans who supported Clexa. She wrote, "Since everyone I followed seemed to think the show had the best representation of any show ever, I thought 'maybe it's just me. maybe since it eventually had great LGBT representation, it's ok? maybe representation gets better? maybe i'm just being sensitive'" (distressedcinnamonroll 2017).

Such self-questioning and doubt regarding concerns about the ways in which nonwhite characters are treated in narratives that ostensibly offer good representation in terms of (white) queerness are recurring elements in media fandom communities. As seen in the noted quote, fans of color often must choose between participating in an assumedly universal joy or outrage over certain characters or pairings or risk being labeled as people who bring drama into fandom spaces, harsh people's squee, or seek to impose purity tests on fannish behavior.

We also want to extend this discussion to the ways in which these debates structure offline fandom spaces. Another effect of the outrage over *The 100* was the birth of ClexaCon, an annual convention in Las Vegas that had its third iteration in 2019. The convention describes itself as "the first and largest multi-fandom event for LGBTQ women and allies, [and] ClexaCon brings together thousands of diverse LGBTQ fans and content creators from around the world to celebrate positive representation for LGBTQ women in the media" (ClexaCon n.d.). The convention is also promoted as a safe space for all fans who would like to celebrate such representation. ClexaCon has had pretty significant success, with over 4,000 attendees from all over the United States and from multiple other countries in 2018.

However, at the same event, the fissures within these safe spaces were made evident around the reception of Nafessa Williams, who plays the character of Anissa Pierce or the superhero Thunder on the CW show *Black Lightning*. In the show, Anissa joyfully flirts with, kisses, breaks up with, and makes up with multiple women and has a well-written romantic arc with the character of Grace Choi (Chantal Thuy), but there has been very little traction for the show in media fandom terms. In contrast to the fanworks for *The 100*, there are only a little over a hundred fan fics listed with the "Anissa/ Grace" pairing tag on Archive of Our Own. This disjunct was also manifested within the physical space of the convention as nonwhite fans were confronted by the clear evidence of her exclusion from the squee generated by other attendees. Tweets from attendees (which were then taken up by fans not at the event as well) pointed out that not only were the panels about *Black Lightning* less well attended than the others, fewer fans queued up to meet Williams during the meet-and-greet event (adenaelamin 2018; gaythunders 2018). This disjunct was also reflected in write-ups by attendees, one of whom also noted the lack of nonwhite fans in the space at all (Marquette 2018). It must be noted that the programming for the convention did include panels on topics like queer women of color in media, where creators were invited to discuss their experiences.

It could be argued, as is often done within fandom spaces, that the discrepancy in fan excitement around characters like Anissa could be attributed to factors apart from race, such as a possible lack of fandom tropes in her portrayal or the fact that compared to a show like *The 100*, *Black Lightning* had not been on the air long enough for viewers to be familiar with it. In the same vein, in response to the criticism, some attendees asserted that they chose to devote their time to the actors, characters, and character pairings they felt the deepest connection with. They objected to complaints that "called them racist" for these choices in an otherwise celebratory environment (HereIsShir 2018).

It would be an error to analyze this incident in isolation. However, when the patterns within femslash fandoms as a whole are taken into account, the sidelining of Williams in a space that should have been geared toward centering her is not surprising (Navar-Gill and Stanfill 2018; Pande and Moitra 2017). These patterns include the dismissal of the concerns of nonwhite fans as policing of pleasure and the demand that they should create their own fanworks and fan spaces. This trend is also evidenced by the narratives of fans of color in femslash spaces, as recorded by Mel Stanfill. As one fan, Leo, points out, "I see a lot of folks in fandom try and say that having a canon white gay couple is a win for the entire community. But when queer or trans people of color try and point out that many of us don't feel represented, we're told to create our own stories or to be happy with the little progress that's been made so far" (Stanfill 2019).

While it might seem self-evident that online patterns are repeated in offline spaces, it is vital to note that these exclusions occur within spaces already marked by the language of representation and inclusion. That is, queer fans of color are often called upon to support such spaces and movements through such labor as supporting hashtags, creating fanwork, and contributing to campaigns to buy billboards as well as through their emotional investments by the promise of representation. However, when they find these spaces to be, once again, structured by the logics of white supremacy, their discomfort and disappointment are seen to be the problem within the fannish space. These logics are highlighted only in moments of conflict but must be seen as a constant context within which fans of color have to operate even as they seek modes of contingent and tenuous representation.

—Sanctioned Fandom: Negotiating Racial Scripts and Representation in *Supergirl*

The second thread that we will examine in this essay on the question of adding dimensionality will be through the CW's *Supergirl*, which has a dedicated following of femslash fans and often earns plaudits for its diverse casting. When *Supergirl* moved from CBS to its sister network the CW for its second season in 2016, the showrunners announced a flurry of new characters—one of which would generate considerable fannish buzz after the revelation that DC Comics' Maggie Sawyer (played by Floriana Lima) would become a series regular. Originally introduced in a 1987 issue of *Superman*, Maggie Sawyer was one of the first openly lesbian characters in the DC universe and continues to be one of its few LGBTQ+ characters. Her casting was welcomed as a progressive step; as Shannon Carlin wrote in Bustle: "It's no surprise this casting move would be the next step for Supergirl in her switch from CBS to The CW, which has made sure its superhero's worlds look more like the real world." Carlin quotes the show's executive producer, Greg Berlanti, who spoke of inclusive casting: "I wanted to contemporize these comics that I loved growing up and have them reflect the society that we live in now. . . . It's still about working in some of those very real qualities so that everyone feels represented" (2016).

Berlanti had earlier been part of an announcement that the CW would be introducing a gay character in one of its superhero shows, revealing no further information at the time except that it was a "significant character" and that the network wanted "the audience to enjoy the character development" (Wagmeister 2016). Fandom speculation zeroed in on Alex Danvers (played by Chyler Leigh), Supergirl's sister and a major character in her own right. This speculation, as hindsight shows, was not off the mark—Alex and

Maggie were to meet within the first few episodes of the second season of *Supergirl*, plunging Alex into a heart-wrenching journey of self-discovery that would eventually lead to a coming out.

Alex's coming out was met with an overwhelmingly positive reception from critics and fans alike. Lena Wilson wrote that as someone who came out as an adult, she felt that Alex's narrative was "uniquely honest and realistic." Wilson felt that Alex's story was one that sought to go beyond "simplistic 'born this way' origin [stories]" and instead sought to explore what it might mean to grow up in a world shaped by compulsory heteronormativity (2016). In an intensely personal piece, Riley Silverman talked about having called her mother, who is a *Supergirl* viewer, to show her the truth of her own experience:

> Alex represents those of us in the very specific generation for whom the gradual mainstreaming of LGBT identities seemed to land right in the middle of our adolescence. She lives in the space between that trickle of dignity that started to arrive and the shadow of a childhood when it was something we just didn't talk about. The end result of this combination is a specific generation of kids who academically understood that being gay was okay, but just couldn't make that step toward giving ourselves permission to accept who we are. (2017)

This note of personal identification was a common strand in the responses to Alex's coming-out story—it was seen as a triumph for viewers who had struggled with their sexual identity as adults, not quite able to claim it for themselves even as they witnessed its slow mainstreaming over the years in the United States, especially following the legalization of same-sex marriage by a landmark Supreme Court verdict in 2015. With the showrunners making it perfectly clear that they had no intention of reiterating the "bury your gays" trope, it seemed that fans of *Supergirl* had hit the jackpot with Sanvers, as the "Alex/Maggie" pairing is popularly known. Executive producer Andrew Kreisberg said, "Well, [Alex and Maggie are] not dying, either of them, so we're really not thinking about that right now" (Wilson 2016). In a fandom that already had a growing femslash contingent—mostly fans of "SuperCat," as the pairing featuring Melissa Benoist's Supergirl and Calista Flockhart's Cat Grant was known—this was met with considerable approval. Sanvers continues to be a popular pairing with 4,943 fanworks in Archive of Our Own, despite Alex and Maggie's eventual split and Floriana Lima's departure from the show at the end of its third season.

What could have been a story of triumphant representation—the sort of canon that femslash fandom had always asked for—is, however, made far more complex by the fact that Andrew Kreisberg had also stated in a pre-season interview with *Entertainment Weekly* that Maggie Sawyer "says in her introductory episode that growing up gay and Latina in Nebraska made her ideally sympathetic to people who are different and people who don't quite fit in" (Abrams 2017). *Supergirl* had been frequently criticized in its first season for its white feminism—that is to say, its purported claim to champion women and women-centered story lines despite its lack of LGBTQ+ representation or women of color in the main cast. Kreisberg's statement seemed to suggest that by including Maggie Sawyer, a canonical lesbian character, as well as racebending her as a Latina (the character in her comics avatar is unequivocally white), the showrunners were making an attempt to address this criticism by adding diversity to their main cast. This, however, ran into problems soon enough. Sharon Leal's Miss Martian, the show's only Black woman, was found to have a disappointing lack of screen time, with most of her onscreen presence being as a green alien. Mehcad Brooks's Jimmy Olsen, another racebent character, was demoted from a love interest for Supergirl in favor of Chris Wood's Mon-El. In later seasons, too, the show continues to display a lack of direction for Olsen as a character, despite his romantic relationship with Katie McGrath's Lena Luthor.

The central problem, however, was none other than the casting of Floriana Lima as Maggie Sawyer, whose character did indeed tell Alex Danvers that "growing up a non-white, non-straight, girl in Blue Springs, Nebraska," was a difficult experience for her (Abrams 2017). Maggie's character was promoted as a strong supporter of alien rights, which in *Supergirl* tend to stand in for the show's commentary on immigrant rights in the context of the charged immigration debates and anti-immigrant crackdowns in the present-day United States. Maggie's statement was meant to be an affirmation for growing up closeted in a hostile atmosphere, but there was one problem: Floriana Lima, though dark-skinned, was not Latina, even though Andrew Kreisberg had promoted her as such in his interview.

An article written by Desiree Rodriguez in *The Nerds of Color* pointed out the irony of this situation for queer Latino fans, for whom Maggie Sawyer's presence and her frank speech about the difficulties she faced growing up with dual identities should have been a "powerful moment" of representation (2016). That *Supergirl* is a genre show would have made Maggie's inclusion even more significant, because of the historical lack of representation of people of color and LGBTQIA people in science fiction and fantasy narratives. There is a sense of loss and betrayal in Rodriguez's words when she talks about Maggie Sawyer in the repeated use of the past tense—"would have been"—which stands in sharp contrast with the heartwarming responses from fans to Alex's story line. Rodriguez sums it up when she writes that "Floriana Lima is of Italian-American heritage; in her own words, her ethnic identity is a mix of 'Italian, Irish, English, Spanish, Portuguese. I'm a mutt'" (2016).

Rodriguez went on to argue that Lima's casting was simply part of a long tradition of Hollywood casting Italian American actors in Latino roles, including celebrated roles such as that of Al Pacino in *Scarface* or *Carlito's Way* or Jennifer Esposito in *Crash*, at the cost of Latino actors who continue to struggle to find roles. A study by USC's Annenberg School for Communication and Journalism, "Inclusion or Invisibility? A Comprehensive Annenberg Report on Diversity in Entertainment," found that out of nearly 11,000 characters surveyed in film and TV, only 5.8 percent were Latino characters with speaking parts compared to 17.4 percent in the US population (Smith, Choueiti, and Pieper 2016). *Supergirl* would in fact go on to add to this trend by casting Carlos Bernard, of Polish and Spanish heritage, as Maggie's homophobic Mexican father in the third season of the show.

Added to that was the problem of persistent stereotypes, both in the types of roles Latino actors were asked to perform and in terms of an aesthetic that erases the sheer diversity of the Latino community. Gina Torres, in a 2013 interview, had spoken of this when she said, "When I became an actress I quickly realized that the world liked their Latinas to look Italian, not like me. So I wasn't going up for Latina parts. I was going up for African-American parts" (Levine 2013). By promoting Maggie Sawyer as a queer Latina, as Andrew Kreisberg had done, only to cast Lima in the role was seen as nothing but a cynical attempt to cash in on Latino fans' support without initiating actual change. Desiree Rodriguez put it succinctly, "When Maggie told Alex she struggled being both non-white and queer, it feels like a trick. Lima is able to adopt the identity for various roles but does not have to live with the reality of being Latina in America. Or the struggle of being a Latina actress in Hollywood" (2016).

Rodriguez's article was received positively by a certain section of fans, even as others felt the criticism was unnecessary. Some commentators sought to add nuance to the discussion, pointing to the fact that Latino identity cannot be reduced to skin color alone. Teresa Jusino wrote in the Mary Sue that despite her disappointment about Lima's casting, "the character of Maggie Sawyer is still Latina," because that is "how she's being played and written and advertised" (2016). While Jusino argued in favor of granting the benefit of the doubt to the show's casting directors—who could not necessarily have known of the actor's ethnic background, pointing to past roles taken up by Lima, which were often of Latina characters—this only served to highlight Hollywood's tendency to cast actors who appear appropriately brown-skinned in Latino roles to the exclusion of a vast spectrum of people who constitute the Latino communities in the United States.

This argument was also taken up by a section of fans themselves. In a series of often cited tweets by Sanvers fans, Twitter user deathtodickens argued that Floriana Lima's "brown hair, eyes, and skin" would have made her a target of racism in the US Midwest, where she grew up: "I'm not saying the show didn't fuck up by labeling her Latinx in the one interview where they did," but addressing the same could not come "at the expense of a WOC that an audience has decided isn't a WOC" (2016). ("WOC" stands for "woman of color.") On Tumblr, itssupersomethings sought to discuss the nuances of "white-passing," arguing that "Floriana Lima is clearly not considered white by the entertainment industry, or she would be getting auditions and parts for white roles and we wouldn't even be having this conversation in the first place"; this discussion of the "arbitrary and political nature of how racial and ethnic categories are defined in the US" and the structural whiteness of the US entertainment industry sought to defuse fannish anger over Lima's casting, calling it the scapegoating of one actor (2016).

It is worth noting that both sides of the debate included self-identified fans of color, with one set of fans feeling the need to defend their enjoyment of the relationship, in the process ending up negating the anger of other fans. Structured by the logics of white supremacy, their interactions could exist only by undermining those seen as either harshing the squee or endorsing problematic things. This stood in sharp contrast to the uncomplicated pleasure that fans were able to express at Alex's story line. This debate, one that continues to rage well after Floriana Lima's departure from *Supergirl*, in many ways emphasizes the fault lines within femslash fandom underneath the celebratory narratives of canonical representation in an era where a more inclusive canonship is no longer an impossible dream.

As our case studies of *The 100*, *Black Lightning*, and *Supergirl* fandoms highlight, the possibility of canonical queer representation—for a very long time a distant fannish dream—does not necessarily resolve the problems of visibility, representation, and authenticity. Even as queer relationships become part of authorized canons, fans grapple with a host of problems. A crucial one is the question of supporting noncanonical character pairings in texts where queer characters and relationships exist. This is also seen in *Supergirl* with regard to the character pairing known as SuperCorp, which involves Kara Danvers and Lena Luthor. At the time we wrote this chapter, the popularity of the noncanonical SuperCorp (with 12,407 fan fics on Archive of Our Own) far outstrips that of the canonical pairing of Sanvers (5,629 fics). This causes conflicts, as fans of the canonical pairing often accuse those who choose the nonauthorized one of being delusional. Ironically, similar charges were once hurled at *all* slash fandoms by supporters of canonical heterosexual pairings. Fans also learn to live with the knowledge that increased queer visibility might still not mean more than one queer character or relationship on a mainstream television show. In the words of Kylie, at once celebrating Sanvers on *Supergirl* and mourning the potential loss of hope for SuperCorp: "Sadly, wlw representation tends to be a zero-sum game, and it seemed as though the writers were positioning Kara to act as a straight sounding board for her sister" (2016; "wlw" stands for "women who love women").

The moments of fannish conflict discussed throughout this essay, often centering around queer women of color—be they characters, actors, or fans themselves—offer clear insights into what remains perhaps one of the most fraught aspects of representation: the racialized dimensions of the same. Even the presence of nonwhite queer bodies onscreen does not necessarily lead up to the generation of squee for reasons that have to do with the structures of whiteness that define cultural production in the US and UK entertainment industries as well as the structures of whiteness within fandom spaces, both online and offline.

11. Jane the Virgen or Virgin?

The Dis-United States of (Latino) Fandom

JENNI M. LEHTINEN

IN A HIGHLY MEMORABLE SCENE in episode 11 of season 1 of the CW's comedy-drama series *Jane the Virgin* (2014–2019), Rafael Solano dines for the first time in the home of his then-girlfriend, Jane Villanueva. Throughout dinner with Jane's inquisitive mother, Xiomara, and grandmother, Alba, Rafael excels at saying all the right things about hard work and ethical behavior as keys to professional and personal success, thanks to the fact that Jane has carefully coached him for the occasion. Xiomara, who knows her daughter well, can see through Rafael's performance; turning to Jane, she mockingly observes in Spanish, "Lo preparaste bien, no soy tonta" (You prepared him well, I am not stupid). However, to Xiomara's and Alba's great surprise, on hearing these words Rafael answers back jovially, "Claro que no es tonta" (Of course you are not stupid). Rafael's ability to utter this phrase in fluent Spanish makes a lasting impression on the highly critical Xiomara and Alba. With a close-up that captures their approving smiles, the protective facade that has kept Rafael outside the family unit begins to crumble.

Knowledge of the Spanish language, as the scene of Rafael's first dinner with the Villanuevas highlights, forms part of the selection criteria for being accepted into this Latino family. (Building on the *Oxford English Dictionary* definition, I use the words "Latino" and "Latina" to refer to "a Latin American inhabitant of the United States," thus distinguishing Latin Americans living in North America from those living south of the border.) Further instances throughout the series reiterate the connection between being able to speak Spanish and being welcomed into Jane's family. Indeed, it is Michael's willingness to learn his wedding vows to Jane in Spanish, regardless of his strong American accent, that marks his official inclusion into the family in the finale of season 2. Moreover, Jane herself regards knowledge of Spanish as an extremely desirable characteristic in a potential suitor, as is demonstrated in episode 33 of season 2 when she contemplates whether to date her college adviser. Jane tries to convince herself that, despite their student-teacher dynamic, Professor Chávez is worth pursuing because he ticks all the boxes on her mental checklist for a perfect match, including the box about speaking Spanish. These narratives of Jane's potential suitors are contrasted interestingly with that of her long-lost father, the famous telenovela star Rogelio De La Vega, who is never portrayed as an outsider in the family unit despite being absent for over twenty years. Owing entirely to his Mexican background and his bilingualism, he is able to integrate seamlessly into the family upon resurfacing after a lengthy period of time.

As shown in reference to the vetting of Jane's suitors and the ease with which Rogelio finds his way back into the Villanueva family, inclusion into the family is granted selectively and only after a baptism by fire. This routinely consists of Xiomara and Alba carefully evaluating the potential suitors' ability to understand and incorporate the Villanueva family's traditions, ethics, and beliefs with their own. Throughout the series Jane, her mother, and her grandmother form a close-knit exclusively female family unit, drawn together not only by shared memories but by their mutual Latino culture and the Spanish language, which act as barriers against intruders. Whereas Alba, who speaks only Spanish on the show, is revealed at the beginning of season 2 to be illegally in the United States, Xiomara and Jane are perfectly assimilated into American society. Irrespective of their integration, though, both women selectively embrace aspects of Latin American popular heritage by binge-watching telenovelas and indulging in their traditional cuisine. Meanwhile, Latino Catholic religiosity, conveyed through Alba's moral teachings, hovers consistently in the background; this is most prominently illustrated by Jane's promise to stay chaste until marriage.

Yet the fact that knowledge of Spanish is repeatedly singled out in *Jane the Virgin* as a criterion for inclusion is clearly at odds with the reality that the series itself is filmed in English. Moreover, the emphasis that the series puts on being able to communicate in Spanish strikes a further discord with the way in which some of the series' main Latino cast members, most notably actor Gina Rodríguez as Jane, have come under fire by some for not being Latino enough, specifically because their Spanish cannot be considered fluent. As Rodríguez put it in a 2015 HuffPostLive interview when addressing criticisms about her limited knowledge of Spanish, it is "bananas" to assume that one needs to speak the language of one's ancestors in order to be proud of one's cultural and ethnic heritage.

Rodríguez's claim that fluency in Spanish should not be regarded as a prerequisite of belonging to the Latino community clearly contradicts the way *Jane the Virgin* establishes knowledge of Spanish as a condition for being accepted into her Latino family. However, although Rodríguez might be arguing the exact opposite from the narrative of the series in which she stars, her words call out to the central role of the Spanish language in debates regarding inclusion or exclusion from Latino communities. In some ways, her comments regarding how knowledge of Spanish is not what makes a person truly Latino make it easier to comprehend why official *Jane the Virgin* fan communities give preferential treatment to speakers of English rather than Spanish, thus taking for granted the Latino viewers' ability and willingness to communicate in English.

In this chapter I will explore how ethnicity and language determine who is included, as well as who is excluded, from mainstream *Jane the Virgin* fandom. This will be accomplished by analyzing fan comments as displayed on the official *Jane the Virgin* Facebook page, @cwJanethevirgin, and those on the unofficial *Jane the Virgin* Latino Facebook page, @JaneTheVirginLatino, which caters specifically to Spanish-speaking Latin American fans of the series. (As the activity on the unofficial Facebook page reveals, the word "Latino" refers not to Latino individuals but to Latino Spanish, the collective name given to the Spanish spoken by people in Latin America as opposed to the Spanish spoken in Peninsular Spain.) I will argue that in a manner that strikes a discordant note with the series' repeated emphasis on the knowledge of Spanish as a criterion for inclusion, it is the Spanish-speaking *Jane the Virgin* fans who are marginalized. My analyses of select fan comments from the two Facebook pages will pinpoint the hierarchies and tensions that exist within the *Jane the Virgin* fan communities, in particular how these discrepancies among fans are by and large closely connected to questions of language and ethnicity. I will further demonstrate that although fan communities can potentially provide a safe and harmonious haven for fans, they can nevertheless also mimic conflicts in the wider society or even create new ones, drawing on the ideological and thematic framework of the specific fandom.

In carrying out my research into the role that language and ethnicity play in determining the dynamics within the *Jane the Virgin* fan communities, I have relied mainly on ethnographic observation of the selected Facebook pages. I chose these two pages not only because they provide a good indication of fan activity but also because they often reveal the ethnic backgrounds of the posters. I archived and analyzed all the relevant fan comments that appeared on the pages between January and May 2017, a period that coincided with the broadcasting of the second half of season 3. Whereas the main emphasis of my essay is on fan engagement with the series, I also occasionally make relevant references to the screen text of *Jane the Virgin*, as information relating to the story line often casts light on why fans react to their fan object in a particular way. By analyzing the fan comments and the screen text through the prism of ethnicity and the language linked to this ethnicity, my methodology resembles significantly the contextual approach, a research methodology that locates "the phenomenon it is studying with the wider social, political, and even global, context" (Saukko 2003, 21).

As a researcher, I am aware that analyzing fan comments found on Facebook pages comes with a range of ethical implications, even more so when dealing with questions of race and ethnicity. To begin with, as Heidi McKee and James Porter note, it is often difficult to answer the question, "What is public versus private information on the Internet?" (2009, 1). Whereas in forums participants can hide their true identities behind usernames and avatars, ethical issues become decidedly more pressing with Facebook's blurred lines of privacy. Despite the fact that individuals can make their profiles private, they often post on publicly open pages (such as fan pages), thus displaying to other users their names and profile pictures and, depending on security settings, parts of their profiles.

Although posting on public pages can be read as a sign of implied consent, I have adopted Amy Bruckman's principle of light disguise in order to provide additional privacy to the posters (Bruckman 2000; Reid 1996). While I use verbatim quotes, I have removed names and usernames, labeling the posters simply by numbers. I follow this way of labeling even when the posters have explicitly signed their posts with their names. Overall, because the exclusion of certain groups of fans within the *Jane the Virgin* fan communities is implicit and connected by and large to the knowledge of Spanish, the comments are rarely openly hostile in nature. Thus, if someone directly linked the posters to their comments, it would not cause them any personal or professional harm. Furthermore, when translating the posts into English, I tried to adhere as closely as possible to the Spanish-language expressions in order to capture the emotions behind the comments as well as the general atmosphere of the communities. All English-original quotes are reproduced exactly without any corrections.

—Dis-United Communities

The positive, creative, and constructive effects of fandom, in particular fandom communities, have been well documented by such leading scholars of fandom studies as Henry Jenkins and Matt Hills. Lynn Zubernis and Katherine Larsen have gone as far as to suggest that, aside from uniting individuals from different backgrounds, for many fans the realm of fandom can have an essentially therapeutic function. Yet despite the possibly overwhelming positive effects of fandom, scholars have also come to acknowledge that fan communities are not altogether harmonious entities. Apart from the obvious minor frictions within fan communities, which are born out of alliances to specific characters or romantic pairings, scholars have also identified more serious discrepancies that undermine the solidarity of many fan communities. Derek Johnson and Jonathan Gray have noted that these discrepancies display obvious social hierarchies among fans. Whereas some fans simply police the opinions of others, there are also outright attacks of fan-tagonism against specific sectors within the fandom. In Johnson's words, fan-tagonism "operates discursively to constitute hegemonies within factionalized fan communities" (2007, 298).

More specific though still limited research has focused on gender as a factor that can exclude individuals from a particular fandom. For example, in her essay on female sports fans, Victoria Gosling notes that "women's marginal position within sports fan cultures means that their legitimacy as sports is often questioned" (2007, 260). Similarly, questions of race and ethnicity can be identified as factors that cause frictions within fandom communities. As Rukmini Pande explains, the roles and positions of racial, ethnic, and cultural minorities in fandoms were originally overlooked because "the foundational studies of media fandom communities saw them comprised of mainly heterosexual, cisgender, white, middle class American women" (2016b, 209).

Aside from Pande's research into race and fandom, pioneering works of critics such as Bertha Chin and Lori Morimoto, alongside the increased importance of global and transnational fan communities, which are thriving thanks to social media platforms, have triggered scholarly interest in the role that race plays within fandom communities. Yet as Pande observes, despite the growing literature on transnational fandom, the literature tends to be predominantly anglophone, focusing primarily on English-language fan communities. For instance, as Maria Immacolata Vassallo de Lopes notes in her exploration of how fans of the Brazilian telenovela *Passione* communicate on Facebook, "the practices of transmedia reception still represents a novelty in the Ibero-American countries" (2012, 114).

Similarly, when it comes to fan products of transnational circulation, aside from Dani Madrid-Morales and Bruno Lovric's 2015 article on K-pop and K-drama communities in Latin America, fans of Latin American heritage have been overlooked by the existent scholarship. Likewise, as Pande also notes, scholars have barely acknowledged the fact that fandom communities are "not immune to hierarchies structured by privilege accruing to income, class, racial, ethnic, and cultural identity, disability, etc." (2016b, 210). While online testimonials by cosplayers and gamers document openly racist demeanor toward minorities within fandom communities—see Eddy 2013, for example—at other times, as I will illustrate with reference to the *Jane the Virgin* fan communities, the discrimination toward the marginalized groups can be far subtler and, at least to some extent, almost accidental.

—Globalizing the Telenovela

Something that cannot be overlooked when analyzing fan responses to *Jane the Virgin* is that telenovelas are traditionally believed to have a unifying power comparable to that of fandoms. Illustratively, in *Jane the Virgin*, the Villanueva women gather daily on the couch in their living room to watch their favorite telenovelas. This gathering remains a constant factor over the years in their otherwise changing lives; in fact, a number of flashbacks show the Villanueva women watching telenovelas when Jane is just a small girl. Moreover, these moments of watching telenovelas bring Jane, Xiomara, and Alba together despite any disagreements they might occasionally have. Indeed, scholars and critics alike have praised telenovelas specifically for their ability to bring together audience members of different social, cultural, ethnic, and generational backgrounds. Much like the newspapers in Benedict Anderson's seminal *Imagined Communities: Reflections on the Origin and Spread of Nationalism*, telenovelas are consumed simultaneously by large groups of spectators and create a sense of imagined communities among otherwise diverse audiences.

Yet whereas Anderson's study focused on how newspapers were able to form a sense of unity among the population of a particular nation, the imagined communities created by telenovelas further expand far beyond national, cultural, and linguistic boundaries, as is illustrated by the enthusiastic reception of telenovelas even as far away as Europe and Asia (Havens 2005). As Ana Uribe explains in her study of Mexican telenovelas and the Mexican and Latino audiences that consume them, telenovelas in particular are apt tools for creating imagined communities because they identify—and then appeal to—audiences' shared values and interests (2009). According to Ana López, even the telenovelas produced for the US Spanish-speaking market are able to create the illusion of nation "where there is no coincidence between nation and state" (1995, 266).

As Rodrigo Gómez, Toby Miller, and André Dorcé note in their excellent essay on cultural convergence in Latino media, television networks such as Telemundo and Univisión specifically aim to create a sense of community across Latino generations and ethnic backgrounds with their programming; their "pan-Latino novelas" especially help build bridges among the spectators, hiding the existing erasures and inequalities. Accordingly, even Latino productions posing as local—that is to say, inherently Latino—are intentionally mainstreamed to respond to transnational demands. Telenovelas, which unarguably dominate Latino broadcasting, can especially be regarded as what these scholars term "glocalized" products: thanks to the combination of their local and universal components, they are equally attractive to US-based Latino audiences and their Latin American counterparts. In fact, telenovelas specifically employ a "multi-Latin" crew with actors from different Latin American origins in order to attract wider Latino audiences (2014, 45, 47). Moreover, these Spanish-language telenovelas carry English-language subtitles, thus reaching out not only to third-generation Latinos, many of whom consider English to be their native tongue, but also to non-Latino North Americans.

Before we consider the tensions and hierarchies in *Jane the Virgin* fan communities as well as how these are at odds with the traditionally unifying agenda of the telenovelas, we need to bear in mind the fans' general reactions to *Jane the Virgin*'s self-declared status as a telenovela. The series no doubt tries hard to pose as a telenovela, as can already be seen from the narrator's persistent exclamations of "like straight out from a telenovela" when highlighting the extraordinary and exaggerated plot twists. Overall, the series offers an appeasingly hybrid depiction of Latinidad, with very few actual references to the original ethnic backgrounds of the diverse Latino characters, consequently mimicking the unifying nature of telenovelas. Apart from highlighting the fact that Alba originally immigrated to the United States from Venezuela and Rogelio comes from Mexico, the rest of the Latino characters are simply identified in terms of their Latinidad. Moreover, the telenovelas in which Rogelio stars often replicate and mirror, although in a hyperbolic manner characteristic of telenovelas, the topics, issues, and dilemmas explored by the wider series narrative, accordingly contributing tongue in cheek to the series' self-identification as a telenovela. On top of this, despite its glossy and clichéd surface, just like telenovelas, which according to Ana López individualize the social world, "locating social and political issues in personal and familial terms," (1995, 261) *Jane the Virgin* deals with numerous serious social issues, including immigration, racial and gender discrimination, and abortion (1995, 261).

However, *Jane the Virgin* ultimately unravels as a satire of the genre that it is celebrating and borrowing from. By addressing and highlighting the hyperbolic conventions of the telenovela through the plot twists, burning passions, multiple hidden identities, and scandalous secrets of its main protagonists, *Jane the Virgin* ridicules everything that makes the telenovela a telenovela. Furthermore, the melodramatically narcissistic Rogelio, a telenovela star himself, can be interpreted as the very embodiment of all the pompousness that characterizes the genre. Yet poking fun at the genre is not what undermines the status of *Jane the Virgin* as a telenovela—after all, the series' satirical tone consistently shows affection for the genre and the very conventions that it is critiquing. On the contrary, what compromises *Jane the Virgin*'s self-identification as a telenovela is its questionable status as a telenovela or, at least, as a telenovela in the more traditional sense. Dictionary definitions emphasize both the genre's inherent Latin Americanness and its peculiar format, which makes it different from the English-speaking soap opera and standard television series. Whereas the *Oxford English Dictionary* simply identifies the telenovela as a Latin American soap opera, *Merriam-Webster* expands this definition by describing it as "a soap opera produced in and televised in . . . Latin American countries," while *Collins* goes into even more detail by pointing out that one of the defining features of the telenovela is that it often has "a limited number of episodes."

More thorough definitions of the telenovela are offered by scholars. For instance, before plunging into his discussion of the fluidity of the genre, Timothy Havens identifies the traditional generic format of the telenovela by stating that "unlike their northern cousins, telenovelas have distinct beginnings, middles, and ends, though a single telenovela can last as long as a year" (2005, 259). Apart from the fact that *Jane the Virgin* is filmed in English rather than Spanish, the series follows the typical format of US television series, being divided into separate seasons, each consisting of approximately twenty to twenty-two episodes. Unlike the fast-paced, shorter-lived telenovelas, a specifically Latin American genre, which are broadcast at least five times a week, the narrative of *Jane the Virgin* unravels far more gradually, with viewers having to settle for a weekly dose of the adventures of Jane and her companions. Yet while it is evident that numerous formal factors align *Jane the Virgin* more closely with US television series than with traditionally Latin American telenovelas, it should nevertheless be acknowledged that the telenovela is a genre that is constantly evolving, particularly in response to its increasing global popularity. As Havens puts it:

> The era of global commercial television has sped the pace of change for genres such as telenovelas that seem uniquely suited to global program trade, as these genres split, merge, and transform due to the multiple duties they perform in settings around the globe and the constant search for new ways to target increasingly differentiated multinational audience segments. (2005, 258)

Unlike critics who have simply lamented that the telenovelas have lost their local flavor as their international sales have increased, Havens highlights the way in which the genre is successfully reinventing itself in response to the demands of the expanding audiences. The way that telenovelas produced by networks such as Telemundo repackage the originally Latin American genre in order to appeal to Latino audiences can already be seen as an illustration of this type of reformulation. Meanwhile, even Netflix has joined the endeavor of mainstreaming the genre by reinventing the telenovela for millennial audiences with the help of the Mexican telenovela *La Casa de las Flores*. When we take these examples of the fluidity of the telenovela genre into account, it also becomes easier to accept the generic hybridity of *Jane the Virgin*. Ultimately, *Jane the Virgin* can best be understood as a mutation or an alteration of the telenovela genre, which in its search for wider audiences has partly adopted the formal conventions of US television series.

Despite *Jane the Virgin*'s obvious affinities with US television series, the numerous fan posts highlight the fans' uncritical acceptance of its self-declared status as an actual telenovela. As fan activity on the official *Jane the Virgin* Facebook page illustrates, the fans' way of overlooking the complexities surrounding the show's genre dictates to a significant degree viewer expectations of the show. Indeed, as the subsequent discussion of fan activity on the official Facebook page pinpoints, audience members over and over again try to make sense of the show's characters and narrative by resorting exclusively to telenovela conventions and jargon. The Latino and anglophone audience members' unquestioning acceptance of *Jane the Virgin* as a telenovela points to its status as a telenovela adapted and appropriated for the tastes of viewers more accustomed to consuming US television series.

Significantly, unlike their North American—both Hispanic and non-Hispanic—counterparts, the predominantly Latin American fans on the unofficial *Jane the Virgin* Latino Facebook page, who thanks to their

Spanish-language skills have access to a wide repertoire of actual telenovelas, barely try to make sense of the plot of *Jane the Virgin* by resorting to the generic conventions of telenovelas. Whereas there is obviously no one accurate or authentic way to engage with *Jane the Virgin,* and the hybrid format of the series in fact encourages diverse interpretations, this fundamental difference in the way the fans approach the series nevertheless divides *Jane the Virgin* fans into two camps. Moreover, as a closer look at the two Facebook fan communities illustrates, issues relating to knowledge of English further sharpen this division. Indeed, whereas exclusively Spanish-speaking Latin American fans are likely to be privileged in terms of their familiarity with telenovelas, they are disprivileged when it comes to participating in fandom communities.

—Language, Privilege, and Exclusion

As Inger-Lise Kalviknes Bore and Rebecca Williams show in their 2010 study of transnational *Twilight* fandom, English is the preferred language of even those *Twilight* fans who are nonnative speakers of English. In point of fact, many fans from nonanglophone countries see communicating in English on social media, as well as consuming fan products in English, as a way of belonging to the wider fan community. Yet assuming that nonanglophone fan communities are nonexistent, unimportant, and peripheral means misinterpreting and overlooking the very nature of transnational fandom. As Anne Kustritz puts it:

> The term *fan* . . . mediates between local and international media and audiences; it encapsulates a broad range of diverse activities, histories, and practices, which become invisible by attending only to English-language fan spaces, or by assuming that because conversations there take place in English, the participants all come from Anglophone countries. (2015, 3.1)

The fans' adherence to the English language even when discussing an object of fandom that is as blatantly bilingual as *Jane the Virgin* works to illustrate the fact that for better or worse fans view English as the lingua franca of fandom. Moreover, a quick scroll down the official *Jane the Virgin* Facebook page reveals the consistent participation of numerous individuals with distinctively Hispanic surnames (e.g., Oliveros, Martínez, Paz, Criollo), who are nevertheless posting their comments, even when communicating among themselves, in English. A further click on the profiles of those participants with Hispanic-sounding names whose profiles are open to the wider public highlights that these participants are generally Latinos living in the United States. What is more, the private profiles of these fans disclose that while they are posting in English on the official *Jane the Virgin* Facebook page, the vast majority post also in Spanish on their individual Facebook pages. Meanwhile, Spanish-language posts or even comments written in Spanglish are strikingly scarce on the official *Jane the Virgin* Facebook page and altogether fail to attract responses from other fans; during my period of observation, there were only two brief comments written in Spanish and one post that mixed English and Spanish.

Overall, there seem to be very few differences in terms of the content of the comments posted by fans with anglophone and Hispanic surnames. As is usually the case with television series that focus specifically on the romantic relationships of the main protagonist, fans are mainly concerned about declaring their support for either "team Rafael" or "team Michael." Many fans express their discontent with the fact that Jane's husband, Michael, was written off the third season due to his death from a mysterious heart failure. In trying to make sense of the dramatic and unexpected plot twists, such as Michael's death, fans by and large evoke the series narrator's reasoning, according to which these types of events are to be expected because *Jane the Virgin* is a telenovela. In discussing *Jane the Virgin* as a telenovela, fans with Hispanic-sounding surnames clearly show a more thorough familiarity with the conventions of telenovelas than do those with anglophone backgrounds. Some of these Latino fans rather explicitly illustrate and at times even brag about their familiarity with the genre-specific expectations:

> Please make [Michael] come back as a ghost. Or maybe he has amnesia and they swapped him by accident at the hospital and he's been living the last three years in Pensacola as Bob Jones, Ballroom Instructor. Or his long lost twin brother shows up. It is a telenovela for crying out loud ... you can do anything ... clone? (Poster 1)
>
> People who complain about Michael's death don't know what Telenovelas are. (Poster 2)

Rather than simply restating the assumption that *Jane the Virgin* should be interpreted as a telenovela, Poster 1 provides a comprehensive summary of the typical dramatic plot twists of telenovelas. Meanwhile, Poster 2 ridicules the numerous (mainly non-Hispanic) posters who feel disillusioned and surprised by the fact that Michael was killed off, while further implying that some viewers (like her) possess a superior understanding of the telenovela genre. Other Latino viewers, meanwhile, use what they regard as their privileged position as expert viewers of telenovelas to educate less knowledgeable fans, enlightening them about potential narrative developments: "In the Venezuelan version (original Jane the Virgin) Juana (Jane) and Mauricio de la Vega (Rafael) they end up together . . . I really hope this happens in this version tooo" (Poster 3). Not only does Poster 3 make fellow viewers aware of the earlier Venezuelan version, *Juana La Virgen,* she patiently answers the ensuing inquiries by explaining that this original version was broadcast in the 1990s and can be viewed on YouTube.

All in all, by assuming to be in possession of superior knowledge of telenovelas, these fans from Hispanic backgrounds seem somewhat successfully to raise themselves above other *Jane the Virgin* fans posting on the official Facebook page. However, while showing their familiarity with telenovelas, these Latino fans completely overlook the fact that *Jane the Virgin*'s status as a telenovela is not unproblematic. Meanwhile, the circumstance that these Latino fans choose to communicate in English rather than in Spanish can be brushed aside, as after all it is only in English that they are able to share their privileged knowledge, assumedly gained from viewing Spanish-language telenovelas, with anglophone viewers. Yet despite the fact that *Jane the Virgin* is indeed a series about a Latino family and there is a strong presence of Latino fans on the series' official Facebook page, the *Jane the Virgin* fan communities do not provide an altogether safe and friendly refuge for the otherwise often discriminated against Latinos. Especially, the plotline that reveals that Alba has been living in the United States undocumented for years gives rise to heated debates and even openly discriminatory and racist comments. Some anglophone fans seem to resent the way in which *Jane the Virgin* begins to tackle sensitive issues of immigration in the direct aftermath of the introduction of President Trump's highly restrictive policies:

> PLEASE KEEP YOUR POLITICAL THOUGHTS TO YOURSELVES . . . THIS IS ONE OF MY FAVOURITE SHOWS . . . however, if your green card, ICE views keep up, I will forget to watch the show period . . . I am sorry but you hollywood people don't understand that we are paying for thier houses, phones and food as taxpayers . . . GO back to ENTERTAINING PLEASE. Love [name omitted for ethical reasons] xxxx (Poster 4)

As both the demands regarding keeping the story line apolitical and the direct assaults on undocumented immigrants demonstrate, this poster does not shy away from expressing her point of view. What is more, she even signs the post with her first name, although as default her name already appears at the beginning of the post, thus emphasizing that she is proud of her opinion. While a couple of fans more discreetly agree with the poster that *Jane the Virgin* should not become too political, the general consensus of the fans is to denounce the discriminatory words of Poster 4. Poster 5, a woman from a Native American background, highlights particularly well the obviously racist undertones of Poster 4's words:

> The show's producers don't care if you watch. The point is you get their message in that episode. Also, this is comming from a white woman? Please educate yourself and also keep in mind your white ancestors were not wanted. You are the illegals. Now play nice, be nice to others and have a nice day. (Poster 5)

Fans, whether Hispanic or anglophone (or representatives of other ethnic groups), almost unanimously rally together to launch a direct attack against Poster 4's misconceptions of undocumented immigrants and her underlying snobbish belief in white supremacy that can be read between the lines of her statements.

Although the open-minded, more pro-immigration fans seem to have the final word in this instance, the very presence of individuals with such reactionary views regarding immigrants highlights the underlying tensions and power struggles of the *Jane the Virgin* fan communities. Yet the most pressing type of discrimination faced by *Jane the Virgin* fans from Hispanic backgrounds has nothing to do with the bitter words of a handful of white fans who do not view immigrants kindly. In point of fact, a number of fans living outside the United States in Latin American countries are consistently excluded from the real-time viewing experience enjoyed by English-speaking Latino and anglophone fans in the United States. Many have trouble accessing episodes that are broadcast weekly by the CW: "ello! I am relly Jane's fan. . . . But I'm so cofused because I watched all the series online from Colombia, where I live, Yesterday I watched episode 20 from season 3 and I'm not sure where is the next episode and when. Could you please help me? Where can I watch episode 21 and 22?" (Poster 6).

On the most obvious level, Poster 6's comments reveal the laborious detective work that a Latin American viewer has to carry out in order to track down each episode. Meanwhile, the various errors in Poster 6's English work as yet another reminder of the language-based exclusion that characterizes the *Jane the Virgin* fandom and occurs even in the series narrative itself. For those who, unlike Poster 6, do not possess at least a working knowledge of English, the viewing experience is further complicated by the laborious efforts of finding subtitled or dubbed episodes. Whereas the Telemundo network caters also to those Latinos who no longer consider Spanish to be their native tongue with the easily accessible Telemundo in English, the dubbed versions of *Jane the Virgin* can be accessed only through the Second Audio Program, an auxiliary audio channel available only in the United States, Canada, and parts of Mexico. No significant efforts are thus made to distribute *Jane the Virgin* to viewers from Latin American countries aside from Mexico.

The unofficial *Jane the Virgin* Latino Facebook page provides a supportive and benevolent community for those fans struggling to access episodes in Spanish. The profiles of the active participants reveal that despite the page's somewhat misleading name, the fans participating in this Spanish-language fan community live in Latin America, with the majority of the posters being Bolivian, Peruvian, Colombian, and Mexican. While it is not unusual for more specific fan groups connecting fans within a certain country or region to exist within the wider fan community, what makes the *Jane the Virgin* Latino Facebook page stand out is that it is devoted almost exclusively to sharing subtitled or dubbed episodes. No doubt the Facebook page also provides a platform for Spanish-speaking fans to discuss their object of fandom in their native language, and the administrators of the page in fact at points encourage fans to speculate about the plot twists through fruitful prompts, such as the translation into Spanish of the letter written by series creator Jennie Urman on the eve of Michael's dramatic death.

Interestingly, the Latin American fans communicating on the Latino Facebook page do not make a single reference to *Jane the Virgin*'s telenovela status, even when discussing melodramatic narrative developments, including Michael's death, the rekindling of the romantic flame between Rafael and Petra, and Rogelio and Xiomara's chaotic wedding. In fact, while there are no direct comments suggesting that *Jane the Virgin* is not a "real" telenovela, fans on this Latino fan page refer over and over again to *Jane the Virgin* as *la serie* (the series), a word choice that is not likely to be accidental. Moreover, any debates among fans regarding their favorite pairings, characters, and plot twists are overshadowed by the genuine hunger for new episodes in Spanish.

In general, posts by the administrators are limited to announcing the availability of links to new episodes. Many of these posts further clarify whether the episodes are subtitled or not. Even though the majority of the fans are grateful for the administrators' efforts to post *Jane the Virgin* episodes in Spanish, that is, with Spanish subtitles, they are nevertheless openly discontented if the administrators fall behind in their task. A particularly good example of fan reactions to such delays can be found in a post dating back to March 2, which announces the delay of the availability of the subtitled version of episode 55 in season 2, which had already aired in English on February 13. As with similar cases, the administrators very appropriately apologize for the inconvenience the delay might cause fans and promise to post the episode in question as soon as they can acquire it. Overall, fan reactions to this particular announcement range from concern about whether the episode will be posted at all to outright impatience:

> Gracias ya me había asustado creí que no los iban a dejar seguir publicando.
> (Thank you I was already afraid that they would not allow you to continue posting them.)
> (Poster 7)
> ¿Todavía no sale el capítulo con traducción?
> (Is it true that the translated episode is still not available?) (Poster 8)
> Quiero verlo subtitulado al español!!! Siempre días dsp ...
> (I want to watch it with Spanish subtitles!!!! Always days later ...)
> (Poster 9)

As Poster 7's comment regarding her fear that the administrators might be stopped from publishing the subtitled episodes of *Jane the Virgin* reveals, in addition to often having to wait a significant period of time before viewing the subtitled episodes, the Spanish-speaking fans have access to these episodes only through websites that pirate them. Indeed, the administrators point Spanish-speaking fans to websites such as Streamin.to, Vidto.me, and Uploaded.net for streaming and downloading the episodes. As is to be expected from these sites, the quality of viewing experience on offer is satisfactory at best, and accordingly the administrators of the *Jane the Virgin* Latino page urge fans to report any links that are not working properly. Indeed, fans are very quick to note any deficiencies in the quality of the links posted; for instance, numerous fans point out with disappointment and anger that the links posted on March 28 to episode 59 all cut off at thirty-three minutes, leaving them in suspense with regard to the ending of the episode. During such moments of heightened despair, fans further try to reach out to other fans in the hopes that they will be able to point them to better links.

Moreover, although the majority of fans seem pleased with the subtitled episodes, there are also a handful of posters who keep inquiring about *Jane the Virgin* episodes dubbed into Latino Spanish, despite the administrators' repeated reminders that only the first season is available in a dubbed version. As one of these fans asking about the dubbed versions explains, "A mí normalmente me gustan las series en su idioma original, pero esta me gusta más en español latino" (Normally I like series in their original language, but this one I prefer in Latino Spanish) (Poster 10). As these inquiries about dubbed episodes of *Jane the Virgin* illustrate, it is impossible for the administrators of the page to accommodate the diverse palates of the Spanish-speaking fans. More importantly, however, despite their best efforts to facilitate fan access to *Jane the Virgin* episodes in Spanish, the administrators fail to re-create the same quality of viewing enjoyed by the English-speaking fans. By guiding fans to low-quality, often illegal websites, the administrators in fact unwillingly further reassert the already peripheral position of the Spanish-speaking Latin American fans.

Although exclusion based on knowledge of a specific language can appear significantly less derogatory than that based on the color of someone's skin, it often conceals a further marginalization of a specific ethnic or cultural group, a group for whom the language in question is not readily accessible. Apart from being unable to participate in conversations posted on mainstream *Jane the Virgin* sites, such as the official Facebook page, non-English-speaking Latin American *Jane the Virgin* fans are further blocked from their actual object of fandom because of the lack of easily available subtitled or dubbed versions of the series. Yet despite these obvious adversities, Latin American fans continue to be drawn to *Jane the Virgin*. This is indeed not a great surprise considering the fact that the appeal of *Jane the Virgin* comes from its generally uplifting tone as well as its ability to continue the work of its most significant predecessor, *Ugly Betty*, in undoing the stereotypical portrayals of women of Latin American descent as exaggeratedly sexual housewives or villainesses (Esposito 2009; González and Rodríguez y Gibson 2015).

However, regardless of the obvious fact that Latin American viewers form a large potential viewer group, no significant efforts have been made to woo further Latin American viewers or to invite already existing Latin American *Jane the Virgin* fans to participate in regulated, official fandom spaces. Although following the example of networks such as Telemundo, it should have been relatively easy to construct a sense of (imagined) community between the Latin American and the Latino viewers, who after all share a common cultural heritage, the Latin American fans seem to fall outside the CW's target audience for *Jane the Virgin*. As indicated by the format of the series as well as the activity on the official *Jane the Virgin* Facebook page, the show ultimately repackages the telenovela genre and the concept of Latinidad in a manner digestible to North American viewers—both Latino and anglophone. Essentially, *Jane the Virgin*, a show that poses as a Latin American telenovela yet adheres to the formal episodic constraints of North American television series, is as hybrid, bicultural, and bilingual as the Latino fans and actors who discuss it repeatedly in English. In point of fact, even though on the narrative level *Jane the Virgin* depicts a microcosm of a multiethnic United States, populated by people who are essentially immigrants from Latin American (and also European) backgrounds, almost all these characters are also already alienated from their country of origin and Americanized. Latin American heritage and the Spanish language, as the series suggests, have been relegated to the domestic sphere, to the type of dinner table conversations where the Villanuevas critically weigh the merits of individuals wishing to be accepted into their family unit. In the final analysis, Latin America, as this case study of *Jane the Virgin* illustrates, is becoming for Latinos, both fictional and real, increasingly like Venezuela for Jane's grandmother: a still important yet distant memory with blurring borderlines.

12. "Not My Captain America"

Racebending, Reverse Discrimination, and White Panic in the Marvel Comics Fandom

MCKENNA JAMES BOECKNER, MONICA FLEGEL,
AND JUDITH LEGGATT

IN 2015, MARVEL COMICS REBRANDED itself under the slogan "All-New, All-Different." This rebranding aimed both to refresh its superhero stable and to diversify its roster along gender and race lines, including highlighting recently introduced characters such as Kamala Khan as Ms. Marvel and Miles Morales as Spider-Man and passing the mantles of many of Marvel's white male superheroes to diversity characters such as Sam Wilson as Captain America and Amadeus Cho as the Hulk. In 2014, for example, Marvel had launched an app intended "to expand readership by providing content in readers' native languages" ("Go Global with Marvel Digital Comics" 2014). These changes reflected a deliberate strategy on Marvel's part; in a March 31, 2017, story on editor-in-chief Axel Alonso, *Fortune* enthused: "In an industry historically dominated by caucasian males, Alonso is breaking the laminated seal of stodgy tradition by adding people of every ilk to the brand's roster of writers and dramatis personae. Under his watch, the Marvel universe has expanded to accommodate costumed crimefighters of myriad ethnicities." *Fortune* and Alonso were quick to point out that the "rush to diversify characters has more to do with business than politics," an "organic" change reflecting an increasingly globalized world and efforts to engage a new audience of younger, more diverse readers, primarily in Western nations but internationally as well (Hackett 2017).

Ironically, the same day that *Fortune* published its praise for Marvel's new direction, Marvel's vice president of sales, David Gabriel, elicited a storm of criticism by claiming that Marvel's sales were waning because "people didn't want any more diversity" (Griepp 2017). (Notably, he was responding to comments from only two retailers at a retailers' summit.) Subsequent online responses from the comics fandom were divided in their reactions to Gabriel's comments. Many defended more diverse representation in superhero comics and blamed the drop-off in sales on everything from reader exhaustion with endless events to a weakness in Marvel's talent pool to the high cost of comics, causing readers to shift away from buy-ing single physical issues. However, a significant number of fans confirmed Gabriel's claims by complaining that Marvel's pursuit of diversity was, in fact, driving them away. As we will discuss, these fans often proclaimed that their dislike of Marvel's diversity was rooted not in misogyny or racism but in an aversion to Marvel's form of diversity, seeing it as a shallow marketing ploy that sought to bring in new fans at the expense of the old.

In this chapter, we examine how these antidiversity fans' rhetoric, particularly their strong rejection of any accusations of racism, still reveals a desire to preserve white privilege. We argue that what is taking place in online comics culture is an alignment of fandom with the divisive politi-cal culture in the United States, one that has seen a rise in white suprema-cist activity since the election of Donald Trump in 2016. Comicsgate, as this battle over diversity has been labeled—linking it to Gamergate, a "2014 hashtag campaign, ostensibly founded to protest about perceived ethical failures in games journalism" that involved harassment of women and peo-ple of color by those who perceived diversity as a threat to the online gam-ing community (Lees 2016)—represents the latest iteration of the culture wars in the United States, with the direction taken by Marvel Comics being read by fans and onlookers on both ends of the political spectrum as a lit-mus test for the state of the social and political sphere, particularly in terms of social justice.

Our analysis focuses on the responses to Gabriel's claim at the retail-ers' summit across three major online platforms: established newspapers and journals, blogs, and YouTube. Many of the blogs and news sites pro-vided the same sparse details, though some did offer their own interpreta-tions of Gabriel's statement as well as opinions on the issue of diversity in Marvel Comics (Asher 2017; Hoffman 2017; Weldon 2017). But in all cases, the full picture of the controversy emerged in the comments sections, which provided space for people from across the political spectrum to voice their interpretations of the politics and their definitions of diversity in contem-porary American culture. From June to August 2017, we performed close readings of the comments sections, some current and some dating back to April of that year, in order to identify patterns and recurring themes. Using discourse analysis, we then identified the underlying ideological subtext of these comments to explain why this particular incident—a brief statement from a marketing executive in response to two retailers—elicited such widespread debate. Although many of the commenters addressed gender and sexuality as well as race, our focus here is on how those on both sides of the debate link transformations in Marvel's superhero lineup to contemporary racial politics. While we acknowledge that there are problems with how Marvel markets and exploits the concept of diversity, we will demonstrate that even apparently legitimate arguments about the preservation of the canon can indicate fears about the waning of white supremacy.

In our discussion of the controversy, we attempt to avoid the academic exploitation of fans. Although posted publicly, fan communications have long been subject to an ethnographic analysis from scholars that Ruth Deller worries runs the risk of reproducing negative representations of fandom, as seen in early fan scholarship by Joli Jenson and Henry Jenkins, both of whom focused on how the fan was pathologized within normative frameworks; as Jenson observes, "Fandom is seen as a psychological symptom of a presumed social dysfunction . . . in an unacknowledged critique of modernity" to support "elitist and disrespectful beliefs about our common life" (1992, 9, 10). Cecile Cristofar and Matthieu Guitton highlight that most fan discussions are not meant to be taken as "citable references in an academic context"; nevertheless, they make exception for fan discourse that is meant to garner the attention of audiences outside specific fan communities, citing "opinion blogs" as one such example (2017, 722). Following their lead, we assert that comments from fans posted on mainstream news sites such as the *Guardian* and *io9* are similarly intended to communicate their concerns to the broader public, rather than to members of their own fan communities.

Furthermore, the extent to which pop culture has been caught up in political debates means that many nonmembers of subcultural fan communities are participating in these discussions. Angela Nagle describes how diverse groups of commenters "from critics of political correctness to those interested in the overreach of feminist cultural crusades" coalesced in similar discussions during Gamergate (2017, 24). This mainstreaming of subcultural issues means that even sites that may appear fan-centric, such as the YouTube channel Diversity & Comics, engage in and promote broad political debates to attract a viewership that exceeds comics fan communities. This is not to say that the comments we analyze cannot tell us anything about comics fandom; rather, they inevitably emphasize how fandom overlaps with and increasingly plays a significant role in contemporary politics.

—It's Not about Racism; It's about Forced Diversity!

Nevertheless, many of the commenters do identify as fans. In this chapter, we distinguish between antidiversity fans and prodiversity fans.

Many fans, particularly those who position themselves as being against diversity, claim simply to speak for comics fans as a monolith, with the implication (and sometimes the stated opinion) that this refers to white male adult fans. We want to avoid this assumption: some fans who reject diversity-driven agendas in comics identify as nonwhite and/or female; some fans who welcome diversity identify as white male adults. Our chosen terminology therefore labels fans according to their positioning in this specific controversy: against or for diversity, with diversity specifically being linked to liberal, progressive politics. Antidiversity fans, in this context, are both those who openly oppose diversity in all forms and those who claim to support diversity *in principle* but oppose the particular diversity of Marvel's 2015–17 lineup. We identified four common arguments from the antidiversity fans about Marvel's methodological changes: focusing on diversity resulted in comics that privileged politics over storytelling; using diversity as a marketing gimmick demonstrated a preference for new audiences over existing ones; ticking boxes to cover all diversity groups led to undeveloped or stereotyped characterization; and embracing diversity sidelined existing beloved characters.

Many fans argued that the introduction of diverse characters needed to be organic rather than forced. While this criticism took a number of different forms, a primary theme was that Marvel's deliberate promotion of diversity represented a kind of aesthetic affirmative action that hurt the quality of the story lines and the characters. For example, one antidiversity fan comments on *io9* that most of "this generation of diversity . . . is so forced and awkward that it makes the stories painful and disjointed," while another complains to readers of the *Guardian* that "I used to be fascinated by diverse characters, but now my initial reaction is to move away from them, because they're most likely shitty" (VonOhlnhausen in Elderkin 2017; Yovenven in Cain 2017). These fans argue that *deliberate* diversity has displaced strong characterization, interesting plotlines, and high-quality writing and art. Pursuing diversity instead of good storytelling, they argue, has backfired, resulting in readers who are wary of new and more diverse characters.

Many antidiversity commenters linked this failed diversity to Marvel's focus on social justice, which they perceived as a form of virtue signaling—a term widely used in the conservative blogosphere—to attract new audiences. In such a scheme, antidiversity fans argue, diversity has become merely "a gimmick, and one that didn't bring anything of value or interest to the table unless you were interested in the comics solely from the SJW viewpoint" (VonOhlnhausen quoted in Elderkin 2017). ("SJW" stands for "social justice warrior," a pejorative term used to denote those who supposedly promote social justice in aggressive and tiresome ways, though in practice it is often used to label anyone who espouses liberal values.) As one fan summed up: "I see entire marketing efforts on twitter focused on who the creators are instead of what the book is about. Just sell me a cool story without trying to earn diversity points" (Joe quoted in Macdonald 2017). This idea that Marvel's focus on diversity is just an example of SJW pandering came up constantly, with fans complaining that Marvel's "gimmicky" pushing of diversity "was a poor attempt at building a bigger fan base on the pre-existing characters, but it alienated their core audience. White guys" (Spottysword quoted in Schedeen 2017). Repeatedly, antidiversity commenters position white male adults as representative comic fans in opposition to new, younger, and more ethnically and racially diverse fans.

Furthermore, antidiversity fans lamented that rich characterization was being displaced by mere box ticking. Daemonick claims that "historically, [Marvel] introduced some of the best 'diverse' characters, like Black Panther, Storm, Luke Cage—when they weren't introducing them as part of a box-ticking exercise. These latest additions are weakly-written, obvious attempts to fight off accusations of whatever -ism is fashionable this week" (in Shepherd 2017). Jimmy Dabosh comments, "I'm all for having strong black characters, strong gay and lesbian characters, but there has to be a point to them being there, no? Diversity for diversity sake doesn't really help anyone" (in Hughes 2017). Another fan jokingly suggests that the inevitable result of such box ticking will be a "gay latino transgender vegan non-binary genderfluid demiqueer foxkin amputee character" (mertinaik quoted in Schedeen 2017). Clearly, one of the things these fans object to is the idea of intersectionality, perceiving this central theory of social justice, which argues for "the need to account for multiple grounds of identity when considering how the social world is constructed," as simply a politically correct exercise in representation that rings hollow (Crenshaw 1991, 1245). Rather than seeing intersectionality as something that complicates singular identity politics, antidiversity commenters instead represent it as a market-driven aim to create the most oppressed or complex identity, as seen in characters like America Chavez (Latina and lesbian) and in multiethnic teams like the Champions.

However, the most virulent responses to Marvel's promotion of diversity came from those who felt that women and people of color were being foregrounded "at the expense of classic characters" by taking on the mantles of Spider-Man, Captain America, Iron Man, Thor, Wolverine, and the Hulk (WhatHuh quoted in Hughes 2017). The fact that these mantle passings were never likely to be permanent did nothing to assuage these fears. There is a long history of mantle passing in the Marvel Comics universe; temporary replacements include Bucky Barnes as Captain America and War Machine as Iron Man. The "All-New, All-Different" diversity replacements were also temporary, with most core superheroes returning to their original white male iterations by mid-2018. YouTube commenter John Ramsey argues that "instead of replacing old core characters I would have liked to see brand new diverse characters" (in Potter 2017). Some argue that these changes are a disservice to both the old and the new characters. Reddit commenter Yak-Yonson specifically critiques African American hero Sam Wilson becoming Captain America, reading it as a sign that Marvel "didn't trust that Falcon was a good enough character to stand on his own" (in "Marvel Executive Says Emphasis…" 2017); this comment predates the creation of the first solo Falcon series as part of the Legacy lineup.

In addition, many comments, like the following by Speak Geek Unlimited, suggest that Marvel should reintroduce dormant diverse heroes from the past and thus prove that diverse heroes can have legacies of their own: "They Killed War Machine, Blade hasn't had an ongoing series in years, bring back Miguel O'Hara, give Luke Cage a solo series, make storm the leader of an X men team again" (in Potter 2017). Showcasing heroes of color with a long history within their own comics, as Marvel did with Ta-Nehisi Coates's Black Panther, does demonstrate that such heroes can be as successful as the "classic" white heroes. But such successes were, for these antidiversity fans, overshadowed by the loss of "their" Iron Man, Hulk, and Thor. Furthermore, altering Steve Rogers's Captain America timeline so that he is a Nazi-like villain in the 2017 Secret Empire event, with the African American Sam Wilson as the "good" Captain America, arguably led fans to perceive the diversity effort as an attack on them, framing their desire for their favorite characters to return as inherently evil.

Not all the complaints can be entirely dismissed as examples of racist backlash. Even those fans who embraced diversity noted that in recent years Marvel has lost talent to brands like Image that allow greater creative control and the freedom of working outside existing, often restrictive universes. While the perceived lack of talent at Marvel is not specific to those working on diversity characters, one could argue that weak writing might result in diversity being done poorly, with an overreliance on stereotyping. As Booinyoureyes points out, "if you make it a corporate goal to add as much diversity as possible to the cast of characters, you are bound to get many wrong" (in Schedeen 2017). We applaud Marvel's attempts to actively increase diversity in its comics but recognize that if this agenda is indeed largely market-driven, it might result in rushed, ill-thought-out creative choices.

There is also some merit to the claim that Marvel misrepresents the complexity of identity by emphasizing ethnicity in marketing its new lineup. While the increase in diverse characters also included some increased diversity in the creative teams—most notably Coates writing the Black Panther series—Marvel's creators remain predominantly white and majority male, although it increased the diversity of its creative teams during the "Fresh Start" campaign that began in 2018 by bringing in widely recognized Black writers from other media to launch solo series for diverse characters, such as Rodney Barnes to write Falcon, Nnedi Okorafor to write Shuri, and Eve Ewing to write Ironheart. Because many of the diverse characters do not have creators who speak from their experiences, this can lead to potentially contrived or stilted characterizations. Reddit commenter Switchfall, for example, argues that "wanting to base your minority characters entirely around the fact that they are a minority runs dangerously close to being VERY racist" and that Marvel should instead try "treating a minority superhero like any other superhero without calling attention to it" in order to "normalize the idea and say anyone can be [a] hero" (in "Marvel Executive Says Emphasis . . ." 2017). For these fans, deliberately writing characters as examples of diversity makes them problematically representative of their sex and ethnicity in ways that white male superheroes are never required to be.

Pursuing diversity primarily as a corporate goal means that it may also be abandoned at the first sign of controversy. Just weeks after Gabriel's comments, Marvel canceled Black Panther and the Crew, a series that followed established Black superheroes and addressed police brutality in Harlem, which author Ta-Nehisi Coates saw as "an opportunity to get inside [the characters] as black people" (in Opam 2017). The title was canceled after just two issues as a result of low sales, which some prodiversity commenters blamed on Marvel's failure to promote the title. Betty Boop observed that "it's sad that the first time i heard of this comic was because it was getting cancelled." Sherrie Ricketts explained, "If I don't see marketing, I can't add it to my pull list. If I don't add it to my pull list, the comic shop doesn't order as many. If the shop doesn't order as many, Marvel doesn't get enough sales. If they don't get enough sales, they cancel the comic. Grrr" (both in Jusino 2017). While this lack of marketing might be a problem for many of Marvel's titles, those titles specifically attempting to reach new readers or convert old ones might face an uphill battle, and if diversity is used mostly for the sake of marketing, it can be sidelined just as quickly if it is believed to be a liability.

—White Panic, "Reverse Racism," and the Rhetoric of Social Justice

While there are legitimate reasons for fans of all political stripes to find fault with Marvel's diversified titles and characters, it is important to recognize that many of these complaints, even those that claim to not be about diversity, rely on and reinforce white privilege. For example, Kyryllo's claim that "most people rooting for 'diversity' aren't part of a core audience" situates this "core audience" in terms of race, gender, and generation (in Cain 2017). Jusbish states that "Marvel just needs to know their audience. The vast majority of collectors (like it or not) are adult white males. This isn't a racist statement, it's a fact" (in Schedeen 2017). Antidiversity statements such as this rely on what Mel Stanfill has identified as the "structural whiteness" of fandom, a narrative perpetuated by fans and fan scholars alike (2018, 305). Rukmini Pande supports Stanfill's claim when she observes, "In my own research on how media industries constructed the concept 'fan' from 1994–2009, I found that representations of fans imagine them overwhelmingly as white people, particularly white men" (2018b, 311).

This assumption of a white male readership is used to argue that these "majority" readers need white male superheroes "because they relate to them, but also imagine what it would be like to have those super-powers. It is fantasy. If you make a white male character into a black teenage girl . . . you cripple that experience for the audience" (Spottysword quoted in Schedeen 2017). This stance constructs white male readers as alienated, which may be true, but this is, of course, a result of privilege, since these readers usually are not asked to identify with characters different from themselves. But as the language used here also implies, the privileged white male reader is "crippled" by association with Blackness and womanhood precisely because both are perceived to be lesser identities not compatible with "fantasy." As the norm against which all other identities are othered, white masculinity never has to be experienced or expressed *as* an identity and, as such, it gets to occupy an apolitical space.

We must therefore understand that complaints about forced diversity come from a position that *always* sees diversity as forced, never as organic. Those who complain about the invasion of politics into their comic books deny both the political nature of their own identities and the political nature of comic book characters. Marvel has always engaged in contemporary politics, as seen when SpiderHyphenMan reproduces a "late 60s early 70s" response from Stan Lee to a complaint about racial politics in comics: "we felt we could do something . . . to change things just a bit for the better" (in Schedeen 2017). Captain America comics have long dealt with issues of racism, starting with Steve Rogers punching Hitler on the cover of the first issue, but a number of YouTube commenters, such as Kobe Bonhomme, criticize the overt political engagement of Sam Wilson's Captain America: "Why would Sam even waste his time with Black Lives Matter? It's destructive and enforces its whole ideology on the grounds of a lie along with misinformation" (in Paladin 2017). Sam Wilson is involved in a fictional group that loosely allegorizes the Black Lives Matter movement in the Marvel universe by protesting against the aggressive policing and police brutality that are clearly depicted in the comics themselves. Furthermore, Sam Wilson addresses this movement because it deals specifically with issues that the character faces as a person of color in Marvel's America. Sam Wilson openly struggles with the fact that he cannot be apolitical in the same way that Steve Rogers, a white man, can. Prodiversity fans were quick to demonstrate the relevance of Sam Wilson's position, as YouTube commenter Sollie Walker IV sarcastically points out: "Yeah why should a Black man in America be interested in Black Lives Matter?" (in Paladin 2017).

To ignore race and culture when producing diversity characters would be to fall into what Kenneth Ghee refers to as "White heroes in Black face" with "little or no reference to a sustaining Black family, a viable Black community, continuity with Black history or Black culture and . . . represented as Black in *color only* while operating in an all White cultural context and worldview" (2013, 232). Asking that writers create minority characters who do not directly deal with the issues of their race suggests that the antidiversity fan base is fine with persons of color as long as they continue to engage with issues that center whiteness and avoid those that reference their own specific racial or cultural heritage. Given that Sam Wilson and Steve Rogers fought white supremacists in the past together, this complaint arguably also betrays a fear of battles against white supremacy that are led by Black men and Black communities: with Steve Rogers wearing the mantle, the white audience could identify with him, but with Sam Wilson aligning with a Black Lives Matter type of movement, white audiences might be forced to see themselves as the bad guys.

Complaints about box ticking, as we have discussed, betray a simplistic rejection of intersectionality as a concept. Many fans seem to believe that a Black lesbian is less realistic than a crime-fighting orphaned scion from a wealthy white family. For example, Riri Williams, who took on the Iron Man mantle as Ironheart, is vilified by antidiversity fans, with one on Reddit, Chadly-Chadwick, scathingly describing her as a "black lesbian sexualized teenager" (in "Marvel Executive Says Emphasis . . ." 2017). Importantly, Riri Williams is not a lesbian, and fan complaints about her being sexualized originated from those who critiqued advance images for participating in racist tropes of Black women, making this box-ticking exercise one primarily within fans' minds rather than in the comic itself (Darden 2016).

Furthermore, antidiversity fans often betray the assumption that Black and gay characters must always demonstrate some point to being there, a requirement never leveled against white characters. For example, *io9* commenter Not the end of the world people! suggests that "when every new character is a POC, Woman or LGBTQ people get tired" (in Elderkin 2017). ("POC" stands for "people of color.") The implicit assumption is that "people" are white, and that diversity representation is a burden to their sensibilities. There is an obvious double standard here, as another fan, collex, points out: "So, when every new character is a POC or Woman or LBTQ people get tired. But when every character is a straight white guy, nobody gets tired? In what world is that logical?" (in Elderkin 2017). The world in which that is logical, we argue, is the current world of entertainment, which by and large still relies on white supremacy.

Thus, the argument that fans would be fine with diversity, as long as Marvel made new characters, is unconvincing. The King Elessar points out, "Riri is new. Amadeus is (relatively) new. Miles is relatively new" (in Jefferson 2017). America Chavez is also a new character who does not threaten the legacy of any established character, but that did not stop commenters from complaining that "there is not a single comic character made since 2010 that is worse than America Chavez" (Dick Butt quoted in Paladin 2017). America Chavez, introduced in 2011 but given her own series in 2017, is a Latina LGBTQ character written by a Latina LGBTQ novelist and, as such, is targeted with many box-ticking complaints. Even in more nuanced comments, America Chavez's diversity is overemphasized: "the comic is incredibly preachy, a[n]d more concerned with pushing an agenda than telling a good story" (KidAnarchy 2105 quoted in Paladin 2017). Ironically, America Chavez is just what many commenters claim they would love: a new character whose diversity does not come at the expense of an established hero. If her presentation of diversity is still being critiqued, it is hard to take the comments asking for Marvel to leave their favorite heroes alone, the ones promising success for diverse characters who take on their own unique mantles, as anything other than a desire for segregation of people of color and their lives from the mainstream media.

The fear of losing white privilege is possibly best illustrated by the ways in which some antidiversity fans adopt arguments associated with social justice to construct *themselves* as the oppressed group. Such fans position themselves as true fans and claim that changing "their" comics and "their" heroes is akin to cultural appropriation. In order to do so, fans argue that diversity "does not mean 'POC/Women' solely. . . . It's about a difference in THOUGHT and concepts" and that the new characters with diverse backgrounds "all sound the same. They all pound the same boring messaging that comes from their mostly highly political writers who all think everyone agrees with them" (Jason Smith quoted in Hoffman 2017). For these commenters, true diversity includes the views that combat racial inclusivity and social justice, views that Marvel is deliberately attacking. YouTube commenter Surrealnumber even depicts this in genocidal terms as "the purging of characters because they had the wrong skin and sex," arguing that "Marvel attacked their fans and then tried to shame them for not liking the new normal" (in Potter 2017). By taking up social justice rhetoric and positioning themselves as misunderstood victims of SJW bullies, these commenters demonstrate that they are clearly not against politics in comics: they just position their own politics as apolitical and such politics as the genre's norms.

The categorization of a fan as someone with a marginalized identity has its basis in early fan scholarship; however, this construction of fandom as "a vector of inequality . . . often ignores the ways fans may (or may not) experience marginalization on the basis of race, class, language, and other structures" (Stanfill 2018, 305). For example, Rebecca Wanzo argues that early fan scholarship from the 1990s tended to view fandom as inherently "antiracist and progressive," even while "sexism, racism, and xenophobia are routinely visible in fan communities." She further illustrates how this assumption of fans as outsiders by fan scholars is itself a concept skewed by white-centric analysis: "the emphasis on cult fans encourages a narrowness of what constitutes a fan. . . . Moreover, the framing of fans as in opposition to normative practices of consumption and to culture more broadly talks about othering in a manner that valorizes people who have claimed otherness for themselves, as opposed to having otherness thrust upon them" (2015, 1.4, 2.3).

Works such as Henry Jenkins's 1992 *Textual Poachers* and concepts such as Derek Johnson's 2017 fan-tagonism track a continual pushback against the greater power of corporations and creators. But such a focus on the fan as activist does not always account for which fans are positioned as more problematic than others, particularly within fan communities themselves. When fighting with producers to ensure that their show is safe from cancellation or that their favorite characters receive the character development they are perceived to deserve, fans might be embraced as "engaged audiences who leverage their personal networks in order to boost support for particular causes" (Pande 2018b, 322). But when underserved fans of color organize to battle structural racism within fan communities or demand better representation within fan texts, their activism can be constructed within the fandom itself as an unwelcome invasion of politics into the sphere of pop culture.

The racial politics of these constructed norms becomes visible in this particular debate when fan commentary attempts to delineate just what constitutes a true fan. Throughout all the comments sections, commenters—both for and against the changes and identifying as white or another race or ethnicity—consistently establish their fan credentials. For example, Freeordie, complaining about the limitations of Miles Morales, notes, "I'm latino and as a nerdy coke bottled kid in brooklyn I loved Peter Parker as Spiderman," suggesting that his outsider status as a bespectacled nerd links him to Parker in ways that his ethnicity does not link him to Morales (in Del Arroz 2017). Likewise, when Ronzero, a fan identifying as Black, agrees with the complaints about diversity, Jusbish welcomes him into the community: "I fully understand obviously everyone from all ethnic backgrounds collect . . . it's a great medium for everyone & shouldn't just be solely for 'adult white males.' Don't wanna come off as some racist a hole" (in Schedeen 2017). This interchange suggests that fan intersectionality is accepted insofar as it supports white-centric fannish norms.

When intersectional fans challenge those norms, however, the exchanges are more fraught. For example, one fan, who identifies as "an african american guy," suggests that the changes Marvel has been making have brought the two identities closer together, both for older fans who have a history with the characters and for the next generation: "I think it's freaking awesome to see a few of the superhero characters I was once in awe of as kid, look like me. I have an 8 year old son. I think it's a great thing for him to see superheroes that look like himself" (unxounceed quoted in Schedeen 2017). But this heartfelt appeal to the needs of this one African American eight-year-old is rejected by another commenter on behalf of the "Majority":

> If they are not publishing the characters we want to read about we as the primary consumer base are well within our rights to cease buying their books and tell them why we have stopped reading. The Majority of us seem to want our classic characters more than these new ones. We do not owe Marvel or your son anything if we wish to stop buying Marvel until they give us back what we want then we have every right to do so. (dracoguardian29 responding to unxounceed in Schedeen 2017)

The repeated use of the exclusionary first-person plural—"we," "our," and "us" are used eleven times in three sentences—delineates a primary fan community both from the third-person plural of the corporation, the "they" that produce the mass culture texts, and from the prodiversity fans who welcome the changes, such as unxounceed and his son. By combining an eight-year-old comics fan with the corporate entity of Marvel, dracoguardian29 casts the child as the oppressor who is obstructing "every right" of the "Majority."

Tied in with this issue of authenticity are the consumers' source of comics—comic book store, mainstream bookstore, online—and the format in which they read them—monthly issue, trade paperback, digital. The stereotype of the white male nerd hanging out at the local comic book store with a pull list of regular purchases is one that continues to be endorsed by those who identify with the persona. Notably, the perceived slump in Marvel sales that set off the 2017 debate is based solely on sales of single issues distributed through comic book stores (Asher 2017). Prodiversity fan Dictatortot points out that "a lot of the 'diversity-unfriendly' and stereotypically fanboyish feedback seems to come disproportionately from the monthly consumers . . . and results in a lot of creative choices that the trade market tends to find disappointing, unambitious, or downright icky" (in Asher 2017). While there are comic book stores that cater to diverse audiences, white males are still the primary customers of some stores, which become safe spaces for those fans. Upsetting these spaces with texts and issues that do better online and in graphic-novel-style trade paperbacks or with prodiversity fans is constructed by antidiversity fans as an invasion and—because of the self-perpetuating nature of discourse within these safe spaces—it can seem to traditional fans as if the diversity-focused stories are not serving the needs of *any* fans.

It is true that many of the mantles traditionally worn by white male characters were temporarily worn by a more diverse group of heroes during Marvel's "All-New, All-Different" rebranding. While passing on the mantle of a superhero identity has long taken place in the genre, we argue that these transitions are taking place in a population that is increasingly constructing whiteness as being under attack. Therefore, comments like those by Will Linn are not uncommon:

> People engage stories to live vicariously through the heroes, for this reason they are compelled by the stories that best enable this projection, and it's easiest to project into characters like yourself. It's not

about disliking heroes of different genders or races, it's about how much easier it is for people to project into heroes more like themselves . . . Everyone deserves to have heroes to project into that are like themselves. (in Elderkin 2017)

This comment suggests that there are no more white male superheroes for white male audiences to idolize; however, white characters are not suddenly a minority in Marvel's lineup. As Hal Jordan points out: "Most of the X-Men, Inhumans, Deadpool, Daredevil, Punisher, Iron Fist, Star Lord, Dr. Strange, Johnny Blaze Ghost Rider, Peter Parker Spider-Man, Logan Wolverine, and others are still white. Even the new Female Thor and Wolverine are white" (in Potter 2017). In other words, the fear that white readers are now as disadvantaged as readers of other races have been does not hold up. In fact, many of these diverse titles have since been canceled, including *Red Wolf*, featuring an Indigenous lead; *America*, featuring America Chavez; *Iceman*, featuring a gay lead; and *Black Panther: World of Wakanda*, focused on both women and people of color (note, however, that titles are frequently canceled). In addition, Marvel's 2018 "Fresh Start" campaign saw the remaining white male superheroes returning to their traditional roles. Nevertheless, Comicsgate raged on, with antidiversity fans upset about Ta-Nehisi Coates taking on the writing role for Captain America in July 2018.

Rather than presenting legitimate complaints of oppression, the antidiversity fans are, we argue, explicitly evoking the reversed rhetoric "of conservative pundits" who claim to be "the true victims of liberal media and progressive politicians" while "the so-called liberal forces of education, media, and politics are represented as the true victimizers" (Samuels 2009, 5–6). Such constructions are apparent in comments such as "let's get this clear it is you sjw who are showing intolerance, not us. trying to spin this into 'we don't like diversity' meaning we're 'intolerant' is also cover for the fact that you are intolerant" (2old4disshi quoted in Schedeen 2017). The commenters align Marvel's editorial decisions with the imagined liberal elite, which allows them to say they are attacking corporate power, not women or minorities. In doing so, they mirror how current conservative rhetoric displaces attacks on "the women's movement, the civil rights movement, and the workers' rights movement" and instead claims to be for those people but against "an extreme version of postmodern academic culture and criticism" that has coopted their fight for its own elite ends (Samuels 2009, 41). David Gabriel's comments about diversity not selling did pit the corporation against its antidiversity fans by suggesting that, if Marvel pulls back from its commitment to diversity, it is the fault of those fans, creating a zero-sum game in which one audience can win only at the expense of the other.

The battle over diversity in comics parallels conflicts such as Gamergate in 2014 and similar battles over *Ghostbusters* in 2016 and *The Last Jedi* in 2017. Antidiversity fans reject creative works that they identify as SJW propaganda or works produced by people they see as diversity creators; they openly portray such creators and works as an invasion of traditional fan spaces. Those who claim to have legitimate critiques of such works resent being associated with what they portray as the more vocal minority of fans with racist or misogynist leanings. We absolutely agree that any work of pop culture can be subject to criticism on the basis of its quality. However, as we have demonstrated, many of those who claim to care only about quality betray the extent to which unconscious white supremacist and masculinist ideologies often underlie those assumptions about quality. Comics have always been both well and poorly written. Marvel has always engaged in contemporary American politics. And characters have always been transformed and replaced by newer and different versions. All that has changed has been the diversity of the characters as well as the toxic nature of the contemporary political climate.

13. Real Love?

Authenticity as Capital in Let's Play Culture

AL VALENTÍN

THIS CHAPTER ANALYZES LET'S PLAYS to argue that discourses of gamer authenticity have gendered and racialized underpinnings that reinforce gamer hegemony and shape gamer humor. While YouTube is built on the premise that anybody can create and share content, the platform's algorithms work alongside existing cultural backlash to create a hostile space where possibility is stifled for content creators who are not white men. Additionally, assumptions of gamer (in)authenticity affect YouTube gaming content success by privileging oppressive constructions of whiteness, maleness, and normative standards of beauty shaped by white supremacy. This virtually prevents content creators who are people of color—POC—women, and queer or trans folks from reaching the same levels of success as their straight white cisgender male peers. Through an analysis of the public personae and success of some key YouTube creators, this chapter identifies how difference can be framed as both liability and advantage in disparate spaces. Even content creators who are members of marginalized groups mobilize normative understandings of gender, race, sexuality, and other forms of difference in order to distinguish themselves and maintain a sense of authenticity within game spaces. Rather than demonizing any one creator, my research investigates how gamers navigate their online personae in the hopes of creating a profitable and loyal fan base, shaping their fans' conceptions of humor, gaming, and society at large through play.

Let's Plays are streamable videos where players record themselves playing a video game with added commentary to share their experiences with other gamers. While Let's Plays are a popular form of media that exist both as artifacts of individual player experiences and as spaces around which new fandoms and communities are created, they are consistently left out of both economic and academic discussions of gaming's impact. Gaming is a huge sector of both the United States economy and the global economy. In 2017, American consumers spent $24.5 billion on gaming content alone, with billions more spent on hardware and accessories (Entertainment Software

Association 2017). In 2017, analysts predicted that global market revenue would grow to $109 billion from $99.6 billion in 2016 (Newzoo 2017).

While not usually factored into analyses of the global economic impact of gaming, Google's YouTube and Amazon's Twitch online gaming video platforms have become increasingly profitable sectors within the industry. In addition to their use by game developers and studios, they've become a space for gamers to record themselves playing everything from AAA games developed by big studios to indie sleeper hits. YouTube has enabled gamers around the world to build huge fan bases who faithfully watch and support them. This means millions of subscribers, video views, and dollars in revenue for video game publishers and content creators alike. Similarly, while game studies is a thriving field of research (Bogost 2008, 2010; Flanagan 2013, 2014; Isbister 2016; Juul 2012; Wolf and Perron 2016), YouTube Let's Plays have received little academic attention (Maloney, Roberts, and Caruso 2017; Piittinen 2018; Postigo 2014). This chapter builds on that research alongside growing feminist game studies literature which reveals gaming as a site where conceptions of race, gender, and sexuality are reflected, contested, and reproduced (Enevold and MacCallum-Stewart 2015; K. L. Gray 2016; Ruberg and Shaw 2017; Russworm and Malkowski 2017; Shaw 2015; Wysocki 2015).

—The Question of the Authentic Gamer: Algorithms and Anger

In order to unravel how Let's Plays function to facilitate a hegemonic framing of the gamer, it is essential to consider authenticity. What does it mean to be an authentic gamer? A real gamer? And how is that always shaped by existing structures that delimit access to the category of human by people seen as less than human on the basis of race, gender, sexuality, size, ability, class, and other forms of difference? First, it's important to note that perceptions of who gamers are don't necessarily line up with the reality of who games. Analyses have consistently shown that women and POC make up sizable portions of the gaming audience (A. Brown 2017; Duggan 2015; Entertainment Software Association 2017). One Pew Research Center survey has even shown that Latinos and Black people are more likely to identify as gamers than their white peers (M. Anderson 2015). Despite these findings, the view of the gamer as generally white and male persists (Duggan 2015).

These perceptions shape not just whether people identify as gamers or whether they play at all but also the very games that are produced—most big-budget games have generally assumed a straight white male audience and pandered to that demographic. This assumption prevents gamers who identify as women, who are queer, who are nonbinary or trans, or who are people of color from having the same access to humanity through a refusal to acknowledge their existence and value both in game and out. And it leads to a culture where people of color, women, queer folks, and trans folks are consistently framed as outsiders to the community and assumed to be less knowledgeable about gaming (Gray 2016; Nakamura 2012; Shaw 2015). Their authenticity as gamers is consistently embattled *because* their status as humans with value is embattled.

But while authenticity may be valued, it is a restrictive way to measure one's inner feelings of love or affinity with a group. John Jackson's *Real Black: Adventures in Racial Sincerity* interrogates the performance of race within Black communities in New York to frame authenticity as a rigid and unforgiving metric for inclusion into a group while positioning sincerity as a more nuanced framework for race and racial performance. When people are members of a group, whatever the basis of its affinity, there are scripts that determine who fits in and who doesn't by testing one's authenticity. Jackson writes, "These scripts provide guidelines for proper and improper behavior, for legitimate and illegitimate group membership, for social inclusion or ostracism" (2005, 13). While he's theorizing about racial authenticity and how real Blackness can be disentangled from fake Blackness, this framework offers a useful understanding of how authenticity tests overall work to shape a community and delimit options for people within it. In the context of gamers, the creation of "appropriate" scripts shapes conceptions of what games are valued, who gets to take up space *within* the space, and, as I'll argue later, what is seen as funny.

Furthermore, authenticity tests assume a hierarchy between the two parties built on domination. Jackson writes, "Authenticity conjures up images of people, as animate subjects, verifying inanimate objects. . . . Authenticity presupposes a relation between subjects (who authenticate) and objects (dumb, mute, inorganic) that are interpreted and analyzed from the outside, because they cannot simply speak for themselves" (2005, 14–15). This is particularly relevant because POC, women, queer people, trans people, and disabled people (and those at the intersections of these categories) are not taken at their word about being members of the community and are thus subject to outside tests by men already assumed to be authentic, not in spite of their identity but because of it, regardless of knowledge or experience of gaming (Nakamura 2012). Marginalized people are functionally produced as objects who are unable to speak for themselves or whom others are unwilling to hear. The real-world conditions of structural racism, sexism, heterosexism, cissexism, ableism, sizeism, and classism produce the devaluation and objectification of marginalized gamers and are upheld by the reinforcement of hierarchies within gaming spaces.

Authenticity tests, then, maintain the status quo and its attendant domination of those framed as Other, particularly along the lines of whiteness. As Lisa Nakamura writes, "Gaming space is part and parcel of what George Lipsitz calls the 'white spatial imaginary,' and the stakes for keeping women and people of color out are the same as they were during redlining, blockbusting, and other techniques to police movement and claims to space in America" (2012). Nakamura's invocation of Lipsitz and his emphasis on the spatial nature of domination brings this framework into digital spaces as battles over territory marked as belonging to straight white males. Gaming spaces are extensions of the same white supremacist quest to delimit the movement, access, and power of marginalized groups in physical spaces. And Nakamura's use of the imaginary further emphasizes the importance of combating these assumptions because of how they shape imagined possibility. As adrienne maree brown writes, "I believe that we are in an imagination battle, and almost everything about how we orient toward our bodies is shaped by fearful imaginations. Imaginations that fear Blackness, brownness, fatness, queerness, disability, difference. Our radical imagination is a tool for decolonization, for reclaiming our right to shape our lived reality" (2019, 10).

Representation is certainly not the only goal, as Adrienne Shaw has shown through her analysis of marginalized gamers' desire (or lack thereof) for representation (2015). Yet its importance cannot be understated, for it shapes notions of possibility of who people can be, how we can feel about them, and what our world should be like. The well-known and well-researched harassment of game developers and game journalists seen as outsiders to gaming spaces on the basis of gender and other categories of difference represents one such imagination battle (M. Salter 2017; A. Salter and Blodgett 2017; Vermeulen, Abeele, and Van Bauwel 2016). Harassment campaigns are used to neutralize the seeming threat posed by people who are believed to be inauthentic in their love for games and secretly aim to destroy them.

Additionally, the ongoing backlash against social justice activists and academics in a post-Obama United States and the global reverberations of rising conservatism further reveal authenticity as a means of domination. Conservatives mobilize so-called authenticity to devalue feminist and antiracist work in favor of telling it like it is or not giving in to political correctness. This frames feminist and antiracist work as false consciousness that conservatives, antifeminists, and racists can see beyond. Political correctness becomes a way to demean progressive beliefs through framing them as based only on politics rather than on research. This line of thinking springs from societal debates about meaning and value difference that extend to gaming communities. Rather than their exclusionary tactics being seen as a sort of violence against these already marginalized groups, the "real" or "authentic" site of injury is framed as straight white males who see gaming and game culture as *their* space, one that must be protected from Others.

Rising conservatism and misperceptions of gamer identity are further reinforced through algorithms that determine what sort of content you'll see on YouTube. Prevalent assumptions about gamers' linkages to the alt-right overdetermine the type of content you'll be exposed to in ways that produce gamers as particular types of people with particular types of politics. Both my partner and I have consistently been recommended antifeminist videos because we watch more gaming-related content on YouTube. The algorithm that YouTube uses to suggest additional content to its viewers noted a connection, assuming that we might enjoy videos that attack feminists and social justice warriors because we watch gaming news and commentary.

Algorithms function as feedback loops, both reflecting and reinforcing racism, sexism, and other structural violences as noted by many scholars, including Safiya Noble, Tarleton Gillespie, Cathy O'Neil, and Sara Wachter-Boettcher. YouTube's Creator Academy itself notes, "On home, the selection of videos is based on two things: performance or how well a video has engaged and satisfied similar viewers as well as personalization, based on a viewer's watch and search history" (2017). Thus, YouTube algorithms suggesting antifeminist content to gamers would be a result of others watching both. A link between these communities is algorithmically noted and subsequently reinforced by exposing new viewers to antifeminist content.

It is here, then, that we return to John Jackson to find another mode of group inclusion not built on authenticity with its assumptions of proper behavior and being. Instead, we can move toward a discourse of sincerity that allows us to move away from rigid and essentializing understandings of who belongs in a group. Jackson's work has been taken up by Rukmini Pande in order to conceptualize the intersections of fandom and racialized identity. Pande writes, "Sincerity as an analytical category allows for the examination of how imperfect texts are simultaneously loved and critiqued by members of an engaged audience that are also articulating and rearticulating their own raced, gendered, and sexualized selves in response to the various societal scripts around them" (2018b, 88). Sincerity offers us a way to conceive of group inclusion that isn't built on rigid adherence to the scripts that would normally facilitate inclusion. There are no tests to pass. There are no scripts that need to be followed. Instead, nuance and negotiation are centered. People are allowed to feel and experience games in their fullness and make critiques of what they still enjoy because rigid adherence to straight white cis male standards of value is no longer necessary with sincerity. Thus, sincerity through Jackson and Pande may represent a more useful framework for conceiving of groups that can push past hegemony.

Before analyzing specific YouTube gaming content creators, we must first acknowledge who the major players are and how their success is shaped by normative conceptions of who gamers are. By comparing the differing levels of diversity in lists that rank popular Let's Play channels by Watch-Mojo and Business Insider, we can see that the industry considers what is best based on assumptions about who gamers are in the first place. While there are clearly gaming content creators of color who are popular and successful, as shown in Business Insider, they are not framed as representative of the field of gaming by WatchMojo. This emphasizes how authenticity itself functions as a racialized and gendered form of capital that gives straight white cis males more access to success.

To do this, I first analyze 2014's "Top 10 Let's Play YouTube Channels—TopX Ep. 2" and 2016's "Top Ten Female Gamers on YouTube" from the website and YouTube channel WatchMojo. Both lists are compiled based on user suggestions, views, and subscribers to determine rankings. The 2014 list is overwhelmingly white, nearly all male, all cisgender, and all based in the United States, Canada, or the United Kingdom. Of the ten channels listed, which include both individual streamers and gaming collectives, there are two channels led by men of color—Markiplier, an American YouTuber who is of Korean and German descent, and VanossGaming, a Canadian YouTuber who is of Korean and Chinese descent—with a couple of POC as honorable mentions or parts of collectives. Mari Takahashi, who is Japanese American, of Smosh Gaming is the only woman and the only woman of color listed. The lack of equal representation of gamers of color and the complete erasure of Black and Latino gamers work to reinforce the idea of the default gamer as white and male with few exceptions. While the first list in 2014 has a title that appears gender neutral, the near-complete exclusion of other gender identities upholds ideas that gaming is a space dominated by men. Cis women are cordoned off to their own list, published two years later, and there is no conception of nonbinary or trans gamers at all, firmly entrenching gamers in gender binary. Similarly, in the women's list, all the YouTubers are based in either the United States or the United Kingdom. And like the first list, all the creators are white or white-passing, with the exception of iHasCupquake and Aphmau.

In contrast, Business Insider's 2017 ranking of the top eighteen YouTubers offers a more diverse and globally minded ranking with gamers from El Salvador, Brazil, Chile, Spain, the United States, Ireland, and Sweden included. Ten of the eighteen YouTubers listed are on gaming channels, but none of those gaming channels is represented by women (McAlone 2017). This reinforces the near-complete lack of representation for women and the complete erasure of nonbinary and trans gamers seen in WatchMojo. However, male gamers of color are more represented here, with six of ten gaming channels being represented by men of color. Business Insider's subsequent ranking of YouTube gamers also emphasized diversity, with six men of color making up more than half of the eleven listed (Clark 2018). Additionally, not one of the most popular gaming YouTubers on Business Insider's list is a Black man, and Black women are nonexistent within any of the lists. WatchMojo included one Black male streamer as an honorable mention. The severe underrepresentation of Black people indicates that while there may be successful non-Black POC within the industry, anti-Blackness generally and the specific hatred for Black women described by Moya Bailey's term "misogynoir" further constrain success in the field.

—The Joke's on You: Gamer Masculinity through Humor

It is within this context that gamer masculinity upholds white supremacy, sexism, and homophobia on YouTube through humor. Swedish content creator PewDiePie, boasting YouTube's biggest channel with over 66 million subscribers, has been criticized for anti-Semitic "jokes," such as paying two people to hold up a sign reading "Death to All Jews" (Winkler, Nicas, and Fritz 2017). PewDiePie railed against the media coverage, arguing that news outlets should focus on "real issues" and accusing them of unfairly targeting his humor (Kastrenakes 2017). This reaction frames such jokes as apolitical, misunderstanding that they normalize anti-Semitism. Additionally, in September 2017, PewDiePie was caught using a racial slur on a livestream (Hern 2017). Within the gaming community, PewDiePie has largely been supported by other well-known streamers. *Variety*'s website ran an article highlighting those who defended him with Markiplier (with over 21 million subscribers) listed among them (Thorne 2017). Alternatively, Jacksepticeye (with over 20 million subscribers) was largely attacked and accused of betrayal by fans who believed he should have supported PewDiePie more (Hernandez 2017).

The refusal to hold PewDiePie accountable and the social sanctions imposed on those who try to do so indicate how normalized this type of humor and behavior is within the gaming community. And while PewDiePie's misogyny has been downplayed by some, he's also made content that has been explicitly racist or sexist, something that Marcus Maloney, Steven Roberts, and Alexandra Caruso's 2017 study misses with its small sample of 10 videos out of over 3,000 (see also Ellis 2017; Roberts and Maloney 2018).

Furthermore, Roberts and Maloney indicate that PewDiePie's framing of himself as an amateur comedian means that we should consider his jokes not as an incitement to violence but as a "dubious attempt at provocative humour" (2018). This misunderstands research that finds that jokes work to normalize prejudice and oppression for marginalized groups unless they mock structural oppression itself (Ford 2016). When humor is framed as something that can and should transcend norms of decency or political correctness, it normalizes the hierarchies of value that maintain structural violence and inequality. Humor is not something to be ignored but something to analyze and unpack for what it says about society at large.

While PewDiePie may be one of the most extreme examples, he is not alone in how his humor mobilizes oppressive norms of difference. Dashie-Games, a Dominican American YouTuber with over 4 million subscribers, makes use of gender and sexual norms as a means of comedy even as his status as a Latino gamer may call his authenticity into question. For example, he's known for pointing out male characters' shapely butts, describing them as firm before saying "pause," a racialized version of "no homo" meant to distance someone from perceived queerness. While DashieGames uses "pause" to make his heterosexuality clear, he uses proximity to queerness as a joke. Furthermore, he aligns himself with white content creators who make similar jokes, tapping into normative gamer humor through homophobia.

DashieGames has also frequently engaged in casual sexism with running gags that involve shrill feminine voices chastising him for his failures, evil exgirlfriends, and an objectification of women's bodies through repeated talk of "getting" or "fucking" the "puh" (a euphemism for "vagina"). The point is not that all or even most of these streamers actively support anti-feminist, racist, or homophobic policies or causes. DashieGames has pushed back on normative gender roles in other instances, and his frequent collaborations with Black male content creators on his channel show him connecting viewers to different voices at least on the basis of race. But the commentary enacting casual sexism and casual homophobia still functions to uphold oppressive structures that alienate marginalized folks from the community even if DashieGames himself may be marginalized on the basis of his ethnicity and racial identity.

—Desirability and Authenticity: Policing Femininity on YouTube

While humor is essential for male streamers, female streamers instead have an imperative to be attractive. Some YouTubers opt for videos where their faces are visible, while others simply provide voice-overs. This decision is political because women are affected more by normative standards of beauty than are their male counterparts. Most well-known female streamers who use face cams are normatively attractive and generally thin. SSSniper-Wolf (with over 11 million subscribers) is known for gameplays as well as provocative cosplays. PressHeartToContinue (with over 800,000 subscribers) modeled for *Playboy* in a shoot referencing her geek girl status. *Playboy* even created a gaming channel with attractive women called Gamer Next Door, and iJustine (with close to 5 million subscribers) appeared in a *Maxim* photo shoot. Their modeling indicates how attractiveness can beget popularity and profit, while the involvement of *Maxim* and *Playboy* reflects the mainstream appeal of normatively attractive girl gamers, all of whom are white or white-passing, which further ties perceptions of desirability to whiteness. One notable exception is TheRPGMinx, who was on YouTube for thirteen years before revealing her face and who still primarily uses voice-overs. When she revealed her face in 2017, she called herself "fat" and said she hoped viewers weren't "too traumatized" by her appearance. While TheRP-GMinx is white and thus benefits from white supremacist beauty norms, she understood the imperative of thinness for "proper" femininity and tried to preempt the negative comments she anticipated.

While attractiveness can be central to the success of female content creators, it is also the quality that calls their authenticity into question. In 2013, YouTuber Melonie Mac (with over 300,000 subscribers) discussed the policing of girl gamers in her popular video "Fake Girl Gamers." Rather than pushing back against the legitimacy of authenticity tests for women, the video reflected her own internalized misogyny. While Mac argues against the harassment of women at conferences and online with regard to their self-identification as gamers, she also agrees that there *are* fake girl gamers. Her video frames herself as one of the real girl gamers, making an appeal for her own authenticity while distancing herself from other women. To delineate real and fake gamers, she delineates real and fake games, arguing that "fake geek girls" are those who only "play Tetris on their phones." By creating a list of acceptable types of games one must play in order to be authentic, Mac leaves out a large part of the community and the industry as a means of asserting a few gamers' superiority over other gamers. She appeals to authenticity rather than acknowledging that the sincerity of another gamer's love for Tetris is valid.

But while Mac uses authenticity tests for inclusion, other female You-Tubers perpetuate normative understandings of gender, sexuality, and ability to appeal to masculine scripts of gamer humor. SSSniperWolf, for example, has been accused of attacking other women's appearances and sexual histories, using slurs related to gender, sexuality, size, and ability to attack people and liking racist tweets from fans (FaZe Censor 2017a and b; Kavos 2017). In order to gain popularity, she has adhered to so-called politically incorrect jokes like her male counterparts as a means of seeming like one of the guys while being attractive and desirable. Although Mac and SSSniper-Wolf take very different approaches toward gaining access to authenticity as gamers, they both ultimately center internalized misogyny.

Even as female gamers may make appeals for inclusion on the basis of humor or authenticity, they are not protected from policing at the hands of straight white male cis gamers. On the comments of Mac's video, people attacked not just other female streamers but Mac herself. FlerpyDerp said of Mac, "You wear a tank top in every video except for the one you're trying to prove yourself in. You're not any better. If you were an actual gamer you would focus on gaming and not try to put on make up every time you make a video. You're just as pathetic as the others." SSSniperWolf was also called out for faking her gameplays, with Douche on A Skateboard writing, "Fake girl gamers should be exterminated from this world cough cough SSsniper-wolf." Kavos himself uses misogyny and slurs to attack SSSniperWolf even while calling out her own harassment of others, saying that "all she's good for are them two big tits" (2017). Thus, her attractiveness makes her an object of desire to viewers, but she is reduced to breasts when convenient.

The policing of women in the community is informed by gendered norms of desirability. Women are expected to be attractive, but if they are too attractive, they're framed as inauthentic and desperate for attention. In fact, many of the comments left on videos of popular gaming streamers like Alinity frame her and other female streamers as being manipulative and using their sexuality for money and fame (Cole 2018). Amouranth, another popular Twitch streamer, received threats and harassment after rumors that she was pretending to be single for monetary gain. This move was framed as inauthentic by fans (Alexander 2018). It seems authenticity for women in gaming is also tied to sexual availability. A study analyzing comments on Twitch streaming videos for men and women further reveals this gendered divide, noting that most of the popular words within the comments center on women's bodies or attractiveness (Nakandala et al. 2016). Words like "boobs," "babe," and "hot" were among the most used for women (Pearson 2016). Comments on men's videos had more to do with in-game mechanics, with words like "reset" and "glitch" being among the most popular (Pearson 2016). Competency within gaming is gendered and racialized through the erasure of Black and Brown women and the prioritization of normatively attractive white women.

—The Next Level

In this chapter, I argued that gendered and racialized standards of authenticity for gamers produce uneven terrain for POC, women, and queer people interested in pursuing careers as gaming YouTubers. While it is not fair to say that POC, women, and queer or trans folks *cannot* be successful on YouTube, we can see that society's structural inequalities bleed into YouTube Let's Plays specifically to create barriers to the highest levels of success. Marginalized people experience harassment, microaggressions, and algorithmic disadvantages that make it even harder to grow as content creators, thus constraining the voices of gamers and reinforcing conceptions of authentic members of the community. As this community grows, we must interrogate how streamers' success is shaped by norms of race, gender, and sexuality and how their play reproduces these norms.

However, there is much more to consider. We must have a more comprehensive analysis of larger trends that moves beyond a few case studies to fully grasp this process. Additionally, more attention to disability and size in these spaces is necessary. Having a truly intersectional analysis of difference and a larger scope of study will allow us to expose and combat oppressive concepts of gender, sexuality, and race on YouTube, making it a more inclusive space for all gamers. It would also be useful to do more research into gamers who are trans and nonbinary to further dismantle the binary perception of gamers. Furthermore, subsequent work should consider more seriously the similarities and differences between Twitch and YouTube for a more comprehensive view of streaming.

While Let's Plays may seem like a frivolous route to take to discuss structural violence, they reshape conversations *with* others and conceptions *of* others in gaming. Diversity stands to make the community richer, and I believe that the shift from authenticity to sincerity is key to achieving this. Rather than aiming to test the authenticity of gamers as a means of removing so-called fakes from the community, gamers must learn to move beyond the scripts of "proper" love of gaming defined by straight white cis males that are marked by an apolitical appreciation of gaming without criticism or regard for the value of difference. By centering sincerity's emphasis on innate feelings of love and affinity over imposed metrics of inclusion, gamers can begin to respect other gamers, other ways of gaming, and other ways of being. Instead of authenticity functioning as capital, a focus on love of gaming, however that may look, can be the key to a more inclusive community.

MCKENNA JAMES BOECKNER is pursuing a Ph.D. in English literature, focusing on English romanticism and theater performance, from the University of New Brunswick. As part of this program, he is working toward a Social Sciences and Humanities Research Council–funded critical-creative dissertation titled "Memoirs of a Sodomite: A Queer Historiography of England's Romantic Period." The essay in this collection results from a research internship he completed while attending Lakehead University as an undergraduate.

ANGIE FAZEKAS is a Ph.D. Candidate at the Women and Gender Studies Institute at the University of Toronto. She completed her master's degree at Queen's University in Kingston, Ontario. Her research interests include fan and audience studies, queer adolescent sexuality, and the intersections of race, gender, sexuality, and pop culture. In her doctoral dissertation, she considers how teenage fans interact with erotic fan fiction as a mechanism for exploring and negotiating their sexuality.

MONICA FLEGEL is a professor of English at Lakehead University, where she teaches cultural studies. She publishes on fan fiction, animals in Victorian culture, and child studies. She is the coeditor, with Chris Parkes, of *Cruel Children in Popular Texts* and Cultures and the coauthor, with Judith Leggatt, of the forthcoming *Superhero Culture Wars*.

INDIRA NEILL HOCH is an assistant professor in the Department of Communication Studies and Theater Arts at Concordia College, Moorhead, Minnesota. Her research areas include online boundary maintenance and social construction of technology in new media contexts.

ELIZABETH R. HORNSBY is an assistant professor and the graduate coordinator in the Department of Communication and Media Studies at Southeastern Louisiana University. For over a decade she has taught classes in public speaking as well as gender, interpersonal, family, and small group communication. She graduated in 2016 with a Ph.D. in communication studies; her dissertation was titled "Welcome to Sleepy Hollow: A Critical Investigation of Meaning-Making and Race in Cyberfandom." Her other research interests include investigating the intersections of race, online and offline communities, and sense making. A native of Nashville, Tennessee, she lives in Hammond, Louisiana, with her husband and seven children.

KATHERINE ANDERSON HOWELL is a licensed aesthetician, independent scholar, and entrepreneur in Washington, D.C. She holds a master's degree in English from Boston College, has worked in disability support, and taught college writing for eleven years at a variety of institutions. She is the editor of *Fandom as Classroom Practice: A Teaching Guide* as well as a Pushcart Prize–nominated poet. Her scholarly work can be found in *Pennsylvania English*, the *Journal of Fandom Studies*, and the MediaCommons front page. Her creative work can be found in *On the Issues, Gargoyle*, the *Riveter Review*, and the *Rumpus*, among others.

CARINA LAPOINTE completed her master's degree in English at the University of Saskatchewan. Her thesis was on contemporary representations of elves in *Dungeons and Dragons* and R. A. Salvatore's Legend of Drizzt series. Her current research focuses on contemporary fantasy with regard to racial representations, narrative developments, and cultural applications.

MIRANDA RUTH LARSEN is a Ph.D. candidate in the ITASIA program at the University of Tokyo. She researches male K-pop idols in Tokyo and Japan's place in K-pop worldwide through the lenses of gender and ethnicity. She regularly appears at KCON LA as a special guest. Her research can be found in books such as *A Companion to Media Fandom and Fan Studies* and *The Global Vampire: Essays on the Undead in Popular Culture around the World* as well as in a wealth of digital articles.

JUDITH LEGGATT is an associate professor of English at Lakehead University, where she teaches Indigenous literature and science fiction. She has recent publications on Indigenous speculative fiction; Indigenous comics; *Nowadays*, an independent Canadian graphic novel; and TimeTravellerTM, an Indigenous machinima. She is the coauthor, with Monica Flegel, of *Superhero Culture Wars*, in press.

JENNI M. LEHTINEN completed her doctoral studies in Spanish American literature at the University of Oxford and later obtained a master's degree in screen studies from Birmingham City University. Before joining Nazarbayev University in 2012 as an assistant professor of languages, linguistics, and literatures, she held teaching positions at Oxford University and Exeter University. At Nazarbayev University, she teaches courses on literature, culture, fandom studies, and film, focusing specifically on postcolonial and Hispanic cultural products. She is the author of *Narrative and National Allegory in Rómulo Gallegos's Venezuela* and *Doña Bárbara Unleashed: From Venezuelan Plains to International Screen*.

JOAN MILLER is a doctoral candidate in communication at the University of Southern California's Annenberg School for Communication and Journalism and a transmedia artist with a broadly interdisciplinary approach. Her dissertation, tentatively titled "The Use of Feeling," explores the ways in which empathy and pathos govern our behavior in relation both to our fandom and to our communities at large. She is especially interested in themes of kinship, empathic communication, and anticolonialist approaches to producing media scholarship. Her work on the intersection of fandom and affect was published in *Popular Culture and the Civic Imagination: Case Studies of Creative Social Change*.

SWATI MOITRA is an assistant professor of English at Gurudas College, University of Calcutta. She has taught at Shivaji College and Miranda House, University of Delhi. Her areas of interest include book history and histories of readership, feminist historiography and women's history, nineteenth-century studies, cultural studies, digital cultures, and new media.

SAMIRA NADKARNI teaches undergraduate English literature at a college in Mumbai and is a working international maritime journalist and subeditor, writing primarily about human rights. She serves on the editorial boards of the undergraduate journal *Watcher Junior*, writes reviews for the speculative science fiction and fantasy magazine *Strange Horizons*, contributed to the digital poetry project *i <3 e-poetry*, and has had her creative writing published in *New Writing Dundee, Grund Lit*, and *Causeway*. She is the editor of *War in the Whedonverses*, forthcoming in 2021, as well as publications on the British poet Geoffrey Hill, multimedia adaptations of *Jumanji*, and the musical *Hamilton*.

SAM PACK is a professor of cultural anthropology in the Department of Anthropology at Kenyon College. His research interests address the relationship between media and culture; specifically, he focuses on an anthropological approach to the production and reception of television, film, photographs, and new media. The author of almost fifty articles in a wide variety of peer-reviewed journals and edited volumes, he is currently the resident director of the Japan Study program at Waseda University.

RUKMINI PANDE is an assistant professor of English literature at O. P. Jindal Global University, Haryana. She completed her Ph.D. at the University of Western Australia. Part of the editorial board of the *Journal of Fandom*

Studies, she has published in multiple edited collections, including *A Companion to Media Fandom and Fan Studies* and *The Routledge Handbook of Popular Culture Tourism.* She has also published in peer-reviewed journals such as *Transformative Works and Cultures* and the *Journal for Feminist Studies.* Her monograph *Squee from the Margins: Fandom and Race* was published in 2018.

DEEPA SIVARAJAN has been in fandom since she was fourteen years old; she used to mostly read and write fan fiction, but in recent years she's dabbled in vidding and podficcing as well. In her more public life, she's worked in community outreach and public engagement for nonprofits, electoral campaigns, and government agencies in the Pacific Northwest region of the United States, and she has written for *Racialicious* and *Transformative Works and Cultures.* She is the secretary of the Seattle LGBTQ Commission, a coproducer of the Tasveer South Asian LitFest, and a member of the Coalition of Seattle Indian-Americans. She is, despite any evidence to the contrary, a big fan of *Hamilton.*

AL VALENTÍN is a queer, nonbinary, Boricua Ph.D. candidate in gender studies at Rutgers University. Their research primarily interrogates how feelings like desire, empathy, and fear circulate within video games to make certain avatars and, subsequently, certain people legible as more or less human. In addition to their academic writing, they are also a poet, educator, and artist who has performed and facilitated workshops around New York City. You can find more about their academic and creative work on their website, alvalentin.com.

Abrams, Natalie. 2017. "'Supergirl': Meet the New Faces Joining Season 2." EW.com. March 24. https://ew.com/article/2016/09/09/supergirl-season-2-spoilers.

adenaelamin. 2018. "Never Gonna Stop Saying How Disappointed I Am at the Lack of Nafessa Williams, Isabella Gomez & Stephanie Beatriz Content in the ClexaCon Tag." Tweet. *@adenaelamin* (blog). April 8. https://twitter.com /adenaelamin/status/983171738732199937.

afrosoka. 2016. "I'm So Tired of Watching Oblivious, White *Hamilton* Bloggers Ignore and Argue with Facts™." Tumblr. June 10. https://afrosoka.tumblr.com /post/147218568905/im-so-tired-of-watching-oblivious-white-hamilton.

Ahmed, Sara. 2004. "Declarations of Whiteness: The Non-Performativity of Anti-Racism." *Borderlands* 3 (2). http://www.borderlands.net.au/vol3no2_2004 /ahmed_declarations.htm.

Aibel, Robert. 1976. "Communication, Cognitive Maps and Interpretive Strategies: Filmmakers and Anthropologists Interpret Films Made by Navajo and Anglos." Master's thesis, Annenberg School for Communication, University of Pennsylvania.

Akil, Omari. 2016. "Warning: Pokemon GO Is a Death Sentence If You Are a Black Man." Medium. https://medium.com/mobile-lifestyle/warning-pokemon -go-is-a-death-sentence-if-you-are-a-black-man-acacb4bdae7f.

Albert, Aaron. 2018. "Top Comic Cons." Comicbooks.About.com. April 23. http:// comicbooks.about.com/od/conventionsandevents/tp/Top-Comic-cons.htm.

Alexander, Julia. 2018. "Streamer Amouranth Is Latest Example of 'Twitch Thot' Harassment Problem." *Polygon*. June 27.

"Alpha/Beta/Omega." n.d. Fanlore. https://fanlore.org/wiki/Alpha/Beta/Omega.

Alters, Diane F. 2007. "The Other Side of Fandom: Anti-Fans, Non-Fans, and the Hurts of History." In *Fandom: Identities and Communities in a Mediated World*, ed. Jonathan Gray, Cornel Sandvoss, and C. Lee Harrington, 344–356. New York: New York University Press.

Anderson, Benedict. 1983. *Imagined Communities: Reflections on the Origin and Spread of Nationalism*. London: Verso.

Anderson, L. V. 2016. "Here Are the Original Notices for *Hamilton* from Before It Was a Theater Legend." *Slate*. March 1. http://www.slate.com/blogs/browbeat/2016 /03/01/hamilton_s_original_casting_notices_sum_up_each_character _from_before_they.html.

Anderson, Monica. 2015. "Views on Gaming Differ by Race, Ethnicity." Pew Research Center. December 17. https://www.pewresearch.org/fact-tank/2015/12/17/views-on-gaming-differ-by-race-ethnicity.

Anderson, Tonya. 2012. "Still Kissing Their Posters Goodnight: Female Fandom and the Politics of Popular Music." *Participations: Journal of Audience and Reception Studies* 9 (2): 239–264.

Andrejevic, Mark. 2008. "Watching Television without Pity: The Productivity of Online Fans." *Television and New Media* 9 (1): 24–46.

Asher, Elbein. 2017. "The Real Reason for Marvel Comics' Woes." *Atlantic*, May 24. https://www.theatlantic.com/entertainment/archive/2017/05/the-real-reasons-for-marvel-comics-woes/527127.

AtomicKitKat. 2007. Comment on "Drizzt Do'Urden, Why All the Hate?" Giant in the Playground Forums. www.giantitp.com/forums/archive/index.php/t-30773.html.

Ayres, Edward. n.d. "African-Americans and the American Revolution." History Is Fun. https://www.historyisfun.org/learn/learning-center/colonial-america-american-revolution-learning-resources/american-revolution-essays-time lines-images/african-americans-and-the-american-revolution.

Bacon-Smith, Camille. 1992. *Enterprising Women: Television Fandom and the Creation of Popular Myth*. Philadelphia: University of Pennsylvania Press.

———and Tyrone Yarbrough. 1991. "Batman: The Ethnography." In *The Many Lives of Batman: Critical Approaches to a Superhero and His Media*, ed. Roberta E. Pearson and William Urrichio, 90–116. New York: Routledge.

Bailey, Moya Z. 2010. "They Aren't Talking about Me. . . ." Crunk Feminist Collective. March 14.

———. 2012. "All the Digital Humanists Are White, All the Nerds Are Men, but Some of Us Are Brave." *Journal of Digital Humanities*. March 9. http://journalofdigitalhumanities.org/1-1/all-the-digital-humanists-are-white-all-the-nerds-are-men-but-some-of-us-are-brave-by-moya-z-bailey.

Bakardjieva, Maria, and Andrew Feenberg. 2001. "Involving the Virtual Subject: Conceptual, Methodological and Ethical Dimensions." *Journal of Ethics and Information Technology* 2 (4): 233–240.

Barnard, Ian. 2004. *Queer Race: Cultural Interventions in the Racial Politics of Queer Theory*. New York: Peter Lang.

Barreiro, Paula. 2010. "Understanding *Ugly Betty*: Negotiating Race in a Culturally-Mixed Text." *Divergencias* 8 (1): 34–40.

Baym, Nancy. 2000. *Tune in, Log On: Soaps, Fandom, and Online Community*. Thousand Oaks, CA: Sage.

Beck, Julia, and Frauke Herrling. 2009. "Playing Sue." *Transformative Works and Cultures* 2. doi.org/10.3983/twc.2009.093.

Bell, Derrick A. 1980. "Brown v. Board of Education and the Interest Convergence Dilemma." *Harvard Law Review* 93: 518–533.

———. 1992. *Faces at the Bottom of the Well: The Permanence of Racism*. New York: Basic Books.

Bennett, Lucy, and Paul Booth, eds. 2016. *Seeing Fans: Representations of Fandom in Media and Popular Culture*. New York: Bloomsbury.

Benwell, Bethan, James Procter, and Gemma Robinson, eds. 2012. *Postcolonial Audiences: Readers, Viewers and Reception*. New York: Routledge.

Berg, Lawrence D. 2012. "Geographies of Identity I: Geography–(Neo) Liberalism–White Supremacy." *Progress in Human Geography* 36 (4): 508–517.

Berk, Brett. 2011. "Q&A: Glee's Naya Rivera Talks about Santana and Brittany's 'Shipper.'" *Vanity Fair*. March 15. https://www.vanityfair.com/hollywood/2011/03/playing-lesbian-multiple-choice-with-glees-naya-rivera.

Bernard, Emily. 2005. "Teaching the N-Word." *American Scholar*. https://theamerican scholar.org/teaching-the-n-word/#.W18r1i3MzBI.

Bérubé, Allan. 2001. "How Gay Stays White and What Kind of White It Stays." In *The Making and Unmaking of Whiteness*, ed. Birgit Brander Rasmussen et al., 234–265. Durham, NC: Duke University Press.

Bhushan, Sandeep. 2015. "The Power of Social Media: Emboldened Right-Wing Trolls Who Are Attempting an Internet Purge." *Caravan*, August 28. http://www.cara vanmagazine.in/vantage/power-social-media-emboldened-right-wing-trolls.

Biedenharn, Isabella. 2016. "Making *The Hamilton Mixtape*: Lin-Manuel Miranda Explains the Stories behind the Songs." *Entertainment Weekly*. November 30. https://ew.com/music/2016/11/30/hamilton-mixtape-lin-manuel-miranda -songs.

Bird, S. Elizabeth. 2003. *The Audience in Everyday Life: Living in a Media World*. New York: Routledge.

Bobo, Jacqueline. 1995. *Black Women as Cultural Readers*. New York: Columbia University Press.

Bogost, Ian. 2008. *Unit Operations: An Approach to Videogame Criticism*. Cambridge, MA: MIT Press.

———. 2010. *Persuasive Games: The Expressive Power of Videogames*. Cambridge, MA: MIT Press.

Booth, Paul. 2009. "Fandom Studies: Fan Studies Re-Written, Re-Read, Re-Produced." Ph.D. dissertation, Rensselaer Polytechnic Institute.

———. 2015a. "Fandom: The Classroom of the Future." In "European Fans and European Fan Objects: Localization and Translation," ed. Anne Kustritz, special issue, *Transformative Works and Cultures* 19. doi.org/10.3983/twc.2015.0650.

———. 2015b. *Playing Fans: Negotiating Fandom and Media in the Digital Age*. Iowa City: University of Iowa Press.

Bowman, Sarah-Lynne. 2010. *The Functions of Role-Playing Games: How Participants Create Community, Solve Problems, and Explore Identity*. Jefferson, NC: McFarland.

Brasor, Philip. 2011. "K-pop Takes on the World While J-pop Stays Home." *Japan Times*. February 13. http://www.japantimes.co.jp/news/2011/02/13/national /media-national/k- pop-takes-on-the-world-while-j-pop-stays-home/# .WKPr8NXhBQJ.

Broadway World News Desk. 2015. "HAMILTON to Hold Broadway Auditions This

Month: Read Lin-Manuel Miranda's Character Descriptions!" *Broadway World.* March 12. https://www.broadwayworld.com/article/HAMILTON-to-Hold -Broadway-Auditions-This-Month-Read-Lin-Manuel-Mirandas-Character -Descriptions-20150312.

Broderick, Ryan. 2014. "A Makeup Artist Enraged People on Facebook for Doing a Blackface 'The Walking Dead' Costume." Buzzfeed. October 13. http://www .buzzfeed.com/ryanhatesthis/blackface-walking-dead-makeup-transforma tion#.ut8v4Oj3yG.

brown, adrienne maree. 2019. *Pleasure Activism: The Politics of Feeling Good.* Chico, CA: AK Press.

Brown, Anna. 2017. "Younger Men Play Video Games, but So Do a Diverse Group of Other Americans." Pew Research Center. September 11.

Brown, Brené. 2015. *Rising Strong: The Reckoning. The Rumble. The Revolution.* Random House Audio.

Bruckman, Amy. 2000. "Ethical Guidelines for Research Online." http://www.cc.gate ch.edu/~asb/ethics.

———. 2001. "Studying the Amateur Artist: A Perspective on Disguising Data Collected in Human Subjects Research on the Internet." NYU Web. www.nyu .edu/projects/nissenbaum/projects_ethics.html.

Burgess, Jean, and Ariadna Matamoros-Fernández. 2016. "Mapping Sociocultural Controversies across Digital Media Platforms: One Week of #Gamergate on Twitter, YouTube, and Tumblr." *Communication Research and Practice* 2 (1): 79–96.

Burt, Stephanie. 2017. "The Promise and Potential of Fan Fiction." *New Yorker.* August 23. https://www.newyorker.com/books/page-turner/the-promise -and-potential-of-fan-fiction.

Bury, Rhiannon, et al. 2013. "From Usenet to Tumblr: The Changing Role of Social Media." *Participations: Journal of Audience and Reception Studies* 10 (1): 299–318.

Busse, Kristina. 2013. "Pon Farr, Mpreg, Bonds, and the Rise of the Omegaverse." In *Fic: Why Fanfiction Is Taking over the World,* ed. Anne Elizabeth Jamison, 316–322. Dallas, TX: Smart Pop Books.

——— and Jonathan Gray. 2011. "Fan Cultures and Fan Communities." In *The Handbook of Media Audiences,* ed. Virginia Nightingale, 425–443. Oxford: Wiley-Blackwell.

——— and Karen Hellekson. 2006. "Introduction: Work in Progress." In *Fan Fiction and Fan Communities in the Age of the Internet: New Essays,* ed. Karen Hellekson and Kristina Busse, 5–32. Jefferson, NC: McFarland.

Cain, Sian. 2017. "Marvel Executive Says Emphasis on Diversity May Have Alienated Readers." *Guardian.* April 3. https://www.theguardian.com/books/2017/apr /03/marvel-executive-says-emphasis-on-diversity-may-have-alienated-readers.

Caldarola, Vincent. 1990. "Reception as Cultural Experience: Visual Mass Media and Reception Practices in Outer Indonesia." Ph.D. dissertation, Annenberg School for Communication, University of Pennsylvania.

Calloway, Collin G. 2008. "American Indians and the American Revolution." National Parks Service. December 4. https://www.nps.gov/revwar/about_the_revolu tion/american_indians.html.

Carlin, Shannon. 2016. "Who Is Maggie Sawyer? 'Supergirl's Newest Character Is a Landmark Addition." Bustle. July 13. https://www.bustle.com/articles/172449-who-is-maggie-sawyer-supergirls-newest-character-is-a-landmark-addition.

Carr, Leslie G. 1997. "Color-Blind" Racism. Thousand Oaks, CA: Sage.

Carrington, André M. 2016. Speculative Blackness: The Future of Race in Science Fiction. Minneapolis: University of Minnesota Press.

Chalfen, Richard. 1988. "Navajo Filmmaking Revisited: Problematic Interactions." In Native North American Interaction Patterns, ed. Regna Darnell and Michael K. Foster, 168–185. Quebec: Canadian Museum of Civilization.

Chambers, Ross. 1997. "The Unexamined." In Whiteness: A Critical Reader, ed. Mike Hill, 187–203. New York: New York University Press.

Chander, Anupam, and Madhavi Sunder. 2007. "Everyone's a Superhero: A Cultural Theory of 'Mary Sue' Fan Fiction as Fair Use." California Law Review 95: 597–626.

Chen, Mark. 2009. "Social Dimensions of Expertise in World of Warcraft Players." Transformative Works and Cultures 2. doi.org/10.3983/twc.2009.072.

———. 2012. Leet Noobs: The Life and Death of an Expert Player Group in "World of Warcraft." New York: Peter Lang.

Chess, Shira, and Adrienne Shaw. 2015. "A Conspiracy of Fishes, or, How We Learned to Stop Worrying about #GamerGate and Embrace Hegemonic Masculinity." Journal of Broadcasting and Electronic Media 59 (1): 208–220. doi.org/10.1080/08838151.2014.999917.

Chin, Bertha, and Lori Morimoto. 2013. "Towards a Theory of Transcultural Fandom." Participations: Journal of Audience and Reception Studies 10 (1): 92–108.

Choi, JungBong. 2015. "Hallyu versus Hallyu-hwa: Cultural Phenomenon versus Institutional Campaign." In Hallyu 2.0: The Korean Wave in the Age of Social Media, ed. Sangjoon Lee and Abé Mark Nornes, 31–52. Ann Arbor: University of Michigan Press.

Clark, Travis. 2018. "The 11 Most Popular Gaming YouTube Stars—Some of Whom Made over $10 Million Last Year." Business Insider. February 14.

Clements, Philip Jameson. 2015. "Roll to Save vs. Prejudice: The Phenomenology of Race in Dungeons and Dragons." Master's thesis, Bowling Green State University.

———. 2019. "Dungeons and Discourse: Intersectional Identities in Dungeons and Dragons." Ph.D. dissertation, Bowling Green State University.

ClexaCon. n.d. "Vision." ClexaCon (blog). https://clexacon.com/about/vision.

Cloud, Dana L. 1996. "Hegemony or Concordance? The Rhetoric of Tokenism in 'Oprah' Oprah Rags-to-Riches Biography." Critical Studies in Media Communication 13 (2): 115–137.

Cole, Samantha. 2018. "Pewdiepie Is Teaching His Audience That Women Are Asking for It." Motherboard. May 25. https://www.vice.com/en_us/article/59q98k/pewdiepie-alinity-copyright-feud-twitch-fails.

Coman, Mihai, and Eric W. Rothenbuhler. 2005. "The Promise of Media Anthropology." In Media Anthropology, ed. Eric W. Rothenbuhler and Mihai Coman, 1–12. Thousand Oaks, CA: Sage.

Cooper, Tristan. 2018. "I Watched The Last Jedi's 'De-Feminized' Cut So You Don't

Have To." Dorkly. January 17. http://www.dorkly.com/post/85800/star-wars
-the-last-jedi-mra-edit-no-women.

Coppa, Francesca. 2006. "A Brief History of Media Fandom." In *Fan Fiction and Fan Communities in the Age of the Internet: New Essays*, ed. Karen Hellekson and Kristina Busse, 41–59. Jefferson, NC: McFarland.

———. 2014. "Fuck Yeah, Fandom Is Beautiful." *Journal of Fandom Studies* 2 (1): 73–82. doi.org/10.1386/jfs.2.1.73_1.

Craddock, David. 2014. "'I Want to Rip Your Heart Out': R. A. Salvatore Interview (Part Three)." *Escapist*. www.escapistmagazine.com.articles/view/ video-game /editorials/interviews/12454-R-A-Salvatore-on-the-Impact-of-Death-in-His -Drizzt-Novels.

Creator Academy. 2017. "How YouTube's Home Screen Works." YouTube. August 31. http://www.youtube.com/watch?v=69tpVNunQEU.

Creighton, Millie. 2016. "Through the Korean Wave Looking Glass: Gender, Consumerism, Transnationalism, Tourism Reflecting Japan-Korea Relations in Global East Asia." *Asia Pacific Journal* 14 (April): 1–15.

Crenshaw, Kimberlé W. 1988. "Race, Reform, and Retrenchment: Transformation and Legitimation in Anti-Discrimination Law." *Harvard Law Review* 101: 1331–1387.

———. 1991. "Mapping the Margins: Intersectionality, Identity Politics, and Violence against Women of Color." *Stanford Law Review* 43 (6): 1241–1299.

———. 2017. "Race Liberalism and the Deradicalization of Racial Reform." *Harvard Law Review* 130: 2298–2319.

Cristofar, Cecile, and Matthieu J. Guitton. 2017. "Aca-fans and Fan Communities: An Operative Framework." *Journal of Consumer Culture* 17 (3): 713–731.

Cumberbatch, Chaka. 2013a. "I'm a Black Female Cosplayer and Some People Hate It." xoJane. http://www.xojane.com/issues/mad-back-cosplayer-chaka -cumberbatch.

———. 2013b. "I'm Demanding Better Representation for Black Girl Nerds in Geek Culture." xoJane. http://www.xojane.com/issues/black-girl-nerds -representation.

Daniels, Jessie. 2009. *Cyber Racism: White Supremacy Online and the New Attack on Civil Rights*. Lanham, MD: Rowman and Littlefield.

Darden, Jenee. 2016. "Why I Needed to Confront the Illustrator behind *Ironheart*." Refinery 29. October 26. https://www.refinery29.com/2016/10/127548/riri -williams-sexualization-black-female-superheroes-marvel.

deathtodickens. 2016. "I Have So Many Problems with Fandom Trying to Come for Floma's Skin Tone That I Don't Even Know Where to Begin. With a Drink, Perhaps?" Tweet. @*deathtodickens* (blog). December 13. https://twitter.com /deathtodickens/status/808740538849497089.

de Certeau, Michel. 1988. *The Practice of Everyday Life*. Trans. Steven F. Rendall. Berkeley: University of California Press.

De Genova, Nicholas. 2016. "The European Question: Migration, Race, and Postcoloniality in Europe." *Social Text* 34 (3): 75–102.

De Kosnik, Abigail, and andré carrington. 2019. "Editorial: Fans of Color, Fandoms of Color." *Transformative Works and Cultures* 29. doi.org/10.3983/twc.2019.1783.

Del Arroz, Jon. 2017. "Forcing Political Correctness on Employees and Characters Is Killing Marvel Comics." *Federalist*. April 12. http://thefederalist.com/2017/04 /12/forcing-political-correctness-employees-characters-killing-marvel-comics.

Deller, Ruth A. 2018. "Ethics in Fan Studies Research." In *A Companion to Media Fandom and Fan Studies*, ed. Paul Booth, 123–142. Hoboken, NJ: Wiley-Blackwell.

Dervin, Brenda. 1983. "An Overview of Sense-Making Research: Concepts, Methods, and Results to Date." Paper presented at the International Communication Association annual meeting, Dallas, TX. http://communication.sbs.ohiostate .edu/sensemaking/art/artabsdervin83smovervie.

———. 1998. "Sense-Making Theory and Practice: An Overview of User Interests in Knowledge Seeking and Use." *Journal of Knowledge Management* 2 (1998): 36–46.

———. 2008. "Interviewing as Dialectical Practice: Sense-Making Methodology as Exemplar." Paper presented at the International Association for Media and Communication Research annual meeting, Stockholm.

———, Lois Foreman-Wernet, and Eric Lauterbach, eds. 2003. *Sense-Making Methodology Reader: Selected Writings of Brenda Dervin*. New York: Hampton Press.

——— and Micheline Frenette. 2003. "Sense-Making Methodology: Communicating Communicatively with Campaign Audiences." In *Sense-Making Methodology Reader: Selected Writings of Brenda Dervin*, ed. Brenda Dervin, Lois Foreman-Wernet, and Eric Lauterbach, 233–249. New York: Hampton Press.

Desta, Yohana. 2018. "Kelly Marie Tran Opens Up about Racist Harassment: 'I Went Down a Spiral of Self-Hate.'" *Vanity Fair*. August 21. https://www.vanityfair .com/hollywood/2018/08/kelly-marie-tran-essay-instagram-harassment.

Dickey, Sara. 1993. *Cinema and the Urban Poor in South India*. Cambridge: Cambridge University Press.

distressedcinnamonroll. 2017. "Racism in Fandom: My Experience with *The 100*." Tumblr. January 29. https://distressedcinnamonroll.tumblr.com/post/15654 0860207/racism-in-fandom-my-experience-with-the-100.

Donovan, Robert J., and Nadine Henley. 1997. "Negative Outcomes, Threats and Threat Appeals: Widening the Conceptual Framework for the Study of Fear and Other Emotions in Social Marketing Communications." *Social Marketing Quarterly* 4 (1): 56–68.

Douglas. 2008. Comment on "Whatever Is Wrong with Drizzt?" Giant in the Playground Forums. www.giantitp.com/forums/archive/index.php/t-91244.html.

Duffett, Mark, ed. 2013a. *Popular Music Fandom: Identities, Roles and Practices*. New York: Routledge.

———. 2013b. *Understanding Fandom: An Introduction to the Study of Media Fan Culture*. New York: Bloomsbury.

Duggan, Maeve. 2015. "Gaming and Gamers." Pew Research Center. December 15.

Dutta, Urmitapa, et al. 2016. "The 'Messiness' of Teaching/Learning Social (In)Justice: Performing a Pedagogy of Discomfort." *Qualitative Inquiry* 22 (5): 345–352.

Dyer, Richard. 1997. *White: Essays on Race and Culture*. London: Routledge.

Dyer-Witheford, Nick, and Greig de Peuter. 2009. *Games of Empire: Global Capitalism and Video Games*. Minneapolis: University of Minnesota Press.

Eddy, Max. 2013. "Cosplayers Speak Out on Racism in the Fandom." PCMag India. http://in.pcmag.com/internet/69634/news/cosplayers-speak-out-on -racism-in-the-fandom.

Edwards, Lynne. 2017. "'The Black Chick Always Gets It First': Black Slayers in Sunnydale." In *Joss Whedon and Race: Critical Essays*, ed. Mary Ellen Iatropoulos and Lowery A. Woodall III, 37–50. Jefferson, NC: McFarland.

Elderkin, Beth. 2017. "Marvel VP of Sales Blames Women and Diversity for Sales Slump." *io9*. April 1. http://io9.gizmodo.com/marvel-vp-blames-women -and-diversity-for-sales-slump-1793921500.

Ellis, Emma Grey. 2018. "PewDiePie's Fall Shows the Limits of 'LOL JK.'" *Wired*. January 9.

Enevold, Jessica, and Esther MacCallum-Stewart. 2015. *Game Love: Essays on Play and Affection*. Jefferson, NC: McFarland.

Eng, David. 2010. *The Feeling of Kinship: Queer Liberalism and the Racialization of Intimacy*. Durham, NC: Duke University Press.

Entertainment Software Association. 2017. "2017 Sales, Demographic, and Usage Data: Essential Facts about the Computer and Video Game Industry." www.theesa .com/wp-content/uploads/2017/06/!EF2017_Design_FinalDigital.pdf.

Esposito, Jennifer. 2009. "What Does Race Have to do with *Ugly Betty*? An Analysis of Privilege and Postracial(?)." *Television and New Media* 10 (6): 521–535.

Evans, Andrea E. 2007. "School Leaders and Their Sensemaking about Race and Demographic Change." *Educational Administration Quarterly* 43 (2): 159–188.

Fanon, Frantz. 1967. *Black Skin, White Masks*. New York: Grove Press.

FaZe Censor. 2017a. "The Fall of SSSniperWolf." YouTube. July 26. https://www.you tube.com/watch?v=xg0arOhBvco.

———. 2017b. "My Relationship with SSSniperWolf." YouTube. July 25. https://www .youtube.com/watch?v=_exomKf5qhw.

Feliciano, Claudia, et al. 2015. "Immigrants (We Get the Job Done)." On *The Hamilton Mixtape*. New York: Atlantic Records.

Ferber, Taylor. 2018. "Now Someone Made a 'Last Jedi' Edit without Men—And It Reveals Something Integral to the Film." Bustle. January 19. https://www .bustle.com/p/this-last-jedi-edit-without-men-is-a-response-to-the-sexist-edit -its-actually-quite-revealing-7960087.

Few, April L., Dionne Stephens, and Marlon Rouse-Arnett. 2003. "Sister-to-Sister Talk: Transcending Boundaries and Challenges in Qualitative Research with Black Women." *Family Relations* 52: 205–215.

Fitzgerald, Tom, and Lorenzo Marquez. 2015. "*Sleepy Hollow*: Pittura Infamante." *Tom and Lorenzo*. http://tomandlorenzo.com/2015/01/sleepy-hollow-pittura -infamante.

Flanagan, Mary. 2013. *Critical Play: Radical Game Design*. Cambridge, MA: MIT Press.

———. 2014. *Values at Play in Digital Games*. Cambridge, MA: MIT Press.

Ford, Thomas E. 2016. "Psychology behind the Unfunny Consequences of Jokes That Denigrate." *The Conversation*. June 28.

Fowler, Megan Justine. 2019. "Rewriting the School Story through Racebending in the Harry Potter and Raven Cycle Fandoms." *Transformative Works and Cultures* 29. doi.org/10.3983/twc.2019.1492.

Fox, Helen. 2006. "Afterword." In *Social Change in Diverse Teaching Contexts: Touchy Subjects and Routine Practices*, ed. Nancy G. Barron, Nancy M. Grimm, and Sibylle Grubell, 252–266. New York: Peter Lang.

France, Lisa Respers. 2016. "Zoë Saldaña, Nina Simone, and the Painful History of Blackface." CNN.com. March 4. http://edition.cnn.com/2016/03/04/opinions/zoe-saldana-nina-simone-blackface/index.html.

Frankenberg, Ruth. 1993. *White Women, Race Matters: The Social Construction of Whiteness*. Minneapolis: University of Minnesota Press.

Garcia, Antero. 2017. "Privilege, Power, and *Dungeons and Dragons*: How Systems Shape Racial and Gender Identities in Tabletop Role-Playing Games." *Mind, Culture, and Activity* 24 (3). doi.org/10.1080/1074939.2017.1293691.

Gates, Henry Louis, Jr. 1993. "The Black Man's Burden." In *Fear of a Queer Planet: Queer Politics and Social Theory*, ed. Michael Warner, 230–238. Minneapolis: University of Minnesota Press.

gaythunders. 2018. "A Friend Who Went to ClexaCon Told Me That the Panel for *Black Lightning* Was Empty Compared to the Others and That's Disappointing and Qwhite Interesting Considering How Packed the Others Were and Nafessa Williams/Anissa Pierce Deserve More Support and Recognition Than This." Tweet. @*gaythunders* (blog). April 7. https://twitter.com/gaythunders/status/982784267166990337.

Geertz, Clifford. 1973. *The Interpretation of Cultures: Selected Essays*. New York: Basic Books.

———. 1988. *Works and Lives: The Anthropologist as Author*. Stanford, CA: Stanford University Press.

George, A. A. 2014. "Gaming's Race Problem: GenCon and Beyond." Tor.com. https://www.tor.com/2014/08/13/gamings-race-problem-gen-con-and-beyond.

Geraghty, Lincoln. 2012. "Just Who Is the Passive Audience Here? Teaching Fan Studies at University." In *Fan Culture: Theory/Practice*, ed. Katherine Larsen and Lynn Zubernis, 162–173. Newcastle upon Tyne: Cambridge Scholars.

Gervais, Ricky. 2011. "The Difference between American and British Humour." Time.com. http://time.com/3720218/difference-between-american-british-humour.

Ghee, Kenneth. 2013. "'Will the "Real" Black Superheroes Please Stand Up?!' A Critical Analysis of the Mythological and Cultural Significance of Black Superheroes." In *Black Comics: Politics of Race and Representation*, ed. Sheena C. Howard and Ronald L. Jackson II, 223–237. London: Bloomsbury.

Gibbens, Guillon. 2000. "Univisión and Telemundo: Spanish Language Television Leaders in the United States." In *The Handbook of Spanish Language Media*, ed. Alan B. Albarran, 237–244. New York: Routledge.

Gibson, Timothy A. 2000. "Beyond Cultural Populism: Notes toward the Critical Ethnography of Media Audiences." *Journal of Communication Inquiry* 24 (3): 253–273.

Gilesbie, Tara. 2006. *My Immortal.* https://www.fanfiction.net/s/6829556/8/My
-Immortal (repost).

Gillespie, Tarleton. 2014. "The Relevance of Algorithms." In *Media Technologies:
Essays on Communication, Materiality, and Society,* ed. Pablo J. Boczkowski,
Kirsten A. Foot, and Tarleton Gillespie, 167–194. Cambridge, MA: MIT Press.

Gilliland, Elizabeth. 2016. "Racebending Fandoms and Digital Futurism." *Transformative Works and Cultures* 22. doi.org/10.3983/twc.2016.0702.

"Gina Rodríguez to Those Saying She's 'Not Latina Enough.'" 2015. HuffPostLive.
October 9. https://www.youtube.com/watch ?v=W4KiYi1rtU8.

Giroux, Henry A. 2017. "White Nationalism, Armed Culture and State Violence in
the Age of Donald Trump." *Philosophy and Social Criticism* 43 (9): 887–910.

GLAAD Media Institute. 2018. "Where We Are on TV: 2018–2019." http://glaad.org
/files/WWAT/WWAT_GLAAD_2018-2019.pdf.

"Go Global with Marvel Digital Comics." 2014. Marvel. February 6. https://news
.marvel.com/comics/21901/go_global_with_marvel_digital_comics.

Gómez, Rodrigo, Toby Miller, and André Dorcé. 2014. "Converging from the South:
Mexican Television in the United States." In *Contemporary Latino/a Media:
Production, Circulation, Politics,* ed. Arlene Dávila and Yeidy M. Rivero, 44–61.
New York: New York University Press.

González, Tanya, and Eliza Rodríguez y Gibson. 2015. *Humor and Latino/a Camp in
"Ugly Betty": Funny Looking.* Lanham, MD: Lexington Books.

Gooden, Tai. 2016. "We Need to Talk about Racism and Sexism in the Cosplay Community." Medium. April 12. https://medium.com/the-establishment/unmask
ing-the-cosplay-communitys-sexism-and-racism-problem-3ca9431f58c0.

Gopinath, Gayatri. 2000. "Queering Bollywood: Alternative Sexualities in Popular
Indian Cinema." *Journal of Homosexuality* 39 (3–4): 283–297.

Gordon-Reed, Annette. 2016. "'Hamilton: The Musical': Blacks and the Founding
Fathers." *History @ Work.* April. http://ncph.org/history-at-work/hamilton
-the-musical-blacks-and-the-founding-fathers.

———. 2017. "Sally Hemings, Thomas Jefferson and the Ways We Talk about Our
Past." *New York Times.* August 24. https://www.nytimes.com/2017/08/24
/books/review/sally-hemings-thomas-jefferson-annette-gordon-reed.html.

Gosling, Victoria. K. 2007. "Girls Allowed? The Marginalization of Female Sports
Fans." In *Fandom: Identities and Communities in a Mediated World,* ed. Jonathan
Gray, Cornel Sandvoss, and C. Lee Harrington, 250–260. New York: New York
University Press.

Gotanda, Neil. 1991. "A Critique of 'Our Constitution Is Color-Blind.'" *Stanford Law
Review* 44: 1–68.

Gray, Herman. 2004. *Watching Race: Television and the Struggle for Blackness.* Minneapolis: University of Minnesota Press.

Gray, Jonathan. 2005. "Antifandom and the Moral Text: Television without Pity and
Textual Dislike." *American Behavioral Scientist* 48 (7): 840–858.

———, Cornel Sandvoss, and C. Lee Harrington, eds. 2007. "Introduction: Why
Study Fans?" In *Fandom: Identities and Communities in a Mediated World,* ed.

Jonathan Gray, Cornel Sandvoss, and C. Lee Harrington, 1–18. New York: New York University Press.

Gray, Kishonna L. 2016. *Race, Gender, and Deviance in Xbox Live: Theoretical Perspectives from the Virtual Margins*. New York: Routledge.

Griepp, Milton. 2017. "Marvel's David Gabriel on the 2016 Market Shift." ICv2. March 31. https://icv2.com/articles/news/view/37152/marvels-david-gabriel-2016-market-shift.

Gygax, Gary. 2000. Interview. TheOneRing. www.archives.theonering.net/features/interview/gary_gygax.html.

———. 2004. "Gary Gygax Interview." Gamespy. http://pc.gamespy.com/articles/538/539917p3.html.

Hackett, Robert. 2017. "Meet the Mythmaster Reinventing Marvel Comics." Fortune. March 31. http://fortune.com/2017/03/31/marvel-comics-axel-alonso.

Haile, Rahawa. 2018. "How *Black Panther* Asks Us to Examine Who We Are to One Another." *Longreads* (blog). February 22. https://longreads.com/2018/02/22/how-black-panther-asks-us-to-examine-who-we-are-to-one-another.

Hall, Michael A. 2005. "The Influence of J. R. R. Tolkien on Popular Culture." Honor's thesis, Southern Illinois University.

Hall, Stuart. 1996. "New Ethnicities." In *Stuart Hall: Critical Dialogues in Cultural Studies*, ed. "Hamilton." n.d. TV Tropes. http://tvtropes.org/pmwiki/pmwiki.php/Quotes/Hamilton#.

"Hamilton." 2018. Fanlore. February 10. https://fanlore.org/wiki/Hamilton_(musical).

"*Hamilton* in Sunnydale." 2017–. Tumblr. https://hamiltonsunnydale.tumblr.com.

Han, Min Wha, et al. 2007. "Forced Invisibility to Negotiating Visibility: *Winter Sonata*, the Hanryu Phenomenon and Zainichi Koreans in Japan." *Keio Communication Review* 29: 155–174.

Harris, Cheryl. 1995. "Whiteness as Property." In *Critical Race Theory: The Key Writings That Formed the Movement*, ed. Kimberlé Crenshaw et al., 276–291. New York: New Press.

Havens, Timothy. 2005. "Globalization and the Generic Transformation of Telenovelas." In *Thinking Outside the Box: A Contemporary Television Genre Reader*, ed. Gary R. Edgerton and Brian G. Rose, 257–279. Lexington: University Press of Kentucky.

Hayashi, Kaori, and Eun-Jeung Lee. 2007. "The Potential of Fandom and the Limits of Soft Power: Media Representations of a Korean Melodrama in Japan." *Social Science Japan Journal* 10 (2): 197–216.

Heinsoo, Rob, Andy Collins, and James Wyatt. 2008. *Dungeons and Dragons Player's Handbook: Arcane, Divine, and Martial Heroes*. 4th ed. Renton, WA: Wizards of the Coast.

Hellekson, Karen, and Kristina Busse, eds. 2014. *The Fan Fiction Studies Reader*. Iowa City: University of Iowa Press.

HereIsShir. 2018. "Yes That's Exactly What It Is For. People Who Weren't Even at ClexaCon Got Ridiculously Mad Because the *Black Lightning* Panel Had Less

Attendees Than Some of the Other Panels, Calling Those Who Didn't Attend the Panel or Pay to Meet Nafessa Williams Racists." Tweet. *@HereIsShir* (blog). April 11. https://twitter.com/HereIsShir/status/984152202565517312.

Hern, Alex. 2017. "PewDiePie: YouTube Megastar's N-word Outburst Sparks Developer Backlash." *Guardian*. September 11. https://www.theguardian.com /technology/2017/sep/11/pewdiepie-youtube-racist-developer-campo-santo -backlash-felix-kjellberg.

Hernandez, Patricia. 2017. "YouTubers Are Getting Dragged for Not Supporting PewDiePie 100%." *Kotaku*. February 22.

Hills, Matt. 2002. *Fan Cultures*. New York: Routledge.

———. 2014. "From Dalek Half Balls to Daft Punk Helmets: Mimetic Fandom and the Crafting of Replicas." *Transformative Works and Cultures* 16. doi.org/10.3983 /twc.2014.0531.

Hoffman, Charles Paul. 2017. "No, Diversity Didn't Kill Marvel's Comic Sales." CBR. April 3. http://www.cbr.com/no-diversity-didnt-kill-marvels-comic-sales.

hooks, bell. 1984. *Feminist Theory: From Margin to Center*. Cambridge, MA: South End Press.

Hrisho, Mark T. 2014. "So You Want to Play an RPG? Races and Cultural Depth." *From the Desk of Mark T. Hrisho: Home to Reflections, Opinions, and Beer Reviews*. https://mthrisho.wordpress.com/2014/03/25/cultural-depth.

Hughes, Stephen Putnam. 2011. "Anthropology and the Problem of Audience Reception." In *Made to Be Seen: Perspectives on the History of Visual Anthropology*, ed. Marcus Banks and Jay Ruby, 288–312. Chicago: University of Chicago Press.

Hughes, William. 2017. "Marvel Execs Say Readers Don't Want 'Diversity.'" A.V. Club. April 1. http://www.avclub.com/article/marvel-exec-says-readers-dont -want-diversity-253087.

Hull, Gloria T., Patricia Bell-Scott, and Barbara Smith. 1982. *All the Women Are White, All the Blacks Are Men, but Some of Us Are Brave: Black Women's Studies*. New York: Feminist Press.

Hume, Kathryn. 1984. *Fantasy and Mimesis*. New York: Methuen.

Hutton, Zina. 2017. "Book Review: River of Teeth by Sarah Gailey." Stitch's Media Mix. June 4. https://stitchmediamix.com/2017/06/04/book-review-river -of-teeth-by-sarah-gailey.

"I Love *Hamilton*, but Something about the Way White Fans Engage with the Musical Really Bothers Me." 2015. Fanlore. December 9. https://fanlore.org/wiki /I_love_Hamilton,_but_something_about_the_way_white_fans_engage _with_the_musical_really_bothers_me.

Isbister, Katherine. 2016. *How Games Move Us: Emotion by Design*. Cambridge, MA: MIT Press.

itssupersomethings. 2016. "I Never Said I Was a Role Model." Tumblr. December 13. https://volando-voy.tumblr.com/post/154410102239/the-white-washing-of -maggie-sawyer-and-my-beef.

Jackson, John L. 2005. *Real Black: Adventures in Racial Sincerity*. Chicago: University of Chicago Press.

Japan Association for Refugees. 2014. "JAR Report Fiscal Year 2014." https://www
    .refugee.or.jp/about/postfile/jar-ar_2014_en.pdf.
Jefferson, Rob. 2017. "Is Diversity Killing Comics? (Response to Comicstorian)." You-
    Tube. January 20. https://youtu.be/EAMpprnnouU.
Jenkins, Henry. 1992. *Textual Poachers: Television Fans and Participatory Culture*. New
    York: Routledge.
———. 2006. *Convergence Culture: Where Old and New Media Collide*. New York:
    New York University Press.
———. 2013. *Textual Poachers: Television Fans and Participatory Culture*. Updated
    20th anniversary edition. New York: Routledge.
———. 2019. "Squee from the Margins: Interview with Rukmini Pande (Part I)."
    Henry Jenkins. June 17. http://henryjenkins.org/blog/2019/6/1/interview
    -with-rukmini-pande-part-i-y2hlj.
——— and Suzanne Scott. 2013. "Textual Poachers, Twenty Years Later: A Conversa-
    tion between Henry Jenkins and Suzanne Scott." In *Textual Poachers: Televi-
    sion Fans and Participatory Culture*, by Henry Jenkins, updated 20th anniver-
    sary edition, vii–li. New York: Routledge.
——— and Sangita Shresthova. 2012. "'Up, Up, and Away!' The Power and Potential
    of Fan Activism." *Transformative Works and Cultures* 10. doi:10.3983/twc.2012
    .0435.
Jenson, Joli. 1992. "Fandom as Pathology." In *The Adoring Audience: Fan Culture and
    Popular Media*, ed. Lisa A. Lewis, 9–29. London: Routledge.
Jin, Dal Yong. 2015. "New Perspectives on the Creative Industries in the Hallyu 2.0
    Era." In *Hallyu 2.0: The Korean Wave in the Age of Social Media*, ed. Sangjoon
    Lee and Abé Mark Nornes, 53–70. Ann Arbor: University of Michigan Press.
———. 2016. *New Korean Wave: Transnational Cultural Power in the Age of Social
    Media*. Urbana: University of Illinois Press.
Joanna. 2013. "Fantasy's Race Problem and Racism IRL." *Geekalitarian: Women in
    Geek Culture*. https://geekalitarian.wordpress.com/2013/06/11/fantasys
    -race-problem-and-racismirl.
Johnson, Derek. 2007. "Fan-tagonism: Factions, Institutions, and Constitutive Hege-
    monies of Fandom." In *Fandom: Identities and Communities in a Mediated
    World*, ed. Jonathan Gray, Cornel Sandvoss, and C. Lee Harrington, 285–300.
    New York: New York University Press.
Johnson, Poe. 2019. "Transformative Racism: The Black Body in Fan Works." *Trans-
    formative Works and Cultures* 29. doi.org/10.3983/twc.2019.1669.
Jung, Sun. 2011. "K-Pop, Indonesian Fandom and Social Media." *Transformative Works
    and Cultures* 8, special issue. http://journal.transformativeworks.org/index
    .php/twc/article/view/289.
Jusino, Teresa. 2016. "Being Latinx Is Not about Color: Floriana Lima on *Supergirl*."
    The Mary Sue. December 13. https://www.themarysue.com/floriana-lima
    -latinx-not-about-color.
———. 2017. "Marvel Cancels Black Panther and the Crew Because of 'Poor Sales.'"
    The Mary Sue. May 15. https://www.themarysue.com/marvel-cancels-black
    -panther-and-the-crew.

Juul, Jesper. 2012. *A Casual Revolution: Reinventing Video Games and Their Players.* Cambridge, MA: MIT Press.

Kalviknes Bore, Inger-Lise, and Rebecca Williams. 2010. "Transnational Twilighters: A Twilight Fan Community in Norway." In *Bitten by Twilight: Youth Culture, Media, and the Vampire Franchise,* ed. Melissa A. Click, Jennifer Stevens Aubrey, and Elizabeth Behm-Moravitz, 189–205. New York: Peter Lang.

Kaplan, Sidney, and Emma Nogrady Kaplan. 1989. *The Black Presence in the Era of the American Revolution.* Amherst: University of Massachusetts Press.

Karlan, Sarah. 2017. "How 'Lexa Deserved Better' Became a Rallying Cry for Positive LGBT Representation." BuzzFeed. September 21. https://www.buzzfeed .com/skarlan/for-the-love-of-clexa.

Kastrenakes, Jacob. 2017. "PewDiePie Says the *Wall Street Journal* Is Out to Get Him in Apology for Nazi Jokes." The Verge. February 16. https://www.theverge .com/2017/2/16/14637934/pewdiepie-apology-nazi-jokes-blames-media.

Kavos. 2017. "This Video Will Make You Hate SSSniperWolf." YouTube. July 28. https://www.youtube.com/watch?v=2beIvCgSc6Q.

Kay, Matthew, Cynthia Matuszek, and Sean A. Munson. 2015. "Unequal Representation and Gender Stereotypes in Image Search Results for Occupations." In *CHI EA '15: Proceedings of the 33rd Annual ACM Conference on Human Factors in Computing Systems,* 3819–3828. doi.org/10.1145/2702123.2702520.

Keene, Adrienne. 2016a. "'Magic in North America': The Harry Potter Franchise Veers Too Close to Home." Native Appropriations. March 7. http://native appropriations.com/2016/03/magic-in-north-america-the-harry-potter -franchise-veers-too-close-to-home.html.

———. 2016b. "Where Are the Natives in *Hamilton*?" Native Appropriations. August 5. http://nativeappropriations.com/2016/08/where-are-the-natives -in-hamilton.html.

"Key & Peele—Obama's Anger Translator—I Sunk Your Battleship, Bitch—Uncensored." 2012a. YouTube. October 24. https://youtu.be/mowdr1IBHuY.

"Key & Peele—Obama's Anger Translator—Meet Luther." 2012b. YouTube. January 11. https://youtu.be/-qv7k2_lcoM.

"Key & Peele—Obama Shutdown." 2012c. YouTube. October 17. https://youtu.be /jDpVg-UEGCI.

"Kind Alpha." 2015. Archive of Our Own. June 2.

Kinnear, Penny. 2001. "Setting Assumptions Aside." In *Proceedings of the JALT 26th Annual International Conference,* ed. Robert Long et al., 44–51. Tokyo: Japan Association for Language Teaching.

Kiyoko, Hayley. 2018. "It's Our Year, It's Our Time. To Thrive and Let Our Souls Feel Alive. #20GAYTEEN #expectations2018." Tweet. @hayleykiyoko (blog). January 1. https://twitter.com/hayleykiyoko/status/947894684499636224?lang=en.

Kluckhohn, Clyde, and Dorothea Leighton. 1951. *The Navaho.* Cambridge, MA: Harvard University Press.

Kondabolu, Hari. 2013. "Totally Biased with Kamau Bell: Hari Kondabolu Reports on Sikh Captain America." YouTube. November 7. https://www.youtube.com /watch?v=shUzrgAUqUw.

Kurashina, Yuko. 2005. "Peacekeeping Participation and Identity Changes in the Japan Self-Defense Forces: Military Service as 'Dirty Work.'" Ph.D. dissertation, University of Maryland.

Kustritz, Anne. 2008. "Painful Pleasures: Sacrifice, Consent and the Resignification of BDSM Symbolism in *The Story of O* and *The Story of Obi.*" *Transformative Works and Cultures* 1. http://journal.transformativeworks.org/index.php/twc/article/view/31/66.

———. 2015. "Transnationalism, Localization, and Translation in European Fandom: Fan Studies as Global Media and Audience Studies." In "European Fans and European Fan Objects: Localization and Translation," ed. Anne Kustritz, special issue, *Transformative Works and Cultures* 19. doi.org/10.3983/twc.2015.0682.

kylie. 2016. "*Supergirl* Introduces Korrasami 2.0, but Is It Brave Enough to Also Deliver?" The Fandomentals. December 7. https://www.thefandomentals.com/supercorp-korrasami.

Ladson-Billings, Gloria. 1998. "Just What Is Critical Race Theory and What's It Doing in a Nice Field Like Education?" *Qualitative Studies in Education* 11: 7–24.

Larsen, Katherine, and Lynn Zubernis. 2013. *Fangasm: Supernatural Fangirls.* Iowa City: University of Iowa Press.

Larsen, Miranda Ruth. 2018. "Benefits and Labor: K-pop in Tokyo beyond the Major Groups." The Learned Fangirl. http://thelearnedfangirl.com/2018/01/k-pop-fandom-in-tokyo-beyond-the-major-groups.

LaSala, Jeff. 2018. "The Legacies and Dark Elves of R. A. Salvatore." Tor.com. https://www.tor.com/2018/02/08/the-legacies-and-dark-elves-of-r-a-salvatore.

Lavender, Isiah, III. 2009. "Critical Race Theory." In *The Routledge Companion to Science Fiction*, ed. Mark Bould et al., 185–194. New York: Routledge.

Lee, Hye-Kyung. 2016. "Transnational Cultural Fandom." In *The Ashgate Research Companion to Fan Cultures*, ed. Stijn Reijnders, 207–220. New York: Routledge.

Lee, Soo Im. 2012. "Diversity of Zainichi Koreans and Their Ties to Japan and Korea." *Studies on Multicultural Societies No. 8.* https://afrasia.ryukoku.ac.jp/phase2/publication/upfile/WP008.pdf.

Lees, Matt. 2016. "What Gamergate Should Have Taught Us about the Alt-Right." *Guardian.* December 1. https://www.theguardian.com/technology/2016/dec/01/gamergate-alt-right-hate-trump.

Levine, Sydney. 2013. "LatinoBuzz: You Don't Look Latina! Celebrating Afro-Latina Documentarians for Black History Month." SydneysBuzz. February 20. https://blogs.sydneysbuzz.com/latinobuzz-you-dont-look-latina-celebrating-afro-latina-documentarians-for-black-history-month-24365c88d803.

Lewis, Lisa A., ed. 1992. *The Adoring Audience: Fan Culture and Popular Media.* London: Routledge.

LEXASPINOFF. 2018. "LEXASPINOFF Project Featuring the Grounders." https://www.lexaspinoff.com.

Lie, John. 2016. "Obasan and Kanryu: Modalities of Convergence of Middle-Aged Japanese Women around South Korean Popular Culture and Gender Divergence in Japan." In *Media Convergence in Japan*, ed. Patrick W. Galbraith and Jason G. Karlin, 124–143. Tokyo: Kinema Club.

Lindvall, Helienne. 2013. "How K-pop and J-pop Are Saving Physical Music Sales." *Digital Music News*. April 10. http://www.digitalmusicnews.com/2013/04 /10/kpopjpop.

Linke, Uli. 2010. "Fortress Europe: Globalization, Militarization and the Policing of Interior Borderlands." *TOPIA: Canadian Journal of Cultural Studies* 23: 100–120.

Lipsitz, George. 2006. *The Possessive Investment in Whiteness: How White People Profit from Identity Politics*. Philadelphia: Temple University Press.

López, Ana. 1995. "Our Welcomed Guests: Telenovelas in Latin America." In *To Be Continued . . .: Soap Operas around the World*, ed. Robert C. Allen, 256–275. New York: Routledge.

Lopez, Lori Kido. 2011. "Fan Activists and the Politics of Race in *The Last Airbender*." *International Journal of Cultural Studies* 15 (5): 431–445.

Lorde, Audre. 1984. *Sister Outsider: Essays and Speeches*. Berkeley, CA: Crossing Press.

Lott, Eric. 1993. *Love and Theft: Blackface Minstrelsy and the American Working Class*. New York: Oxford University Press.

Lyons, Andrew P. 1990. "The Television and the Shrine: Towards a Theoretical Model for the Study of Mass Communications in Nigeria." *Visual Anthropology* 3 (1): 429–456.

Mac, Melonie. 2013. "Fake Girl Gamers". YouTube. July 7. https://www.youtube.com /watch?v=WQS7lB8iR-k.

Macdonald, Heidi. 2017. "Marvel: Retailers and Readers 'Turning Their Noses Up at Their More Diverse Titles—UPDATED." Comics Beat. March 31. http:// www.comicsbeat.com/marvel-retailers-and-readers-turning-their-nose-up-at -their-more-diverse-titles.

Madrid-Morales, Dani, and Bruno Lovric. 2015. "'Transatlantic Connection': K-pop and K-drama Fandom in Spain and Latin America." *Journal of Fandom Studies* 3 (1): 23–41. doi.org/10.1386/jfs.3.1.23_1.

Malinowski, Bronislaw. 1922. *Argonauts of the Western Pacific*. New York: E. P. Dutton.

Maloney, Marcus, Steven Roberts, and Alexandra Caruso. 2017. "'Mmm . . . I Love It, Bro!' Performances of Masculinity in YouTube Gaming." *New Media & Society* 20 (5): 1697–1714. doi:10.1177/1461444817703368.

Marquette, Andi. 2018. "Fangirl Friday: ClexaCon Aftermath." *Women and Words* (blog). April 13. https://womenwords.org/2018/04/13/fangirl-friday-clexacon -aftermath.

Marshall, Colin. 2015. "The K-Town Dream: California in Korea, Korea in California." *Boom: A Journal of California* 5, no. 1 (Spring): 14–19.

"Marvel Executive Says Emphasis on Diversity May Have Alienated Readers." 2017. Reddit. https://www.reddit.com/r/books/comments/637jvx/marvel _executive_says_emphasis_on_diversity_may.

Maskovsky, Jeff. 2017. "Toward the Anthropology of White Nationalist Postracialism: Comments Inspired by Hall, Goldstein, and Ingram's 'The Hands of Donald Trump.'" *HAU: Journal of Ethnographic Theory* 7 (1): 433–440.

MasqueofComus. 2012. Comment on "Books and Literature: What Is the Appeal of R. A. Salvatore?" GameFAQs. https://www.gamefaqs.com/boards/202-books -and-literature/62013029.

Matsuda, Mari. 1995. "Looking to the Bottom: Critical Legal Studies and Repara-
    tions." In *Critical Race Theory: The Key Writings That Formed the Movement*, ed.
    Kimberlé Crenshaw et al., 63–79. New York: New Press.
Mbembe, Achille. 2003. "Necropolitics." *Public Culture* 15: 11–40.
McAllister, Marvin. 2017. "Toward a More Perfect *Hamilton*." *Journal of the Early
    Republic* 37 (2): 279–288.
McAlone, Nathan. 2017. "These Are the 18 Most Popular YouTube Stars in the
    World—and Some Are Making Millions." Business Insider. March 7.
McCurry, Justin. 2010. "Rocky Relations between Japan and South Korea Over Dis-
    puted Islands." *Guardian*. August 18. https://www.theguardian.com/world
    /2010/aug/18/japan-south-korea-disputed-islands.
McDonald, Heidi. 2012. "NPC Romance as a Safe Space: Bioware and Healthier
    Identity Tourism." *Well Played Journal* 1 (4): 23–39. http://www.etc.cmu.edu/
    etcpress/content/volume-1-number-4-romance.
McKee, Heidi A., and James Porter. 2009. *Internet Research: A Rhetorical, Case-Based
    Process*. New York: Peter Lang.
McVeigh, Robbie. 2010. "United in Whiteness? Irishness, Europeanness and the
    Emergence of a 'White Europe' Policy." In *Europeanisation and Hibernicisation*,
    ed. Cathal McCall and Thomas M. Wilson, 251–278. Amsterdam: Brill Rodopi.
Mearls, Mike, and Jeremy Crawford. 2014. *Dungeons and Dragons Player's Handbook*.
    5th ed. Renton, WA: Wizards of the Coast.
Mehri, Momtaza. 2018. "Who Is Welcome in Wakanda? On *Black Panther* and Con-
    tradictory Afrofuturisms." Open Space. March 13. https://openspace.sfmoma
    .org/2018/03/who-is-welcome-in-wakanda-on-black-panther-contradictory
    -afrofuturisms.
Melanson, Yvette, with Claire Safran. 1999. *Looking for Lost Bird: A Jewish Woman
    Discovers Her Navajo Roots*. New York: Avon Books.
Mignolo, Walter. 2005. *The Idea of Latin America*. Oxford: Wiley-Blackwell.
Mikhaylova, Larisa. 2012. "Star Trek (2009) and the Russian ST Fandom: Too Many
    Batteries Included." In *Fan Culture: Theory/Practice*, ed. Katherine Larsen and
    Lynn Zubernis, 148–161. Newcastle: Cambridge Scholars.
Mills, Charles W. 2008. "Racial Liberalism." *PMLA* 123 (5): 1380–1397. https://www
    .jstor.org/stable/25501942.
Milner, Ryan M. 2009. "Working for the Text: Fan Labor and the New Prganization."
    International Journal of Cultural Studies 12 (5): 491–508.
Mims, Christopher. 2014. "+2 to Charisma: Everything I Need to Know about Man-
    agement I Learned from Playing *Dungeons and Dragons*." Quartz. https://
    qz.com/171166/everything-i-need-to-know-about-management-i-learned-
    from-playing-dungeons-and-dragons.
Miranda, Lin-Manuel. 2015. "Cabinet Rap Battle #3." On *The Hamilton Mixtape*. New
    York: Atlantic Records.
———— and Jeremy McCarter. 2016. *Hamilton: The Revolution*. New York: Hatchette
    Book Group.
Mitchell-Smith, Ilan. 2009. "Racial Determinism and the Interlocking Economics of
    Power and Violence in *Dungeons and Dragons*." In *Co-Opting Culture: Culture*

and Power in Sociology and Cultural Studies, ed. B. Garrick Harden and Robert Carley, 207–224. Lanham, MD: Lexington Books.

Mohale, Maneo. 2018. "'Who Is More Sci-Fi Than Us?'" The Mail and Guardian Online. February 23. https://mg.co.za/article/2018-02-23-00-who-is-more-sci-fi-than-us.

Mohanty, Chandra Talpade. 1984. "Under Western Eyes: Feminist Scholarship and Colonial Discourses." *Boundary 2* 12/13 (3): 333–358.

Monteiro, Lyra D. 2016. "Race-Conscious Casting and the Erasure of the Black Past in Lin-Manuel Miranda's *Hamilton.*" *Public Historian* 38 (1): 89–98.

Moreton-Robinson, Aileen. 2000. *Talkin' Up to the White Woman: Aboriginal Women and Feminism.* St. Lucia: University of Queensland Press.

Morris, Charles E., and K. J. Rawson. 2013. "Queer Archives/Archival Queers." In *Theorizing Histories of Rhetoric,* ed. Michelle Ballif, 74-89. Carbondale: Southern Illinois University Press.

Morris, Rosalind C. 1994. "Three Sexes and Four Sexualities: Redressing the Discourses on Gender and Sexuality in Contemporary Thailand." *Positions* 2 (1): 15–43. doi.org/10.1215/10679847-2-1-15.

Muñoz, José Esteban. 1999. *Disidentifications: Queers of Color and the Performance of Politics.* Minneapolis: University of Minnesota Press.

———. 2009. *Cruising Utopia: The Then and There of Queer Futurity.* New York: New York University Press.

Murphy, Shaunna. 2016. "'The 100' Fans Just Took Their Fight against Queer TV Deaths a Giant Step Further." Revelist. May 19. https://www.revelist.com/tv/the-100-lexa-billboard/2427.

Murphy-Shigemitsu, Stephen. 2008. "'The Invisible Man' and Other Narratives of Living in the Borderlands of Race and Nation." In *Transcultural Japan: At the Borderlands of Race, Gender, and Identity,* ed. David Blake Willis and Stephen Murphy-Shigemitsu, 282–304. New York: Routledge.

Nagle, Angela. 2017. *Kill All Normies: The Online Culture War from Tumblr and 4chan to the Alt-Right and Trump.* Winchester, UK: Zero Books.

Nakamura, Lisa. 1995. "Race in/for Cyberspace: Identity Tourism and Racial Passing on the Internet." *Works and Days* 25 (26): 13.

———. 2002. *Cybertypes: Race, Ethnicity, and Identity on the Internet.* London: Routledge.

———. 2012. "Queer Female of Color: The Highest Difficulty Setting There Is? Gaming Rhetoric as Gender Capital." *Ada: A Journal of Gender, New Media and Technology* 1. doi:10.7264/N37P8W9V.

Nakandala, Supun, et al. 2016. "Gendered Conversation in a Social Game-Streaming Platform." November 22. https://arxiv.org/abs/1611.06459.

Narayan, Kirin. 1993. "How Native Is a 'Native' Anthropologist?" *American Anthropologist* 95: 671–686.

Nathans, Heather S. 2017. "Crooked Histories: Re-Presenting Race, Slavery, and Alexander Hamilton Onstage." *Journal of the Early Republic* 37 (2): 271–278.

Navar-Gill, Annemarie, and Mel Stanfill. 2018. "'We Shouldn't Have to Trend to

Make You Listen': Queer Fan Hashtag Campaigns as Production Interventions." *Journal of Film and Video* 70 (3–4): 85–100. doi.org/10.5406/jfilmvideo .70.3-4.0085.

netweight. 2013. "The Nonnies Made Them Do It." Archive of Our Own. http:// archiveofourown.org/works/1022303/chapters/2033841.

Newzoo. 2017. "2017 Global Games Market Report." https://resources.newzoo .com/hubfs/Reports/Newzoo_The_2017_Global_Games_Market_Report _Light.pdf.

Noble, Safiya Umoja. 2018. *Algorithms of Oppression: How Search Engines Reinforce Racism*. New York: New York University Press.

"Not." 2012. Archive of Our Own. August 17.

Nyong'o, Tavia. 2009. *The Amalgamation Waltz: Race, Performance, and the Ruses of Memory*. Minneapolis: University of Minnesota Press.

Nyshka, Chandra. 2018. "North Korea Problem Complicated by Tension between South Korea and Japan." January 2. CNBC Online. https://www.cnbc.com /2018/01/02/tensions-south-korea-and-japan-could-impact-north-korea -china.html.

obsession_inc. 2009. "Affirmational Fandom vs. Transformational Fandom." Dreamwidth. June 1. https://obsession-inc.dreamwidth.org/82589.html.

Ohito, Esther O. 2016. "Making the Emperor's New Clothes Visible in Anti-Racist Teacher Education: Enacting a Pedagogy of Discomfort with White Preservice Teachers." *Equity and Excellence in Education* 49 (4): 454–467.

Okabe, Daisuke. 2012. "Cosplay, Learning and Cultural Practice." In *Fandom Unbound: Otaku Culture in a Connected World*, ed. Muzak Ito, Daisuke Okabe, and Izumi Tsuji, 225–248. New Haven, CT: Yale University Press.

Okeyo, Agunda. 2018. "Wakanda: A Nation without Chains." Progressive. February 23. https://progressive.org/api/content/178ab5e6-18ce-11e8-be77 -121bebc5777e.

Omi, Michael. 1989. "In Living Color: Race and American Culture." In *Cultural Politics in Contemporary America*, ed. Ian Angus and Sut Jhally, 111–123. New York: Routledge.

O'Neil, Cathy. 2016. *Weapons of Math Destruction: How Big Data Increases Inequality and Threatens Democracy*. New York: Crown.

Opam, Kwame. 2017. "Ta-Nehisi Coates Black Panther and the Crew Has Been Cancelled." The Verge. May 13. https://www.theverge.com/2017/5/13/15636276/ marvel-black-panther-and-the-crew-cancelled-ta-nehisi-coates.

Pack, Sam. 2006. "How They See Me vs. How I See Them: The Ethnographic Self and the Personal Self." *Anthropological Quarterly* 79 (1): 105–122.

Paladin, Aydin. 2017. "Marvel Has a Pandering Problem NOT a Diversity Problem." YouTube. April 12. https://youtu.be/EsUGm1ATJB4.

Pande, Rukmini. 2016a. "Squee from the Margins: Investigating the Operations of Racial/Cultural/Ethnic Identity in Media Fandom." Ph.D. dissertation, University of Western Australia.

———. 2016b. "Squee from the Margins: Racial/Cultural/Ethnic Identity in

Global Media Fandom." In *Seeing Fans: Representations of Fandom in Media and Popular Culture*, ed. Lucy Bennett and Paul Booth, 209–220. New York: Bloomsbury.

———. 2018a. *Squee from the Margins: Fandom and Race*. Iowa City: University of Iowa Press.

———. 2018b. "Who Do you Mean by 'Fan'? Decolonizing Media Fandom Identity." In *A Companion to Media Fandom and Fan Studies*, ed. Paul Booth, 319–332. Hoboken, NJ: Wiley-Blackwell.

——— and Swati Moitra. 2017. "Racial Dynamics of Online Femslash Fandoms." In "Queer Female Fandom," ed. Julie Levin Russo and Eve Ng, special issue, *Transformative Works and Cultures* 24. doi.org/10.3983/twc.2017.908.

Parc, Jimmyn, and Nobuko Kawashima. 2018. "Wrestling with or Embracing Digitization in the Music Industry: The Contrasting Business Strategies of J-pop and K-pop." *Kritika Kultura* 30: 24–48.

Parker, Laurence. 1998. "Race Is . . . Race Ain't: An Exploration of the Utility of Critical Race Theory in Qualitative Research in Education." *Qualitative Studies in Education* 11: 43–55.

Pearson, Jordan. 2016. "Twitch Commenters Talk about Games on Men's Streams, 'Boobs' on Women's." *Motherboard*. November 23. https://motherboard.vice.com/en_us/article/kb7yqz/twitch-commenters-talk-about-games-on-mens-streams-boobs-on-womens.

Peterson, Mark Allen. 2003. *Anthropology and Mass Communication: Media and Myth in the New Millennium*. New York: Berghahn.

Piittinen, Sari. 2018. "Morality in Let's Play Narrations: Moral Evaluations of Gothic Monsters in Gameplay Videos of Fallout 3." *New Media and Society* 20 (12): 564–580. doi:146144481877975.

Poor, Nathaniel. 2012. "Digital Elves as a Racial Other in Video Games: Acknowledgment and Avoidance." *Games and Culture* 7 (5): 375–396.

Postigo, Hector. 2014. "The Socio-technical Architecture of Digital Labor: Converting Play into YouTube Money." *New Media and Society* 18 (2): 332–349. doi.org/10.1177/1461444814541527.

Potter, Benny. 2017. "Did Diversity Kill Marvel? Well They Seem to Think So. . . ." YouTube. April 4. https://youtu.be/iPUd8GllsJs.

Prins, Harald E. L. 1989. "American Indians and the Ethnocinematic Complex: From Native Participation to Production Control." In *Eyes across the Water: The Amsterdam Conference on Visual Anthropology and Sociology*, ed. Robert M. Boonzajer Flaes, 80–90. Amsterdam: Het Spinhuis.

"Priyanka Chopra as Mary Kom: Is Bollywood Being Racist?" 2014. *Newsminute*. July 17. http://www.thenewsminute.com/article/priyanka-chopra-mary-kom-bollywood-being-racist-20259.

Prudom, Laura. 2013. "What Every TV Show Can Learn from *Sleepy Hollow*." The Week. http://theweek.com/articles/455254/what-every-tv-show-learn-from-sleepy-hollow.

Puar, Jasbir K. 2005. "Queer Times, Queer Assemblages." *Social Text* 23 (3–4): 121–139.

———. 2007. *Terrorist Assemblages: Homonationalism in Queer Times.* Durham, NC: Duke University Press.

———. 2012. "'I Would Rather Be a Cyborg Than a Goddess': Becoming-Intersectional in Assemblage Theory." *PhiloSOPHIA* 2 (1): 49–66.

Puls, Carina. 2018. "The Antithesis of the Traditional Elf: Deconstructing Racial Representations in *Dungeons and Dragons* and R. A. Salvatore's the Legend of Drizzt." Master's thesis, University of Saskatchewan.

Punathambekar, Aswin. 2005. "Bollywood in the Indian-American Diaspora Mediating a Transitive Logic of Cultural Citizenship." *International Journal of Cultural Studies* 8 (2): 151–173.

———. 2007. "Between Rowdies and Rasikas: Rethinking Fan Activity in Indian Film Culture." In *Fandom: Identities and Communities in a Mediated World*, ed. Jonathan Gray, Cornel Sandvoss, and C. Lee Harrington, 198–209. New York: New York University Press.

Puri, Jyoti. 1997. "Reading Romance Novels in Postcolonial India." *Gender and Society* 11 (4): 434–452. doi.org/10.1177/089124397011004004.

quinn. 2014. Comment on "New Rules of Fantasy #1: Evil Is a Choice." *Thoughtcrime.* July 24. http://thoughtcrimegames.net/new-rules-of-fantasy-1-evil-is-a-choice.

Rancière, Jacques. 1999. *Dis-agreement: Politics and Philosophy.* Trans. Julie Rose. Minneapolis: University of Minnesota Press.

———. 2010. *Dissensus: On Politics and Aesthetics.* Trans. and ed. Steven Corcoran. New York: Continuum International Publishing Group.

Rao, Shakuntala. 2007. "The Globalization of Bollywood: An Ethnography of Non-Elite Audiences in India." *Communication Review* 10 (1): 57–76.

Rearick, Anderson. 2004. "Why Is the Only Good Orc a Dead Orc? The Dark Face of Racism Examined in Tolkien's World." *Modern Fiction Studies* 50 (4): 861–874.

Reese, Debbie. 2017. "1) I—a Native Woman/Scholar/Critic—Saw *Hamilton*, Yesterday." Tweet. @debreese (blog). May 11. https://twitter.com/debreese/status/862747703066886144.

Reid, E. M. 1996. "Informed Consent in the Study of On-Line Communities: A Reflection on the Effects of Computer-Mediated Social Research." *Information Society* 12 (2): 169–174.

Reina, Elena. 2018. "'La Casa de las Flores' Reinventa la Telenovela 'Millennial' para Netflix." *El País.* August 10. https://elpais.com/cultura/2018/08/09/television/1533777015_190159.html.

Reinhard, CarrieLynn D., and Brenda Dervin. 2009. "The Application of Dervin's Sense-Making Methodology to Media Reception Studies: Interpretivism, Situationality and the Empowerment of Media Users." Paper presented at the Transforming Audiences conference, London.

———. 2012. "Comparing Situated Sense-Making Processes in Virtual Worlds: Application of Dervin's Sense-Making Methodology to Media Reception Situations." *Convergence: The International Journal of Research into New Media Technologies* 18 (1): 27–48.

Richie, Bryan. 2017. "*Dungeons and Dragons*: A Life Changing Experience." Prison University Project. https://prisonuniversityproject.org/news/dungeons -dragons-a-life-changing-experience-by-brian-richie.

Roberts, Steven, and Marcus Maloney. 2018. "PewDiePie, New Media Stars and the Court of Public Opinion." *The Conversation*. June 27.

Rodgers, A. 2003. "Make Up Your Mind: What Is a Mary Sue?" LiveJournal. http:// alarar.livejournal.com/44440.html.

Rodriguez, Desiree. 2016. "The Disappointing Truth about *Supergirl*'s Maggie Sawyer." *The Nerds of Color* (blog). December 12. https://thenerdsofcolor .org/2016/12/12/the-disappointing-truth-about-supergirls-maggie-sawyer.

Romano, Aja. 2014. "Police Kill Man for Cosplaying While Black." Daily Dot. September 16. http://www.dailydot.com/news/darrien-hunt-shot-by-police -while-cosplaying.

———. 2016. "*Hamilton* is Fanfic, and Its Historical Critics Are Totally Missing the Point." Vox. July 4. https://www.vox.com/2016/4/14/11418672/hamilton-is -fanfic-not-historically-inaccurate.

Rony, Fatimah Tobing. 1996. *The Third Eye: Race, Cinema, and Ethnographic Spectacle*. Durham, NC: Duke University Press.

Rosenberg, Howard. 2003. "History Rewritten to Make Us Feel Good." *Los Angeles Times*. June 30.

Ross, Sharon Marie. 2008. *Beyond the Box: Television and the Internet*. Malden, MA: Wiley-Blackwell.

Roth, Dany. 2016. "Why *The 100*'s Showrunner Just Lost 15K Followers, and Why It Matters." *Blastr* (blog). March 8. http://www.blastr.com/2016-3-8/why-100s -showrunner-just-lost-15k-followers-and-why-it-matters.

Ruberg, Bonnie, and Adrienne Shaw. 2017. *Queer Game Studies*. Minneapolis: University of Minnesota Press.

Ruby, Jay. 1991. "Speaking for, Speaking about, Speaking with, or Speaking Alongside: An Anthropological and Documentary Dilemma." *Visual Anthropology Review* 7 (2): 50–67.

Rumsby, John Henry. 2017. "Otherworldly Others: Racial Representation in Fantasy Literature." Ph.D. dissertation, University of Montreal.

Russworm, TreaAndrea, and Jennifer M. Malkowski. 2017. *Gaming Representation: Race, Gender, and Sexuality in Video Games*. Bloomington: Indiana University Press.

Rytkønen, Helle. 2006. "Whose Knowledge? How Race, Class, Religion, and Gender Intersect and Interfere with 'Our' Intellectual Community." In *Social Change in Diverse Teaching Contexts: Touchy Subjects and Routine Practices*, ed. Nancy G. Barron, Nancy M. Grimm, and Sibylle Grubell, 43–53. New York: Peter Lang.

Salah, Trish. 2014. "Of Activist Fandoms, Auteur Pedagogy, and Imperial Feminism: From *Buffy the Vampire Slayer* to *I Am Du'a Khalil*." In *Muslim Women, Transnational Feminism and the Ethics of Pedagogy: Contested Imaginaries in Post-9/11 Cultural Practice*, ed. Lisa K. Taylor and Jasmine Zine, 152–172. New York: Routledge.

Salter, Anastasia, and Bridget Blodgett. 2017. *Toxic Geek Masculinity in Media: Sexism, Trolling, and Identity Policing*. London: Palgrave Macmillan.

Salter, Michael. 2017. "From Geek Masculinity to Gamergate: The Technological Rationality of Online Abuse." *Crime, Media, Culture: An International Journal* 14 (2): 247–264. doi:174165901769089.

Salvatore, R. A. 1988. *The Crystal Shard*. Renton, WA: Wizards of the Coast.

———. 2011. "Dark Mirror." In *The Legend of Drizzt: The Collected Short Stories*, ed. Philip Athans, 21–57. Renton, WA: Wizards of the Coast.

Samuels, Robert. 2009. *New Media, Cultural Studies, and Literary Theory after Postmodernism: Automodernity from Zizek to Laclau*. London: Palgrave Macmillan.

Sandvoss, Cornel. 2005. *Fans: The Mirror of Consumption*. Cambridge: Polity Press.

———, Jonathan Gray, and C. Lee Harrington. 2017. "Introduction: Why Still Study Fans?" In *Fandom: Identities and Communities in a Mediated World*, 2nd ed., ed. Jonathan Gray, Cornel Sandvoss, and C. Lee Harrington, 1–26. New York: New York University Press.

Saukko, Paula. 2003. *Doing Research in Cultural Studies: An Introduction to Classical and New Methodological Approaches*. London: Sage.

Schedeen, Jesse. 2017. "Between the Panels: Diversity Isn't the Real Problem for Marvel Comics." IGN. April 4. http://ca.ign.com/articles/2017/04/05/between -the-panels-diversity-isnt-the-real-problem-for-marvel-comics.

Scodari, Christine. 2003. "Resistance Reimagined: Gender, Fan Practices and Science Fiction Television." *Popular Communication* 1 (2): 111–130.

———. 2012. "'Nyota Uhura Is Not a White Girl': Gender, Intersectionality, and *Star Trek*'s (2009) Alternate Romantic Universes." *Feminist Media Studies* 12 (3): 335–351.

Serpell, Namwali. 2018. "'Black Panther': Choose Your Weapons." *New York Review of Books* (blog). February 22. https://www.nybooks.com/daily/2018/02/22 /black-panther-choose-your-weapons.

Seung Cheung, Hye. 2015. "Hating the Korean Wave in Japan: The Exclusivist Inclusion of Zainichi Koreans in *Nerima Daikon Brothers*." In *Hallyu 2.0: The Korean Wave in the Age of Social Media*, ed. Sangjoon Lee and Abé Mark Nornes, 195–211. Ann Arbor: University of Michigan Press.

Shank, Dianna Rockwell. 2006. "'I Don't Want to Hurt Anyone's Feelings': Using Race as a Writing Prompt in a Composition Classroom." In *Social Change in Diverse Teaching Contexts: Touchy Subjects and Routine Practices*, ed. Nancy G. Barron, Nancy M. Grimm, and Sibylle Grubell, 125–140. New York: Peter Lang.

Shapiro, Stephen. 2002. "*Lord of the Rings* Labelled Racist." *Scotsman*. December 14. www.scotsman.com/lifestyle/culture/film/lord-of-the-ringslabelled-racist -1-632928.

Sharf, Barbara F. 1999. "Beyond Netiquette: The Ethics of Doing Naturalistic Discourse Research on the Internet." In *Doing Internet Research: Critical Issues and Methods for Examining the Net*, ed. Steven Jones, 43–25. Thousand Oaks, CA: Sage.

Sharpe, Christina. 2010. *Monstrous Intimacies: Making Post-Slavery Subjects*. Durham, NC: Duke University Press.

Shaw, Adrienne. 2015. *Gaming at the Edge: Sexuality and Gender at the Margins of Gamer Culture*. Minneapolis: University of Minnesota Press.

Shefrin, Elana. 2004. "*Lord of the Rings, Star Wars,* and Participatory Fandom: Mapping New Congruencies between the Internet and Media Entertainment Culture." *Critical Studies in Media Communication* 21 (3): 261–281.

Shepherd, Jack. 2017. "Marvel VP of Sales Blames Diversity for Falling Comic Book Sales." *Independent.* April 2. http://www.independent.co.uk/arts-entertain ment/books/news/marvel-comic-book-sales-falling-vp-diversity-women-a76 62771.html.

"Show Me How You Do That Trick." LiveJournal. November 27.

Silverman, Riley. 2017. "A Look Back at Alex Danvers' Coming Out on *Supergirl.*" Syfy Wire. October 9. https://www.syfy.com/syfywire/a-look-back-at-alex -danvers-coming-out-on-supergirl.

Singh, Vishavjit. 2013. "Captain America in a Turban." Salon. September 10. http:// www.salon.com/2013/09/10/captain_america_in_a_turban.

Skud. n.d. "Affirmational Fandom." Fanlore. https://fanlore.org/wiki/Affirmational _Fandom.

Smith, S. E. 2010. "Feminism and Joss Whedon: The Whitewashing of Sunnydale." Meloukhia. December 4. http://meloukhia.net/2010/12/feminism_and _joss_whedon_the_whitewashing_of_sunnydale.

Smith, Stacy L., Marc Choueiti, and Katherine Pieper. 2016. "Inclusion or Invisibility? A Comprehensive Annenberg Report on Diversity in Entertainment." Los Angeles: University of Southern California Annenberg School for Communication and Journalism.

Smith-Shomade, Beretta E. 2013. *Watching While Black: Centering the Television of Black Audiences.* New Brunswick, NJ: Rutgers University Press.

songlin. 2015. "Omegaverse and You." Retrieved from https://www.dropbox.com /s/34lfdgidbcohke4/OverseSurvey.pdf?dl=0.

Staggs, Matt. 2015. "Interview with R. A. Salvatore: The Future of Drizzt, and More." Unbound Worlds: Exploring the Science Fiction and Fantasy Universe. https://www.unboundworlds.com/2015/03/1n-interview-with-r-a-salvatore -the-future-of-drizzt-vengeance-of-the-iron-dwarf-and-more.

Stanfill, Mel. 2011. "Doing Fandom, (Mis)doing Whiteness: Heteronormativity, Racialization, and the Discursive Construction of Fandom." In "Race and Ethnicity in Fandom," ed. Robin Anne Reid and Sarah Gatson, special issue, *Transformative Works and Cultures* 8. doi.org/10.3983/twc.2011.0256.

———. 2018. "The Unbearable Whiteness of Fandom and Fan Studies." In *A Companion to Media Fandom and Fan Studies,* ed. Paul Booth, 305–317. Hoboken, NJ: Wiley-Blackwell.

———. 2019. "Fans of Color in Femslash." *Transformative Works and Cultures* 29. doi .org/10.3983/twc.2019.1528.

Stedman, Kyle D. 2012. "Remix Literacy and Fan Compositions." *Computers and Composition* 29: 107–123.

Stein, Louisa Ellen. 2015. *Millennial Fandom: Television Audiences in the Transmedia Age.* Iowa City: University of Iowa Press.

Stonington, Joel. 2014. "Blackface Is Big in Germany." Vocativ. http://www.vocativ .com/world/germany-world/blackface-big-germany.

Stratton, Jon. 2008. *Jewish Identity in Western Pop Culture: The Holocaust and Trauma through Modernity.* New York: Palgrave Macmillan.

Strehlau, Nelly. 2017. "She's White and They Are History: *Buffy the Vampire Slayer*'s Racialization of the Past and Present." In *Joss Whedon and Race: Critical Essays,* ed. Mary Ellen Iatropoulos and Lowery A. Woodall III. Jefferson, NC: McFarland.

Stubblebine, Allison. 2018. "Watch Black Cosplayers Talk about the Racism in Comic Fandom." Nylon. October 8. https://nylon.com/articles/black-cosplayers -here-video.

Sturtevant, Paul B. 2017. "Race: The Original Sin of the Fantasy Genre." *Public Medievalist.* December 5. https://www.publicmedievalist.com/race-fantasy-genre.

Sura, Oona. 2018. "Anti-Blackness in the Convention and Cosplay Community: An Interview With Cluelessxbelle." *Black Nerd Problems* (blog). June 19. https:// blacknerdproblems.com/anti-blackness-convention-cosplay-community.

Tate, William. 1997. "Critical Race Theory and Education: History, Theory and Implications." *Review of Research in Education* 22: 195–247.

TheRPGMinx. 2017. "The Face Reveal." YouTube. April 1. https://www.youtube.com /watch?v=xyaeQaVo2Ng.

———. 2018. "YouTube Is Making Me Shut Down My Channel." YouTube. May 3. https://www.youtube.com/watch?v=cBOqLB6VZy8.

Thomlison, Natalie. 2012. "The Colour of Feminism: White Feminists and Race in the Women's Liberation Movement." *History* 97 (July): 453–475. doi.org /10.1111/j.1468- 229X.2012.00559.x.

Thorne, Will. 2017. "Prominent YouTubers Rally around PewDiePie in Anti-Semitism Saga." *Variety.* February 18.

"Tokyo's Textbook Rules Spark Protest from South Korea." 2018. *Straits Times.* March 30. https://www.straitstimes.com/asia/tokyos-textbook-rules-spark -protest-from-south-korea.

Tolkien, J. R .R. 1981. *The Letters of J. R. R. Tolkien.* Ed. Humphrey Carpenter and Christopher Tolkien. Boston: George Allen and Unwin.

Trinh, T. Minh-Ha. 1989. *Woman, Native, Other: Writing Postcoloniality and Feminism.* Bloomington: Indiana University Press.

Uribe, Ana B. 2009. *Mi México Imaginado: Telenovelas, Televisión y Migrantes.* Mexico City: Miguel Ángel Porrúa.

Valdivia, Angharad N. 2010. *Latina/os and the Media.* Cambridge: Polity Press.

Vassallo de Lopes, Maria Immacolata. 2012. "A Case Study on Transmedia Reception: Fandom on Facebook and Social Issues in the Brazilian Telenovela *Passione.*" *Anàlisi Monogràfic:* 111–132.

Vermeulen, Lotte, Mariek Vanden Abeele, and Sofie Van Bauwel. 2016. "A Gendered Identity Debate in Digital Game Culture." *Press Start, Negotiating Gamer Identities* 3 (1): 1–16.

Wachter-Boettcher, Sara. 2018. *Technically Wrong: Sexist Apps, Biased Algorithms, and Other Threats of Toxic Tech.* New York: W. W. Norton.

Wagmeister, Elizabeth. 2016. "The CW's Superhero Shows to Feature Character 'Exploring Sexuality and Coming Out.'" *Variety* (blog). August 11. https://

variety.com/2016/tv/news/gay-character-arrow-flash-supergirl-legends
-of-tomorrow-cw-1201835641.

Walden, Corey Ryan. 2015. "'A Living and Breathing World . . .': Examining Participatory Practices within *Dungeons and Dragons*." Ph.D. dissertation, Auckland University.

Want, Kaori Mori. 2016. "*Haafu* Identities Inside and Outside of Japanese Advertisements." *Asia Pacific Perspectives* 13 (2): 83–101.

Wanzo, Rebecca. 2015. "African American Acafandom and Other Strangers: New Genealogies of Fan Studies." *Transformative Works and Cultures* 20. doi.org/10.3983/twc.2015.0699.

Warner, Kristen J. 2015a. "ABC's *Scandal* and Black Women's Fandom." In *Cupcakes, Pinterest, and Ladyporn: Feminized Popular Culture in the Early Twenty-First Century*, ed. Elana Levine, 32–50. Urbana: University of Illinois Press.

———. 2015b. *The Cultural Politics of Colorblind TV Casting*. New York: Routledge.

———. 2017. "Plastic Representation." *Film Quarterly* 71 (2). https://filmquarterly.org/2017/12/04/in-the-time-of-plastic-representation.

Warnes, Christopher. 2005. "*Baulder's Gate* and History: Race and Alignment in Digital Role Playing Games." Paper presented at the Digital Games Research Association conference, Vancouver. http://summit.sfu.ca/item/253.

Waskul, Dennis. 1996. "Ethics of Online Research: Considerations for the Study of Computer-Mediated Forms of Interaction." *Information Society* 12 (2): 129–140.

WatchMojo. 2014. "Top 10 Let's Play YouTube Channels—TopX Ep. 2." YouTube. November 12. http://www.youtube.com/watch?v=jHMmSYIweME.

———. 2016. "Top 10 Female Gamers on YouTube." YouTube. April 30. http://www.youtube.com/watch?v=3vvpQs5dYzU.

Weicker, Susanne. 1993. "Anthropology and Television: Ethnographic-Ethnological Topics on German Television." *Visual Anthropology* 6 (3): 271–283.

Weldon, Glen. 2017. "Beyond the Pale (Male): Marvel, Diversity and a Changing Comics Readership." NPR. April 8. http://www.npr.org/2017/04/08/523044892/beyond-the-pale-male-marvel-diversity-and-a-changing-comics-readership.

"Wells Jaha." n.d. The 100 Wiki. https://the100.fandom.com/wiki/Wells_Jaha.

Wildman, Stephanie M. 1996. *Privilege Revealed: How Invisible Preference Undermines America*. New York: New York University Press.

Willis, Ika. 2006. "Keeping Promises to Queer Children: Making Space (for Mary Sue) at Hogwarts." In *Fan Fiction and Fan Communities in the Age of the Internet: New Essays*, ed. Karen Hellekson and Kristina Busse, 153–170. Jefferson, NC: McFarland.

Wilson, Lena. 2016. "Alex Danvers, Coming Out and *Supergirl*'s Quiet Revolution." ScreenRant. November 28. https://screenrant.com/supergirl-alex-lesbian-coming-out-maggie.

Winkler, Rolfe, Jack Nicas, and Ben Fritz. 2017. "Disney Severs Ties with YouTube Star PewDiePie after Anti-Semitic Posts." *Wall Street Journal*. February 14.

Wolf, Mark J. P., and Bernard Perron, eds. 2016. *The Routledge Companion to Video Game Studies*. New York: Routledge.

Woo, Benjamin. 2017. "The Invisible Bag of Holding: Whiteness and Media Fandom." In *The Routledge Companion to Media Fandom*, ed. Melissa A. Click and Suzanne Scott, 245–252. New York: Routledge.

Worth, Sol, and John Adair. 1972. *Through Navajo Eyes: An Exploration in Film Communication and Anthropology*. Bloomington: Indiana University Press.

Wynter, Sylvia. 2003. "Unsettling the Coloniality of Being/Power/Truth/Freedom: Towards the Human, after Man, Its Overrepresentation—An Argument." *New Centennial Review* 3 (3): 257–337.

Wysocki, Matthew. 2015. *Rated M for Mature: Sex and Sexuality in Video Games*. New York: Bloomsbury.

Yamazaki, Akiko. 2008. "Otherness through Elves: Into Elfland and Beyond." *Children's Literature in Education* 39 (4): 305–313.

Yeo, Yezi. 2017. "The Good, the Bad, and the Forgiven: The Media Spectacle of South Korean Male Celebrities' Compulsory Military Service." *Media, War and Conflict* 10 (3): 293–313.

Young, Helen. 2010. "Diversity and Difference: Cosmopolitism and *The Lord of the Rings*." *Journal of the Fantastic in the Arts* 21 (3): 351–365.

——. 2015. "Racial Logics, Franchising, and Video Game Genres: *The Lord of the Rings*." *Games and Culture* 10 (1): 1–22. doi.org/10.1177/1555412014568448.

——. 2016. *Race and Popular Fantasy Literature: Habits of Whiteness*. New York: Routledge.

Zabus, Chantal. 2001. "Subversive Scribes: Rewriting in the Twentieth Century." *Anglistica* 5 (1–2): 191–207.

Zawaodniak, Chris. 1997. "'I'll Have to Help Some of You More Than I Want To': Teacher Involvement and Student-Centered Pedagogy." In *Sharing Pedagogies: Students and Teachers Write about Dialogic Practices*, ed. Gail Tayko and John Paul Tassoni, 25–32. Portsmouth, NH: Boynton/Cook.

Zubernis, Lynn, and Katherine Larsen. 2012. *Fandom at the Crossroads: Celebration, Shame, and Fan/Producer Relationships*. Newcastle upon Tyne: Cambridge Scholars.

Queerbaiting and Fandom: Teasing Fans through Homoerotic Possibilities
edited by Joseph Brennan

Gaming Masculinity: Trolls, Fake Geeks, and the Gendered Battle for Online Culture
by Megan Condis

Emo: How Fans Defined a Subculture
by Judith May Fathallah

Johnny Cash International: How and Why Fans Love the Man in Black
by Michael Hinds and Jonathan Silverman

Fandom as Classroom Practice: A Teaching Guide
edited by Katherine Anderson Howell

Straight Korean Female Fans and Their Gay Fantasies
by Jungmin Kwon

Aussie Fans: Uniquely Placed in Global Popular Culture
edited by Celia Lam and Jackie Raphael

Austentatious: The Evolving World of Jane Austen Fans
by Holly Luetkenhaus and Zoe Weinstein

Sherlock's World: Fan Fiction and the Reimagining of BBC's Sherlock
by Ann K. McClellan

Star Attractions: Twentieth-Century Movie Magazines and Global Fandom
edited by Tamar Jeffers McDonald and Lies Lanckman

Fandom, Now in Color: A Collection of Voices
edited by Rukmini Pande

Squee from the Margins: Fandom and Race
by Rukmini Pande

Disney's "Star Wars": Forces of Production, Promotion, and Reception
edited by William Proctor and Richard McCulloch

Everybody Hurts: Transitions, Endings, and Resurrections in Fan Cultures
edited by Rebecca Williams